# MINING TECHNOLOGY HANDBOOK

# MINING TECHNOLOGY HANDBOOK

**BY**

**HALENA NEWMAN**
**AMELIA WALKER**

KNOWLEDGE
BAKERS

KNOWLEDGE BAKERS

ISBN: 978-81-975594-6-4



*Published by* : **Knowledge Bakers**
Pune, India
*Email: info@knowledgebakers.com*

# PREFACE

Mining technology stands as a cornerstone of modern industry, providing essential tools and methodologies for extracting valuable minerals and resources from the Earth's crust. From underground mines to open-pit operations, mining technologies have evolved significantly over the years, driven by innovations in machinery, automation, safety practices, and environmental stewardship. As the mining industry continues to adapt to changing market dynamics, regulatory requirements, and sustainability challenges, there is a growing demand for comprehensive resources that provide insights into the latest trends, best practices, and emerging technologies in mining. As we embark on this exploration of mining technology, we delve into a realm where engineering, innovation, and sustainability converge, uncovering the principles, tools, and techniques that define success in this dynamic field.

This book, titled "Mining Technology Handbook," is crafted to serve as a comprehensive reference guide for professionals, researchers, and students in the field of mining and mineral engineering. Through collaboration with leading experts, practitioners, and academics in the mining industry, we aim to offer readers a multidimensional and insightful journey through the complexities of mining technology.

As editors of this volume, we have curated a collection of chapters that cover a wide range of topics in mining technology, including mine planning and design, drilling and blasting techniques, equipment selection and operation, mineral processing, environmental management, safety practices, and emerging trends such as digitalization and sustainable mining practices. Each chapter is designed to provide practical insights, case studies, and real-world examples to empower readers to navigate the challenges and opportunities of modern mining operations.

Furthermore, this book seeks to highlight the importance of sustainability and responsible mining practices in the mining industry. By examining the principles of sustainable mining, community engagement, and environmental stewardship, we aim to inspire readers to adopt innovative approaches and collaborative strategies to minimize the environmental footprint of mining operations and maximize the benefits for local communities and stakeholders.

As we embark on this enlightening journey through the world of mining technology, we extend our gratitude to the contributors whose expertise and dedication have enriched this handbook. We hope that the "Mining Technology Handbook" serves as a valuable resource for mining professionals, educators, policymakers, and researchers alike, empowering them to leverage the latest advancements in mining technology to drive efficiency, safety, and sustainability in the global mining industry.

**Halena Newman | Amelia Walker**

# CONTENTS

# CHAPTER-1

# INTEGRATING THE SAFETY MANAGEMENT OF TAILINGS FACILITIES TO THE ISO MODEL AND TO THE GLOBAL INDUSTRY STANDARD ON TAILINGS MANAGEMENT

## 1. INTRODUCTION

Mining companies (notably large ones) have structured management according to the ISO model. It is a fact that the tailings management in these companies usually has a 'life of its own' and is not part of the ISO model. In an article recently published in the journal Mine Water and Environment entitled 'Integrated Risk Management in Mine Tailings Facility' "see [1]", the authors presented a way to integrate the two aspects of management above.

The management of Quality, Environment, Safety and Occupational Health of mining companies already follows, for the most part, the ISO model. Tailings management, on the other hand, does not follow (in principle and in a general assessment) a pre-established model. In the article, the authors sought the best (and most consolidated) technical reference in tailings management, represented by Mining Association of Canada (MAC), in order to facilitate this integration. MAC itself recognizes that its model, expressed in the so-called Tailings Guide "in [2] A Guide to the Management of Tailings Facilities", is based on the ISO 14001 standard "in [3] ISO 14001:2015 Environmental Management Systems — Requirements with Guidance for Use". The ISO 14001 standard "see [3]" (as well as all the ISO management systems standards), in turn, as of 2015, started to follow a unique structure defined by ISO, represented by the so-called Annex SL. Add to this the fact that, in the article mentioned above, a specific approach was developed in terms of Quality management, aimed at design and construction.

In August 2020, the Global Industry Standard on Tailings Management "see [4]" was published, developed through an independent process (Global Tailings Review), jointly organized by the United Nations Environment Program (UNEP), the Principles for Responsible Investment (PRI), and the International Council on Mining and Metals (ICMM). This became a benchmark for the mineral sector. The so-called Global Standard is comparable to Towards Sustainable Mining® (TSM®), an externally verified performance system for sustainable mining, adopted by MAC, in which tailings management is inserted. TSM® is composed of several protocols, one of which is represented by MAC's Tailings Guide "see [2]" (and, subsidiarily, by Developing an Operation, Maintenance, and Surveillance Manual for Tailings and Water Management Facilities - OMS Guide "in [5] Developing an Operation, Maintenance, and Surveillance Manual for Tailings and Water Management Facilities"). The Tailings Guide "see [2]" guides how the company should organize a Tailings Management System (TMS) which, according to the Global Standard itself, represents its central element.

The Global Standard "see [4]" also says that the TMS and its various elements need to interact with other systems, such as the Environmental and Social Management System (ESMS), the operations management system as a whole and the regulatory system, and that this interaction between systems is essential for the Standard to be effectively implemented.

## 2. DIFFERENCES BETWEEN THE MAC GUIDES AND ISO STANDARDS

In the text of the article entitled 'Integrated Risk Management in Mine Tailings Facility' "see [1]", can be found the most notable differences and main points of attention between the guides published by MAC (Tailings Guide, Third Edition, released in February 2019 "see [6]"; OMS Guide, Second Edition, released in February 2019 "see [7]") and the ISO 9001 "in [8] ISO 9001:2015 Quality Management Systems, Requirements", ISO 14001 "see [3]" and ISO 45001 "in [9] ISO 45001:2018 Occupational

Health and Safety Management Systems, Requirements with Guidance for Use" management system standards.

In March 2021, MAC published version 3.2, which is an update to the third edition of the Tailings Guide, dated February 2019. Changes were made due to the launch in August 2020, of the Global Industry Standard in Tailings Management (the Standard), thus aiming to improve the alignment between the tailings management component of MAC's TSM® program and the Standard. For the same reason, also in March 2021, MAC published version 2.1, which is an update of the second edition of the OMS Guide, dated February 2019.

In sequence, an analysis is made of the possible impacts of these changes on the differences and points of attention mentioned above, between the two guides published by MAC and the three ISO standards for management systems considered.

## 2.1 Accountability and responsibility

In Version 3.2 of the Tailings Guide "see [2]", the level of detail in the descriptions of the roles and responsibilities of the Accountable Executive Director has been increased over the previous version.

This greater detail, seeking to clarify the roles and responsibilities of this executive, and greater alignment with the Standard's requirements, in no way impacts the analysis carried out previously and the perspective of integration of the management mechanisms.

## 2.2 Critical controls

As part of a redistribution of requirements that made up the "Plan" element of the Plan-Do-Verify-Act (PDCA) cycle in Version 3.1 of the Tailings Guide "see [6]", the Critical Controls requirement was repositioned in Version 3.2 "see [2]", becoming part of the Risk Management process.

In terms of content, just highlighting the addition made to the text, incorporating two stakeholders (regulatory bodies and COI) into the process of defining high-consequence events. This in no way impacts the analysis made previously and the perspective of integrating management mechanisms.

## 2.3 Quality management

As part of a redistribution of requirements that made up the "Plan" element of the Plan-Perform-Verify-Act (PDCA) cycle in Version 3.1 of the Tailings Guide "see [6]", the Quality Management requirement, which was subordinated to Controls, which in turn was included in the Management Process, it was repositioned in Version 3.2 "see [2]", moving up the hierarchy to becoming one of the components of the "Plan" element of the PDCA cycle.

In terms of content, the text of Version 3.2 of the Tailings Guide "see [2]" incorporated the assertion that quality management must address a wide range of aspects related to tailings facilities, considering the initial and ongoing construction, including specifications for materials and construction procedures (e.g. material compaction), OMS activities such as calibration of surveillance instruments, and Quality Assurance and Quality Control related to the closure plan implementation.

### 2.4 Emergency preparedness

The text added in Version 3.2 of the Tailings Guide "see [2]", over the previous one, reinforced this document's alignment with ISO standards by including what is apparently obvious in terms of what it means to be prepared for an emergency: assessing the range of potential emergency scenarios that could occur, and potential impacts; maintaining the necessary capacity (e.g., personnel, equipment, supplies) to respond; maintaining a state of readiness to respond, in collaboration with external parties (e.g., local first responders) that would be involved in responding to an emergency; developing plans for emergency preparedness; and conducting training and exercises/tests of the plans for emergency preparedness.

## 3. ADDITIONAL DIFFERENCES BETWEEN MAC GUIDES AND ISO STANDARDS

We will now analyze other changes promoted in Version 3.2 of the Tailings Guide "see [2]", and also in Version 2.1 of the OMS Guide "see [5]", and their potential impact on the ease of integration between management models advocated in the article 'Integrated Risk Management in Mining Waste Facility' "see [1]", mentioned earlier in this text.

### 3.1 Policy and commitment

To highlight, in the text added in Version 3.2 of the Tailings Guide "see [2]", in relation to the previous one, the emphasis given to the need for the Owner of the tailings facility to demonstrate commitment to a culture that promotes the early recognition of problems, and also with the response to emergencies and participation in post-incident recovery, in collaboration with authorities and communities of interest (COI).

This in no way impacts the analysis made previously and the perspective of integrating management mechanisms.

### 3.2 Managing change

To highlight, in the text added in Version 3.2 of the Tailings Guide "see [2]", in relation to the previous one, the emphasis given to the Engineer of Record (EoR) succession plan.

This in no way impacts the analysis made previously and the perspective of integrating management mechanisms.

## 3.3 Control of documented information

The most significant change promoted in version 2.1 of the OMS Guide "see [5]" was precisely the transfer of the text existing in the second edition of this guide, then called 'Control of Documented Information', to the Tailings Guide. The text, in addition, was enriched in content, renamed 'Information Management', in turn subdivided into two requirements: 'Information to be Documented' and 'Control of Documented Information'. The text has been transferred from the OMS Guide to the Tailings Guide because the latter is applicable to documented information that goes beyond that contained in OMS manuals.

The text of the new 'Information to be Documented' requirement even spells out what information must be documented and updated throughout the tailings facility lifecycle, and references to the new Appendix 6 (Information to be Documented to Support Responsible Tailings Management) and Appendix 8 (Technical Considerations) of the Tailings Guide "see [2]", specifically with regard to the closure plan.

In terms of correspondence with the text of the ISO standards, the new text of the Tailings Guide presents itself as more aligned in the richness of details, containing specific characteristics of a specific management system for mining tailings facilities.

## 3.4 Training and competence

To highlight, in the text added in Version 3.2 of the Tailings Guide "see [2]", in relation to the previous one, the importance given to the traceability of evidence of competence, in order to ensure that all relevant personnel receive the appropriate training.

This in no way impacts the analysis made previously and the perspective of integrating management mechanisms.

## 3.5 Communications

Section 3.1.2 of the OMS Guide - second edition "see [7]", discussing Communications, was deleted and incorporated into Version 3.2 of the Tailings Guide "see [2]". The associated appendix (Appendix 7: Factors in Effective Communications, Governance, and the "Human Element" of Tailings Management) was also moved to the Tailings Guide, even with the same numbering.

The three ISO standards do not go as deep as the Tailings Guide on Communications aspects and, in a common way, define the need for the organization to establish, implement and maintain the necessary processes for internal and external communications, including: a) about what to communicate; b) when to communicate; c) with whom to communicate; d) how to communicate; e) who should communicate. The ISO 14001 "see [3]" and ISO 45001 "see [9]" standards also emphasize the need to take into account legal obligations and ensure that the information communicated is consistent with that generated within the scope of the management system, and that it is reliable.

The Tailings Guide "see [2]", for its part, emphasizes the fact that timely communication of potential problems can be essential to achieving the goal of minimizing harm, and cites two main mechanisms for establishing a corporate culture that encourages people to report problems: establishing a confidential process to promptly receive, investigate and resolve issues; and the development and implementation of whistleblower protection mechanisms to ensure there are no retaliations.

It is also important to cite the content of the aforementioned Appendix 7, which presents a summary of 14 lessons learned on governance and communications, applicable to tailings management and dam safety, extracted, according to the Tailings Guide "see [6]", from the publication Martin, T. (2001) - Pearl Harbor: Lessons for the Dam Safety Community (presented at the annual conference of the Canadian Dam Association).

## 3.6 Management review for continual improvement

The Tailings Guide text "see [2]" incorporated, as one of the inputs to periodic management reviews, the integration of tailings management activities with site-wide systems, such as, where applicable, a site-wide environmental and social management system.

This requirement meets the idea of integration of management mechanisms advocated by the authors.

Another addition made in version 3.2 of the Tailings Guide "see {2]" was the requirement that management review describe the current conditions related to the tailings facility, including a summary of construction activities since the last review, as well as any significant changes that have taken place since the last management review, including: an assessment of whether the tailings facility is continuing to meet the design intent; and a summary of any deviations from the design or expected conditions since the last management review, including an assessment of the cumulative impacts of those deviations.

Finally, to highlight an item added in version 3.2 of the Tailings Guide "see [2]", the list of changes that should be considered for the continuous improvement of the tailings management system: relevant new or emerging technologies, practices or knowledge related to tailings management.

Such particularities found in the Tailings Guide text in no way compromise the analysis made before and the perspective of integration of management mechanisms.

From the "Do" element of the Plan-Do-Check-Act (PDCA) cycle in version 3.1 of the Tailings Guide "see [6]", Section 5.3 was deleted, which described a checklist that could assist in the implementation of the tailings management framework throughout the life cycle. Appendix A.5.1 - Considerations for Managing Throughout the Life Cycle of a Tailings Facility, which included, in version 3.1 of the Tailings Guide "[6]", an illustrative sample of a master checklist, to be used as a tool for Owners in implementing the tailings management framework, has been deleted in version 3.2 "see [2]". The checklist has been replaced by MAC in the Tailings Guide by a Table of Conformance, as a reference for Gap Analysis in relation to the TSM® Tailings Management Protocol.

As part of the effort to bring TSM® into line with the standard, MAC has added a new supporting appendix (Appendix 6: Information to be Documented to Support Responsible Tailings Management) on information requirements related to: site characterization; design information; documentation on construction and as-built conditions; and closure plan.

## 4. COMPARATIVE ANALYSIS BETWEEN THE STANDARD AND THE ISO MANAGEMENT SYSTEMS

The Standard developed by the Global Reporting Initiative has 77 requirements for tailings management, covering six thematic areas, which in turn are subdivided into 15 principles. MAC conducted a detailed analysis "in [10] Equivalency Between Requirements for Sustainable Mining and the Global Industry Standard on Tailings Management" of the TSM requirements against the Standard. Considering the form and content of this gap analysis, the authors of this text carried out a comparative analysis of each of the 77 requirements of the Standard with those of the ISO 9001, ISO 14001 and ISO 45001 standards, indicating how the management system(s) of mining companies could be used to implement the requirements of the Standard. The analysis was complemented by the indication of the sections of the Tailings Guide that would support the structuring of this integrated management system. The result of this analysis is embodied in Table 1.

**Table 1. Comparative analysis between the requirements of the Standard and ISO standards.**

| Global Industry Standard on Tailings Management X ISO Standards | |
|---|---|
| **G. I. Standard** | **ISO Standards** |
| TOPIC I: Affected Communities | |
| PRINCIPLE 1: Respect the rights of project-affected people and meaningfully engage them at all phases of the tailings facility lifecycle, including closure. | |
| Requirement 1.1 | Recognize the applicability of the UNGP when determining external and internal issues that are relevant to its purpose and that affect its ability to achieve the intended results of its environmental and OH&S management system (4.1/ISO 14001 + ISO 45001), and also by seeking to understand the needs and expectations of its stakeholders (4.2/ISO 14001 + ISO 45001). Explicitly make this commitment in its policy (5.2/ISO 14001 + ISO 45001; corresponding section in Tailings Guide: 3 - Policy and Commitment), include the UNGP in its compliance obligations (6.1.3/ISO 14001 + ISO 45001; corresponding section in Tailings Guide: 4.4 - Conformance Management) and periodically assess compliance (9.1.2/ISO 14001 + ISO 45001; corresponding section in Tailings Guide: 6 - Performance Evaluation). |
| Requirement 1.2 | Recognize the applicability of the FPIC when determining external and internal issues that are relevant to its purpose and that affect its ability to achieve the intended results of its environmental, OH&S management system (4.1/ISO 14001 + ISO 45001), and also by seeking to understand the needs and expectations of its stakeholders (4.2/ISO 14001 + ISO 45001). Explicitly make this commitment in its policy (5.2/ISO 14001 + ISO 45001; corresponding section in Tailings Guide: 3 - Policy and Commitment), include the FPIC in its compliance obligations (6.1.3/ISO 14001 + ISO 45001; corresponding section in Tailings Guide: 4.4 - Conformance Management) and periodically assess compliance (9.1.2/ISO 14001 + ISO 45001; corresponding section in Tailings Guide: 6 - Performance Evaluation). |
| Requirement 1.3 | When implementing the process of understanding stakeholders needs and expectations (4.2/ISO 14001 + ISO 45001), include the involvement of those affected by the project among the compliance obligations (6.1.3/ISO 14001 + ISO 45001; corresponding section in Tailings Guide: 4.4 - Conformance Management). From there, periodically assess this compliance (9.1.2/ISO 14001 + ISO 45001; corresponding section in Tailings Guide: 6 - Performance Evaluation). From the perspective of ISO 9001, clause 4.2 determines that the needs and expectations of interested parties must be understood in terms of their effect or potential effect on the organization's ability to provide products and services that meet customer requirements, regulatory requirements and applicable bylaws. These needs and expectations must be monitored and reviewed periodically. |

| Global Industry Standard on Tailings Management X ISO Standards | |
|---|---|
| **G. I. Standard** | **ISO Standards** |
| Requirement 1.4 | Emphasize the participation of non-managerial level workers in hazard identification (5.4/ISO 45001), and establish the necessary process(es) to receive and respond (in accordance with the UNGP) to relevant communications from stakeholders (7.4/ISO 14001 + ISO 45001; corresponding section in Tailings Guide: 4.11 Communications, with emphasis on key mechanisms required to ensure confidentiality and protection of whistleblowers), protecting workers from retaliation when reporting incidents, hazards and risks (5.1/ISO 45001). |
| TOPIC II: Integrated Knowledge Base | |
| PRINCIPLE 2: Develop and maintain an interdisciplinary knowledge base to support safe tailings management throughout the tailings facility lifecycle, including closure. | |
| Requirement 2.1 | By establishing the process to determine the external and internal issues that are relevant to its purpose and that affect its ability to achieve the intended results of the environmental and OH&S management system (4.1/ISO 14001 + ISO 45001), ensure that the knowledge is updated at least every 5 years and whenever there is any relevant change in the tailings disposal structure or in the local social, environmental and economic context. Incorporate into this process of analyzing the context and when making commitments in the environmental policy (5.2/ISO 14001) the uncertainties related to climate change (corresponding section in Tailings Guide: 3 - Policy and Commitment). |
| Requirement 2.2 | Whenimplementingrequirements8.3.2ofISO9001(Designanddevelopmentplanning)and8.3.3(Designanddevelopment input), relevant topics such as climatic, seismological, geomorphological, geological, geochemical, hydrological and hydrogeological conditions can be considered as important information for elaboration of the tailings dam project. Tailings Guide - Appendix 6: Information to be Documented to Support Responsible Tailings Management |
| Requirement 2.3 | Ensure that the methodology(ies) established to identify and assess environmental and occupational hazards/risks contemplates plausible failure modes, site conditions and the properties of the slurry (6.1.2/ISO 14001 + ISO 45001; corresponding section in Tailings Guide: 4.1 Risk Management). Ensure that, when flowable materials are present in tailings disposal structures with a consequence classification of "High", "Very High" or "Extreme", according to criteria in Annex 2 of the Standard), the results include estimates of the physical area impacted by a possible failure, flow arrival times, depth and velocities, and material deposition depth. When establishing the planning for response to potential emergency situations, consider the results of the above analysis (8.2/ISO 14001 + ISO 45001; corresponding section in Tailings Guide: 5.2 Emergency Preparedness). Update the risk assessment and response planning whenever there is any relevant change in the tailings disposal structure or in the impacted physical area (8.1/ISO 14001 – 8.1.3/ISO 45001; corresponding section in Tailings Guide: 4.5 Managing Change). |

| Global Industry Standard on Tailings Management X ISO Standards | |
|---|---|
| **G. I. Standard** | **ISO Standards** |
| Requirement 2.4 | Update the risk assessment and response planning contemplated in R 2.3 whenever there is any relevant change in the tailings disposal structure, in the impacted physical area or in the knowledge base. |
| PRINCIPLE 3: Use all elements of the knowledge base - social, environmental, local economic and technical - to inform decisions throughout the tailings facility lifecycle, including closure. | |
| Requirement 3.1 | Keep the identification and assessment of environmental and occupational hazards/risks updated (6.1.2/ISO 14001 + ISO 45001; corresponding section in Tailings Guide: 4.1 Risk Management), as well as the operational control planning (8.1/ISO 14001 + ISO 45001; corresponding section in Tailings Guide: 5.1 Operation, Maintenance, and Surveillance Manual), in view of knowledge about climate change and using the principles of Adaptive Management. Make appropriate adjustments in emergency planning (8.2/ISO 14001 + ISO 45001; corresponding section in Tailings Guide: 5.2 Emergency Preparedness). The knowledge base attributed to climate can be verified both in the planning phase (8.3.2/ISO 9001) and in the requirement regarding changes in projects and development (8.3.6/ISO 9001), applicable throughout the life cycle of tailings facilities. |
| Requirement 3.2 | For new tailings facilities, ensure that in the process of identification and assessment of environmental and occupational hazards/risks (6.1.2/ISO 14001 + ISO 45001; corresponding section in Tailings Guide: 4.1 Risk Management), a multi-criteria analysis of location alternatives, technological and viable strategies for the management of tailings is made in order to minimize risks to people and the environment. The assignment of responsibilities and authorities must ensure the need for approval by the ITRB or an independent senior technical reviewer (5.3/ ISO 9001 + ISO 14001 + ISO 45001, corresponding section in Tailings Guide: 4.3 Accountability and Responsibility). For existing facilities, ensure that the identification and assessment of environmental and occupational hazards/risks (6.1.2/ISO 14001 + ISO 45001; corresponding section in the Tailings Guide: 4.1 Risk Management) is kept up to date in terms of technologies, of the design of the disposal structures and tailings management strategies to minimize risks and improve environmental performance. When considering the requirements of ISO 9001 that can be applied to both new tailings facilities and existing facilities, it is possible to consider the need for risk assessment in 6.1 (Action to address risks and opportunities) which makes reference to item 4.2 (Understanding the needs and expectations of interested parties), in addition to item 8.3.3 (Design and development input), especially with regard to the assessment of potential consequences of failures (paragraph "e"). |

| Global Industry Standard on Tailings Management X ISO Standards | |
|---|---|
| **G. I. Standard** | **ISO Standards** |
| Requirement 3.3 | Implement the process of identification and assessment of environmental and occupational hazards/risks from the stage of conceptual and feasibility studies (6.1.2/ISO 14001 + ISO 45001; corresponding section in the Tailings Guide: 4.1 Risk Management), including the impacts of social and economic nature, and ensuring that, in the case of identification of potential acute or chronic impacts at a relevant level, mitigation measures are established and implemented according to a hierarchy of controls (8.1/ISO 14001 + ISO 45001; corresponding sections in the Tailings Guide: 4.1 Risk Management +4.8 Operation, Maintenance, and Surveillance Manuals +5.1 Operation, Maintenance, and Surveillance Manual). Item 8.3.3 of ISO 9001 (Design and development inputs) provides for the need to assess the potential consequences of failures, in addition to the need to retain documented information, which may consider the uncertainties regarding climate change and its social, environmental consequences and economic, in the scope of tailings facilities. |
| Requirement 3.4 | Ensure that the identification and assessment of environmental and occupational hazards/risks (6.1.2/ISO 14001 + ISO 45001; corresponding section in the Tailings Guide: 4.1 Risk Management) is kept up to date, including as a result of knowledge about climate change or about long-term impacts (8.1/ISO 14001 – 8.1.3/ISO 45001; corresponding section in Tailings Guide: 4.5 Managing Change). |
| TOPIC III: Design, construction, operation and monitoring of the tailings facility | |
| PRINCIPLE 4: Develop plans and design criteria for the tailings facility to minimize risk for all phases of its lifecycle, including closure and post-closure. | |
| Requirement 4.1 | In the environmental and occupational risk assessment process (6.1.2/ISO 14001 + ISO 45001; corresponding section in the Waste Guide: 4.1 Risk Management) consider, for all categories of impacts, the classification of consequences of the highest indicated level in Annex 2, Table 1 of the Standard. |
| Requirement 4.2 | The application of clause 8.3 of ISO 9001 (Design and development of products and services) makes clear the need to evaluate, in the planning phase (8.3.2/ISO 9001), the items referring to the nature, duration and complexity of the project; stages of required processes, including necessary revisions; project verification and validation requirements; definition of responsibilities and necessary authorities; assessment of required resources; interface control; expected level of control, considering the interested parties. |
| Requirement 4.3 | By applying item 8.3.2 of ISO 9001, paragraph "d", it is possible to verify the establishment of responsibilities and authorities involved in the design and development process and, in addition, paragraph "j" determines the need to establish these responsibilities and authorities as documented information for the project. |

| Global Industry Standard on Tailings Management X ISO Standards | |
|---|---|
| **G. I. Standard** | **ISO Standards** |
| Requirement 4.4 | Item 8.3.3 of ISO 9001 (Design and development input) establishes the need to consider issues associated with: functional and performance requirements of the project; verification of similar projects; verification of the need to comply with statutory, regulatory, standards and applicable codes requirements; potential consequences of failures. And, also, to ensure that all information evaluated is considered as controlled. |
| Requirement 4.5 | According to item 8.3.4 of ISO 9001 (Design and development controls), the following control measures must be considered: ensure that the results to be achieved are defined; that reviews are conducted to assess the ability of the results to meet the project's purposes; verification to ensure that the outputs meet the conditions established at the entrance of the projects; determination of the results validation process; guarantee of the solution of the problems identified during the reviews. There is also a need to document all information obtained and decisions made. |
| Requirement 4.6 | In item 8.3.5 of ISO 9001 (Design and development output), measures are defined to: ensure that the project input requirements have been met; that the project is fit for purpose; that monitoring and measurement requirements are defined and that acceptance criteria have been defined; guarantee of project safety. |
| Requirement 4.7 | For existing tailings facilities, item 8.3.6 of ISO 9001 (Design and development changes) can contribute to their adequacy, as it considers: the possibility of revisions, including their documentation; establishing responsibilities and authorities for making necessary changes; and taking actions to prevent adverse impacts. |
| Requirement 4.8 | With regard to the Design Basis Report (DBR), full compliance with clause 8.3 of ISO 9001 (Design and development of products and services) provides that all stages are properly documented, including with the approval of those responsible. |
| PRINCIPLE 5: Develop a robust design that integrates the knowledge base and minimizes the risk of failure to people and the environment for all phases of the tailings facility lifecycle, including closure and post-closure. | |
| Requirement 5.1 | Clause 8.3 of ISO 9001 (Design and development of products and services) makes clear the need to evaluate, in the planning phase (8.3.2/ISO 9001), the items referring to: nature, duration and complexity of the project; stages of required processes, including necessary revisions; project verification and validation requirements; definition of responsibilities and necessary authorities; assessment of required resources; interface control; expected level of control, considering the interested parties. |
| Requirement 5.2 | The same comment made for R 5.1 applies. |

| Global Industry Standard on Tailings Management X ISO Standards | |
|---|---|
| **G. I. Standard** | **ISO Standards** |
| Requirement 5.3 | By integrating items 8.3.2 (Design and development planning) and 8.3.3 (Design and development input) of ISO 9001, relevant topics such as climatic, seismological, geomorphological, geological, geochemical, hydrological and hydrogeological conditions can be considered as important information for the elaboration of the tailings dam project. |
| Requirement 5.4 | The same comment made for R 5.1 applies. |
| Requirement 5.5 | The same comment made for R 4.4 applies.<br>For existing tailings facilities, the same comment made for R 4.7 applies. |
| Requirement 5.6 | The same comment made for R 4.6 applies. It is important that, in implementing the planning and entry requirements (8.3.2 + 8.3.3/ISO 9001), the requirements for closing the tailings facility have been considered. |
| Requirement 5.7 | Clause 8.3 of ISO 9001 (Design and development of products and services) establishes the need to define responsibilities and authorities at the various stages of the process. In addition, paragraph "e" (8.3.3/ISO 9001) establishes the need to assess the potential consequences of failures. |
| Requirement 5.8 | Item 8.3.3 of ISO 9001 (Design and development input) establishes the need to consider statutory, regulatory, standards and codes requirements, thus taking into account the possibility of including international standards. |
| PRINCIPLE 6: Plan, build and operate the tailings facility to manage risk at all phases of the tailings facility lifecycle, including closure and post-closure. | |
| Requirement 6.1 | For the stages of planning, construction and operation of tailings disposal structures, the application of a methodology based on the requirements of ISO 10005 "in [11] ISO 10005:2018 Quality management systems - Guidelines for quality plans" can be considered, which in turn considers the means for process requirements, product, project or contract. |
| Requirement 6.2 | The same comment made for R 6.1 applies. |
| Requirement 6.3 | The same comment made for R 6.1 applies. |
| Requirement 6.4 | The same comment made for R 6.1 applies. |

| Global Industry Standard on Tailings Management X ISO Standards | |
|---|---|
| G. I. Standard | ISO Standards |
| Requirement 6.5 | The same comment made for R 4.7 applies. |
| Requirement 6.6 | The same comment made for R 4.4 applies. |
| PRINCIPLE 7: Design, implement and operate monitoring systems to manage risk at all phases of the facility lifecycle, including closure. | |
| Requirement 7.1 | The same comment made for R 4.4 applies. |
| Requirement 7.2 | The same comment made for R 4.6 applies. |
| Requirement 7.3 | Clause 8.3 of ISO 9001 (Design and development of products and services) establishes the need to define responsibilities and authorities at the various stages of the process. In addition, item "e" of item 8.3.3 (Design and development input) establishes the need to assess the potential consequences of failures. In item 8.3.5 (Design and development output) measures are defined to: guarantee that the project input requirements have been met; that the project is fit for purpose; that monitoring and measurement requirements are defined and that acceptance criteria have been defined; guarantee of project safety. |
| Requirement 7.4 | The same comment made for R 4.4 applies. |
| Requirement 7.5 | The same comment made for R 6.1 applies. |
| TOPIC IV: Management and Governance | |
| PRINCIPLE 8: Establish policies, systems and accountabilities to support the safety and integrity of the tailings facility. | |
| Requirement 8.1 | Ensure the inclusion, in the Environmental and OH&S policies (5.2/ISO 14001 + ISO 45001), of the commitments with the safe management of tailings facilities, with emergency preparedness and recovery from failures. Alternatively, establish a specific tailings management policy in which these commitments are made explicit (Tailings Guide: 3 Policy and Commitment). |

| Global Industry Standard on Tailings Management X ISO Standards | |
|---|---|
| **G. I. Standard** | **ISO Standards** |
| Requirement 8.2 | Establish and implement a tailings management system based on the MAC Tailings Guide, integrated with the management system(s) in the ISO model (4.4/ISO 9001 + ISO 14001 + ISO 45001) that include social aspects, possibly using as references the guidelines of ISO 26000 and the requirements of the SA8000 standard in [12] Social Accountability International. 2014. International Standard SA8000. |
| Requirement 8.3 | Individual performance evaluations linked to compensation mechanisms are beyond the scope of this text. Nevertheless, it is recommended that the determinations of R 8.3 be considered as compensation criteria that are part of the organization's human resources policy. |
| Requirement 8.4 | Ensure that responsibilities and authorities for relevant functions in the management system are assigned, formally communicated and understood at all levels (5.3/ISO 9001 + ISO 14001 + ISO 45001; corresponding section in the Tailings Guide: 4.3 Accountability and Responsibility). |
| Requirement 8.5 | The same comment made for R 8.4 applies. |
| Requirement 8.6 | Determine the necessary competence of professionals whose performance affects the results of tailings management, ensure that these people are competent, based on appropriate education, training and experience and, where applicable, take actions to acquire the necessary competence and assess effectiveness of the actions taken (7.2/ISO 9001 + ISO 14001 + ISO 45001; corresponding section in the Tailings Guide: 4.10 Training and Competence). |
| Requirement 8.7 | Ensure that responsibilities and authorities for relevant functions in the management system are assigned, formally communicated and understood at all levels (5.3/ISO 9001 + ISO 14001 + ISO 45001; corresponding section in the Tailings Guide: 4.3 Accountability and Responsibility - 2.2.3 Independent Review). |
| PRINCIPLE 9: Appoint and empower an Engineer of Record. | |
| Requirement 9.1 | Determine the necessary competence of professionals whose performance affects the results of tailings management, ensure that these people are competent, based on appropriate education, training and experience and, where applicable, take actions to acquire the necessary competence and assess effectiveness of the actions taken (7.2/ ISO 9001 + ISO 14001 + ISO 45001; corresponding section in the Tailings Guide: 4.10 Training and Competence). When considering clause 8.4 of ISO 9001 (Control of externally provided processes, products and services), it is possible to identify three important steps in the acquisition of these specialized services in tailings facilities: the first step is that regarding the approval of possible suppliers, considering the necessary competency criteria; the second step refers to the selection of the supplier; and the third stage refers to the performance evaluation, considering the possibility or not of continuity of service provision. |

**Global Industry Standard on Tailings Management X ISO Standards**

| G. I. Standard | ISO Standards |
|---|---|
| Requirement 9.2 | Ensure that responsibilities and authorities for relevant functions in the management system are assigned, formally communicated and understood at all levels (5.3/ISO 9001 + ISO 14001 + ISO 45001; corresponding section in the Tailings Guide: 4.3 Accountability and Responsibility). |
| Requirement 9.3 | It is possible to consider that the establishment of quality management to ensure the proper operation of a tailings disposal structure can be done through Quality Plans, provided for in ISO 10005 "in [13] ISO 10005:2018 Quality management systems - Guidelines for quality plans", which considers the means to process, product, project, or contract requirements. Tailings Guide: 4.7 Quality Management |
| Requirement 9.4 | The same comment made for R 9.2 applies. When considering clause 8.4 of ISO 9001 (Control of externally provided processes, products and services), it is possible to identify three important steps in the acquisition of these specialized services in tailings facilities: the first step is that regarding the approval of possible suppliers, considering the necessary competency criteria; the second step refers to the selection of the supplier; and the third stage refers to the performance evaluation, considering the possibility or not of continuity of service provision. |
| Requirement 9.5 | When considering clause 8.4 of ISO 9001 (Control of externally provided processes, products and services), it is possible to identify three important steps in the acquisition of these specialized services in tailings facilities: the first step is that regarding the approval of possible suppliers, considering the necessary competency criteria; the second step refers to the selection of the supplier; and the third stage refers to the performance evaluation, considering the possibility or not of continuity of service provision. |
| PRINCIPLE 10: Establish and implement levels of review as part of a strong quality and risk management system for all phases of the tailings facility lifecycle, including closure. | |
| Requirement 10.1 | When establishing the process of identification and assessment of environmental and occupational hazards/risks (6.1.2/ISO 14001 + ISO 45001; corresponding section in the Tailings Guide: 4.1 Risk Management), specify the use of methodologies based on best practices, and establish responsibilities and authorities related to this process (5.3/ISO 9001 + ISO 14001 + ISO 45001; corresponding section in the Tailings Guide: 4.3 Accountability and Responsibility), ensuring that it is carried out by a qualified multidisciplinary team (7.2/ISO 9001 + ISO 14001 + ISO 45001; corresponding section in the Tailings Guide: 4.10 Training and Competence), at the minimum defined frequency. Cover the aspects and impacts of a social and economic nature in the process. Submit the assessment result for scrutiny by the ITRB or an independent senior technical reviewer (Tailings Guide/2.2.3 Independent Review), establishing and implementing a plan to mitigate the risks considered unacceptable (8.1/ISO 14001 + ISO 45001). |

| Global Industry Standard on Tailings Management X ISO Standards | |
|---|---|
| G. I. Standard | ISO Standards |
| Requirement 10.2 | Implement the process of periodic critical analysis of tailings safety management (Tailings Guide: 7 Management Review for Continuous Improvement), integrated with quality, environmental and OH&S management (9.3/ISO 9001 + ISO 14001 + ISO 45001), at intervals settled down. Define responsibilities and authorities related to this process (5.3/ISO 9001 + ISO 14001 + ISO 45001; corresponding section in the Tailings Guide: 4.3 Accountability and Responsibility), ensuring that the analyzes are carried out by senior technical reviewers with the appropriate qualifications and knowledge (7.2/ISO 9001 + ISO 14001 + ISO 45001; corresponding section in the Tailings Guide: 4.10 Training and Competence) and resources (7.1/ISO 9001 + ISO 14001 + ISO 45001; corresponding section in the Tailings Guide: 4.9 Resources). |
| Requirement 10.3 | Conduct internal audits at planned intervals to provide information on the performance of the tailings system integrated with quality, environmental and OH&S management (9.2/ISO 9001 + ISO 14001 + ISO 45001; corresponding section in Tailings Guide: 8 Assurance). |
| Requirement 10.4 | Define responsibilities and authorities related to this process (5.3/ISO 9001 + ISO 14001 + ISO 45001; corresponding section in the Tailings Guide: 4.3 Accountability and Responsibility), ensuring that the analyzes are carried out by the EoR or by a senior independent technical reviewer, with the appropriate qualifications and knowledge (7.2/ISO 9001 + ISO 14001 + ISO 45001; corresponding section in the Tailings Guide: 4.10 Training and Competence), at intervals settled down. |
| Requirement 10.5 | When establishing a process to monitor, measure, analyze and evaluate the performance of tailings management, integrated with quality, environmental and OH&S management, define the need to conduct DSRs at the defined frequency and according to best practices, imposing the restriction on the carrying out consecutive works by the same contracted technical manager (9.1/ISO 9001 + ISO 14001 + ISO 45001; corresponding sections in the Tailings Guide: 6 Performance Evaluation - 8 Assurance). |
| Requirement 10.6 | When establishing a process to monitor, measure, analyze and evaluate the performance of tailings management, integrated with quality, environmental and OH&S management, define the need to conduct DSRs at the defined frequency (9.1/ISO 9001 + ISO 14001 + ISO 45001; corresponding sections in the Tailings Guide: 6 Performance Evaluation - 8 Assurance), allocating responsibilities and authorities as required (5.3/ISO 9001 + ISO 14001 + ISO 45001; corresponding section in the Tailings Guide: 4.3 Accountability and Responsibility), and ensuring that DSRs are conducted by competent professionals (7.2/ISO 9001 + ISO 14001 + ISO 45001; corresponding section in the Tailings Guide: 4.10 Training and Competence). |

| Global Industry Standard on Tailings Management X ISO Standards | |
|---|---|
| **G. I. Standard** | **ISO Standards** |
| Requirement 10.7 | Ensure the provision of the necessary financial resources for the planned closure, early closure, rehabilitation, and post-closure of tailings disposal structures (7.1/ISO 9001 + ISO 14001 + ISO 45001; corresponding section in the Tailings Guide: 4.9 Resources). When establishing the process(es) of external communication (7.4.3/ISO 14001 + ISO 45001; corresponding section in the Tailings Guide: 4.11 Communications), define the obligation of public disclosure with due frequency, in addition to, limited by the provisions of local or national regulations on the matter, seek to influence prospective acquirers to comply with the requirements of the Standard. |
| PRINCIPLE 11: Develop an organizational culture that promotes learning, communication and early problem recognition. | |
| Requirement 11.1 | Making people who carry out work under the organization's control aware of their role in preventing failures (5.1 + 7.3/ISO 9001 + ISO 14001 + ISO 45001; corresponding sections in the Tailings Guide: 3 Policy and Commitment +4.11 Communications + Appendix 7). |
| Requirement 11.2 | When establishing the process that aims to ensure the necessary competence of people whose actions may affect the performance of tailings management, integrated with the management of quality, environmental and OH&S (7.2/ISO 9001 + ISO 14001 + ISO 45001; corresponding section in the Tailings Guide: 4.10 Training and Competence), build a database that integrates workers' experience in planning, design, and operations at all stages of the tailings disposal structure lifecycle. |
| Requirement 11.3 | Make people who perform work under the organization's control aware of the importance of sharing data and knowledge, effective communication, and the proper implementation of management measures (5.1 + 7.3/ISO 9001 + ISO 14001 + ISO 45001; corresponding sections in the Guide Tailings: 3 Policy and Commitment +4.11 Communications + Appendix 7). |
| Requirement 11.4 | When establishing the process(es), including reporting, investigations and taking action, to determine and manage incidents and non-compliances (10.2/ISO 9001 + ISO 14001 + ISO 45001; corresponding section in Tailings Guide: 6 Performance Evaluation), emphasize human and organizational factors. |
| Requirement 11.5 | Making people who carry out work under the organization's control aware of their role in reporting problems or identifying opportunities to improve the management of tailings disposal structures (5.1 + 7.3/ISO 9001 + ISO 14001 + ISO 45001; 5.4/ISO 45001; corresponding sections in the Tailings Guide: 3 Policy and Commitment +4.11 Communications + Appendix 7), protecting them from retaliation (5.4/ISO 45001; corresponding section in the Tailings Guide: 4.11 Communications), in addition to establishing deadlines for response and communication of measures taken and their results. |

| Global Industry Standard on Tailings Management X ISO Standards | |
|---|---|
| **G. I. Standard** | **ISO Standards** |
| PRINCIPLE 12: Establish a process for reporting and addressing concerns and implement whistleblower protections. | |
| Requirement 12.1 | When establishing the internal communication process of relevant information on tailings management, integrated with quality, environmental and OH&S management, between the various levels and functions of the organization, define a formal and confidential process to receive, investigate and respond promptly to the concerns raised by employees and contractors (7.4/ISO 9001 + ISO 14001 + ISO 45001; corresponding section in Tailings Guide: 4.11 Communications). |
| Requirement 12.2 | When establishing the internal communication process of relevant information on tailings management, integrated with quality, environmental and OH&S management, between the various levels and functions of the organization, define a formal and confidential process to receive, investigate and promptly respond to concerns raised by employees and contractors (7.4/ISO 9001 + ISO 14001 + ISO 45001; corresponding section in Tailings Guide: 4.11 Communications), safeguarding the whistleblower from dismissal, discrimination or any retaliation. |
| TOPIC V: Emergency Response and Long-Term Recovery | |
| PRINCIPLE 13: Prepare for emergency response to tailings facility failures. | |
| Requirement 13.1 | Establish, implement and maintain the process(es) necessary to prepare and respond to potential emergency situations, taking actions to prevent or mitigate the consequences arising from these situations, including the case of a catastrophic tailings facility failure, testing the planned response actions at the established frequency, when feasible, and periodically review the process(es) and planned response actions, in particular, after the occurrence of emergency situations or tests (8.2/ISO 14001 + ISO 45001; corresponding section in the Tailings Guide: 5.2 Emergency Preparedness). Provide relevant information and training related to emergency preparedness and response to relevant stakeholders, including emergency response services, government authorities and, as appropriate, the local community. |
| Requirement 13.2 | The same comment made for R 13.1 applies. |
| Requirement 13.3 | The same comment made for R 13.1 applies. |
| Requirement 13.4 | The same comment made for R 13.1 applies. |

| Global Industry Standard on Tailings Management X ISO Standards | |
|---|---|
| **G. I. Standard** | **ISO Standards** |
| PRINCIPLE 14: Prepare for long-term recovery in the event of catastrophic failure. | |
| Requirement 14.1 | When establishing external communications processes (7.4.3/ISO 14001 + ISO 45001; corresponding section in the Tailings Guide: 4.11 Communications), including what to communicate, when to communicate, to whom to communicate, how to communicate, insert in the process(s) public sector agencies and other organizations, including the actions defined in emergency response planning, to mitigate the consequences arising from these situations (8.2/ISO 14001 + ISO 45001; corresponding section in the Tailings Guide: 5.2 Emergency Preparedness). |
| Requirement 14.2 | When critically analyzing, as timely as possible, after the occurrence of a catastrophic failure, the planned response to the previously identified scenario(s), consider the social, economic and environmental impacts caused by the emergency situation (8.2/ISO 14001 + ISO 45001; corresponding section in the Tailings Guide: 5.2 Emergency Preparedness). |
| Requirement 14.3 | When planning and implementing actions to mitigate the consequences arising from emergency situations (8.2/ISO 14001 + ISO 45001; corresponding section in the Tailings Guide: 5.2 Emergency Preparedness) arising from catastrophic failure, involve public agencies and other interested parties in the development and implementation of reconstruction, rehabilitation and recovery plans. |
| Requirement 14.4 | When planning and implementing actions to mitigate the consequences arising from emergency situations (8.2/ISO 14001 + ISO 45001; corresponding section in the Tailings Guide: 5.2 Emergency Preparedness) arising from catastrophic failure, consider, when establishing responsibilities and authorities, the participation of persons affected in the ongoing reconstruction, rehabilitation and rehabilitation works and monitoring activities (5.3/ISO 14001 + ISO 45001; corresponding section in the Tailings Guide: 4.3 Accountability and Responsibility). |
| Requirement 14.5 | When establishing the process(es) for external communications, including who to communicate, what to communicate, when to communicate, to whom to communicate and how to communicate, encompass the public disclosure of post-failure results and adapt these activities according to the results and with feedback received from the parties involved (7.4/ISO 14001 + ISO 45001; corresponding section in Tailings Guide: 4.11 Communications). |
| TOPIC VI: Public Disclosure and Access to Information | |
| PRINCIPLE 15: Publicly disclose and provide access to information about the tailings facility to support public accountability. | |

| Global Industry Standard on Tailings Management X ISO Standards | |
|---|---|
| **G. I. Standard** | **ISO Standards** |
| Requirement 15.1 | Recognize the applicability of the UNGP (and particularly of Principle 21) when determining external and internal issues that are relevant to its purpose and that affect its ability to achieve the intended results of its environmental and OH&S management system (4.1/ISO 14001 + ISO 45001), and also by seeking to understand the needs and expectations of its stakeholders (4.2/ISO 14001 + ISO 45001). Explicitly make this commitment in its policy (5.2/ISO 14001 + ISO 45001; corresponding section in Tailings Guide: 3 - Policy and Commitment), include the UNGP (and particularly of Principle 21) in its compliance obligations (6.1.3/ ISO 14001 + ISO 45001; corresponding section in Tailings Guide: 4.4 - Conformance Management) and periodically assess compliance (9.1.2/ISO 14001 + ISO 45001; corresponding section in Tailings Guide: 6 - Performance Evaluation). When establishing the process(es) for external communications, including who to communicate, what to communicate, when to communicate, to whom to communicate and how to communicate, cover the public disclosure of the content established by Requirement 15.1 of the Standard and the obligation to provide local authorities and emergency services with information from the analysis of breach formation (7.4/ISO 14001 + ISO 45001; corresponding section in the Tailings Guide: 4.11 Communications). |
| Requirement 15.2 | When establishing the process(es) for external communications, including who to communicate, what to communicate, when to communicate, to whom to communicate and how to communicate, define how and when to respond to stakeholder demands (7.4/ISO 14001 + ISO 45001; corresponding section in the Tailings Guide: 4.11 Communications). |
| Requirement 15.3 | By determining external and internal issues that are relevant to its purpose and that affect its ability to achieve the intended results of its environmental and OH&S management system (4.1/ISO 14001 + ISO 45001), and also seeking to understand needs and expectations of its stakeholders (4.2/ISO 14001 + ISO 45001), assume as one of the compliance obligations the commitment to cooperate with plausible global transparency initiatives aimed at creating databases, inventories or other information repositories (5.3 + 6.1.3/ISO 14001 + ISO 45001; corresponding sections in the Tailings Guide: 3 Policy and Commitment +4.4 Conformance Management). |

## 5. CONCLUSION

The recent publication of the Global Industry Standard for Tailings Management prompted some modifications or adjustments to the main MAC reference documents, such as the Tailings Guide "see [2]", but these changes did not have a major impact on the model originally proposed in the article published by authors in the journal Mine Water and Environment entitled 'Integrated Risk Management in Mine Tailings Facility' "see [1]". In a way, however, the Standard induced a different view on the applicability of ISO standards to tailings management, in particular the ISO 9001 standard.

In our previous article, we considered as a differential the use of requirement 8.3 of the ISO 9001:2015 standard, as one of the tools for integrating MAC guides to ISO standards, although the focus was on the design and development of products and services. In line with our purposes, by identifying some works edited by TC 176, the committee responsible for the work on ISO 9001 at ISO, we identified recommendations for using this requirement for process design, as can be seen in the document ISO 9001 Auditing Practices Group - Guidance on: Design and Development Process, "see [13]".

In addition, through the Standard, it was possible to increase the scope of the applicability of ISO 9001, including, in this text, issues associated with the context of the organization, risk mentality and quality plans, which were not previously considered.

Finally, the interpretation of the Standard led us to conclude that its design did not take into account the current models of management systems, making it repetitive in some of the established requirements, and we believe it is appropriate that, in a future revision, the Standard becomes be organized according to the superior structure of Annex SL, used in the ISO standards of management systems and based on the PDCA cycle.

## REFERENCES

1. Ramos Dantés dos Reis G, de Oliveira JC, Abrahão Porto Silva MV. Mint: Integrated Risk Management in Mining Waste Facilities. Mine Water and the Environment (2021) 40:6-15. DOI: 10.1007/s10230-021-00750-w

2. Mining Association of Canada. A Guide to the Management of Tailings Facilities - Version 3.2, March 2021. Available from: MAC-Tailings-Guide-Version-3-2-March-2021.pdf (mining.ca)

3. ISO 14001:2015 Environmental Management Systems — Requirements with Guidance for Use. International Organization for Standardization. Geneva, Switzerland. https://www.iso.org/home.html

4. Global Industry Standard on Tailings Management. 2020. Global Tailings Review. Available from: global-industry-standard_EN.pdf (globaltailingsreview.org)

5. Mining Association of Canada. Developing an Operation, Maintenance, and Surveillance Manual for Tailings and Water Management Facilities - Version 2.1, March 2021. Available from: MAC-OMS-Guide-March-2021.pdf (mining.ca)

6. Mining Association of Canada. A Guide to the Management of Tailings Facilities - Version 3.1, February 2019. Available from: MAC-Tailings-Guide_2019.pdf (mining.ca)

7. Mining Association of Canada. Developing an Operation, Maintenance, and Surveillance Manual for Tailings and Water Management Facilities - Version 2.0, February 2019. Available from: MAC-OMS-Guide_2019.pdf (mining.ca)

8. ISO 9001:2015 Quality Management Systems, Requirements. International Organization for Standardization, Geneva, Switzerland. https://www.iso.org/home.html

9. ISO 45001:2018 Occupational Health and Safety Management Systems, Requirements with Guidance for Use. International Organization for Standardization. Geneva, Switzerland. https://www.iso.org/home.html

10. Equivalency Between Requirements of Towards Sustainable Mining and the Global Industry Standard on Tailings Management - Version date: March 31, 2021 - Available from: Microsoft Word - MAC Assessment of Equivalency between TSM and the Standard - 2021-03-31 (mining.ca)

11. ISO 10005:2018 Quality management — Guidelines for quality plans. https://www.iso.org/home.html

12. Social Accountability International. 2014. International Standard SA8000. https://sa-intl.org

13. ISO 9001 Auditing Practices Group - Guidance on: Design and Development Process. 2016. Microsoft Word - APG-Design&Development2015.doc (iso.org)

## CHAPTER-2

# RADON IN UNDERGROUND MINES

## 1. INTRODUCTION

Radon is a colorless, odorless, and tasteless inert gas. It can only be detected or measured with the help of special detectors. It can travel through cracks of the bedrock, soil, and through groundwater. In underground mines or underground structures, high concentrations of radon may be detected in the absence of adequate ventilation. In underground mines with uranium-bearing mineralization, radium 226 (radium's most stable isotope) is a natural source of radiation. Other isotopes of radon, such as radon 220 and radon 219, also exist naturally; however, because of the small amount and short lifetime, other isotopes are of less concern. Radium 226 decays into radon 222, which in turn decays into its short-lived radioactive daughters in the mine atmosphere. The uranium decay chain can be summarized as shown in Figure 1.

Until the late 1970s, radon and its daughter products were of concern only at uranium mines. A study conducted by Daniels and Schubauer in 2017 shows that the radon exposure varied widely among several working populations, most of whom were employed in industries unrelated to the uranium fuel cycle. With the recent advancement of scientific knowledge, there has been more interest and attention to the hazards in non-uranium mines, underground structures, and residential buildings. In the absence of control measures, occupational exposures outside the uranium fuel cycle (e.g., tourist cave workers, waterworks employees) can exceed those found in most uranium workers [1].

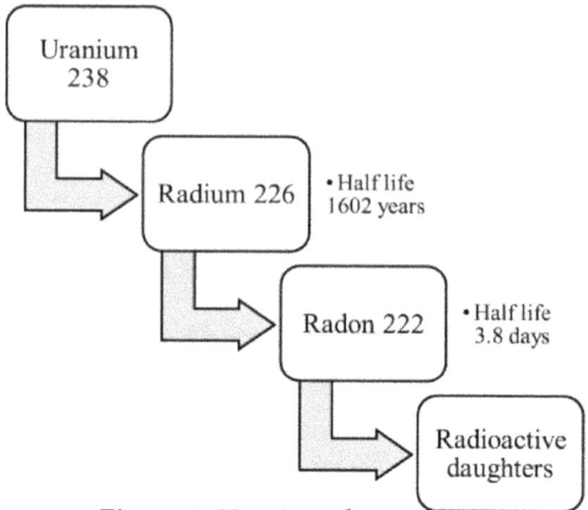


**Figure 1. Uranium decay chain.**

Dehnret [2] reported high radon concentrations in old underground workings in Germany and protective steps taken for miners' safety. Sahu et al. [3] reported the sources of radon, its emanation rate, and measurement techniques, particularly for underground uranium mines. Hu et al. [4] highlighted radon and radon progeny problems in Chinese uranium mines. In the United States, radon has been listed as the second major cause of lung cancer after tobacco [5]. A study of underground miners shows that 40% of lung cancer deaths may be due to radon progeny exposure [6]. MSHA has regulations for radon concentration in underground mines and sampling procedures depending on the concentration.

Considering the short half-life and the high radiation dose of radon gas and its daughter products, its mitigation in the underground environment becomes very important. In the absence of mitigation techniques, both the uranium and non-uranium mines (with uranium mineralization in the orebody) pose a serious threat to the personnel working in the underground environment.

Ventilation plays a significant role by supplying fresh air and removing the contaminated air from the working areas, thereby minimizing the radon concentrations in the mine environment. In addition, an appropriate mining method and well-designed mining sequence can also help control radon gas in the mine atmosphere [4]. In this chapter, the different radon mitigation methods that are specific to the underground mining operations are discussed.

## 2. SOURCES OF RADON

Radium 226 decays into radon 222, which in turn decays into its short-lived radioactive daughters in the mine atmosphere. Common sources of radon emissions in underground mines are summarized in Table 1.

**Table 1. Common sources of radon in underground uranium mines [3].**

| Sources | Remarks |
|---|---|
| Mine walls | In low/medium ore grades, porosity and micro-fractures are dominant factors affecting the rate of radon gas emanation. |
| Broken ore | Fragmented ore provides a source of higher radon emanation due to the increased exposed surface area. |
| Backfill tailings | Radon emanation rate increases with increasing water content up to a certain saturation level, and beyond the saturation level, it decreases with the increase in water content. |
| Mine water | Mine water carries radon from the mineralized rocks to mine openings and transports it to a considerable distance in the mine galleries. |

## 3. RADON MONITORING

The concentration of radon gas is measured in units of picocuries per liter (pCi/L) or becquerels per cubic meter (Bq/m$^3$) of ambient air. Due to difficulties in measuring radon gas concentration, potential alpha particles per liter of air are usually measured. The ratio of all the short-lived radon daughters' activity to the parent radon gas activity is called the equilibrium factor. The equilibrium factor is 1 when both are equal. Radon daughter activities are usually less than the radon activity, and hence, the equilibrium factor is generally less than 1. In artificially ventilated scenarios such as underground mines, the equilibrium factor is in the range of 0.4 to 0.5.

In the United States, radioactivity for radon decay products is measured in terms of Working Level (WL). A WL is defined as the concentration of short-lived radon daughters, representing 1.3 × 105 MeV of potential alpha particle energy while decaying to the stable Pb-210. The worker's prolonged exposure to radon daughters is expressed in Working Level Months (WLM). One WLM is equivalent to 1 WL exposure for 170 hours.

In underground mines as per the Mine Safety and Health Administration (MSHA) regulations, personnel shall not be exposed to air containing concentrations of radon daughters exceeding 1.0 WL. No person shall be permitted to receive exposure over 4 WLM (Working Level Months) in any calendar year. In all mines, at least one sample must be taken in exhaust mine air by a competent person to determine whether concentrations of radon daughters are present [7]. Table 2 provides the radon sampling frequency for uranium and non-uranium mines and households. Gamma radiation surveys shall be conducted annually in all underground mines where radioactive ores are mined. Gamma radiation dosimeters shall be provided to all personnel working in the area where gamma radiation exceeds 2.0 milliroentgens; annual individual gamma radiation exposure shall not exceed 5 Roentgen Equivalent Man [7].

**Table 2. Radon daughter exposure monitoring [7].**

| Type of mine | Radon daughter concentration level (a) | Frequency of monitoring |
|---|---|---|
| Uranium mine | a > 0.1 WL | Radon daughter concentration shall be determined at least every 2 weeks at random times in all working areas. |
| | a > 0.3 WL | Radon daughter concentration shall be determined weekly in that area until the concentration reaches 0.3 WL or less for 5 consecutive weeks. |
| | a < 0.1 WL (exhaust mine air sample) | Radon daughter concentration shall be determined by taking at least one sample in the exhaust mine air monthly. |
| Non-uranium mine | 0.1 WL < a < 0.3 WL | Radon daughter concentration shall be determined at least every 3 months at random times until the concentration is below 0.1 WL in that area and annually thereafter. |
| | a > 0.3 WL | Radon daughter concentration shall be determined at least weekly in that area until the concentration drops to 0.3 WL or less for 5 consecutive weeks. |
| | a < 0.1 WL (exhaust mine air sample) | No further exhaust mine air sampling is required. |
| Houses | a > 0.04 WL (equilibrium factor of 1) | The EPA (Environmental Protection Agency) guidelines recommend the installation of radon mitigation systems. |

## 4. MEASUREMENT TECHNIQUES

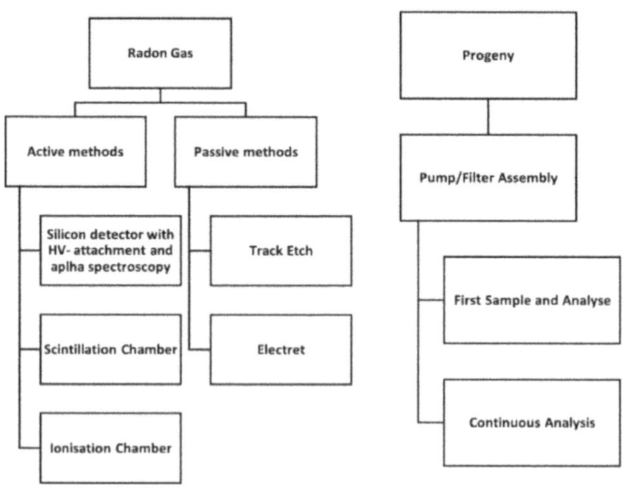


**Figure 2. Radon gas and daughter (progeny) product measurement methods [8].**

The measurement techniques for radon can be classified based on a) whether the technique measures radon gas222 or its daughter products, b) time resolution, and c) radioactive detection of the type of emission resulting from radioactive decay—alpha, beta, gamma radiation. The commonly used methods for measuring radon and its daughter products are shown in Figure 2.

Active methods require electric power for measurements, whereas passive methods require no power. Measurements can be performed at specified intervals and data can be stored and read directly with active methods. In contrast, in the case of passive methods, integrated exposure concentrations can be measured, and data analysis requires special equipment. Time resolution techniques can be classified into three types, as shown in Figure 3.

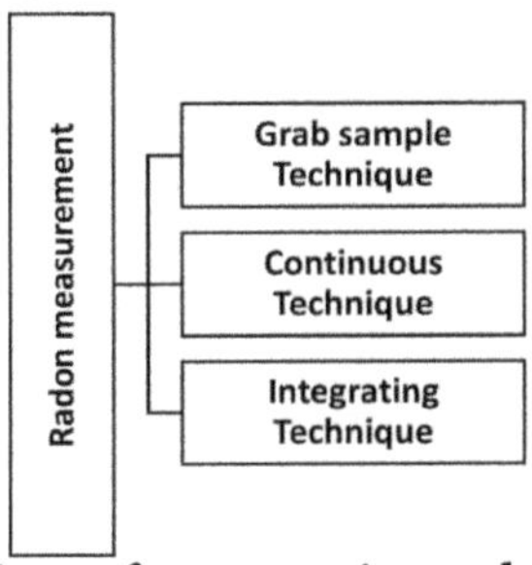


**Figure 3. Time resolution techniques for measuring radon and its daughter products** [8].

Grab sample technique: This technique involves measurement of 222Rn in a discrete sample of air collected over a very short period of time (compared with the mean life of 222 Rn at a single point). Radon measuring instruments such as RAD7 can be used to measure 222 Rn and its daughters. When it is used in "sniffer" mode, in which radon is typically present with minimal growth of its progeny, a large number of measurements can be taken in a relatively less period of time [8].

Grab sampling technique for radon progeny involves drawing a known air volume through a filter and counting the alpha activity during or following the sampling. Usually, a known volume of air is drawn through a filter using an air sampling pump for very short sampling periods usually 5 minutes. Filters are counted for alpha particle emissions during mathematically determined periods after the sample is collected. There are three main methods available for counting these particles, namely the Kusnetz method, where the filter is counted once, and the modified Tsivoglou method, where the filter is counted three times to measure the decay. Another method, named the Rolle method, is quite popular in Canadian mines. It is similar to Kusnetz method but is more rapid, and the procedure differs only in the timing of filter counting after sample collection. Figure 4 shows one of the MSHA recommended instruments for sampling radon progeny that works based on the Kusnetz method.

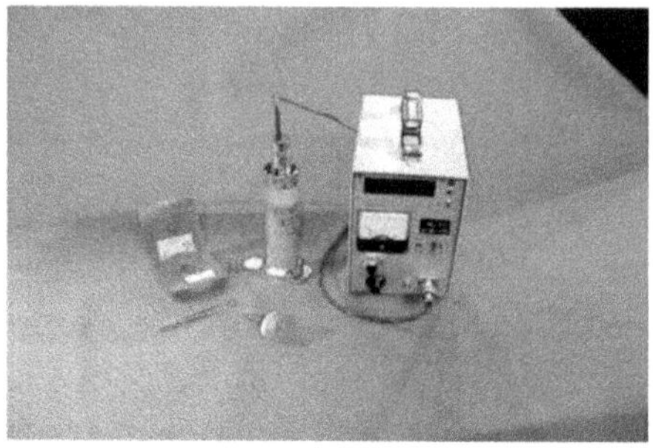

**Figure 4. Ludlum 2000 with accessories.**

Continuous technique: This technique provides time series concentrations of 222 Rnin air samples; in this method, sampling and counting are performed simultaneously. Most of the continuous monitors are portable, and nearly all of those are designed to detect alpha radiation (by an ionization chamber, gross alpha counting, or alpha spectrometry). Specific ionization and scintillation chambers are shown in Figures 5 and 6, respectively.

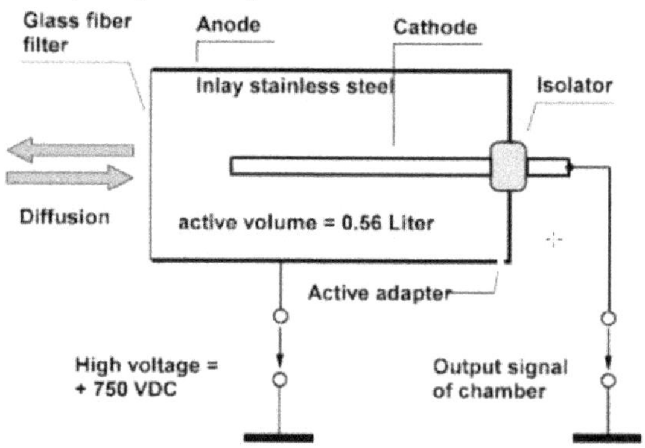


**Figure 5. Schematic diagram of an ionization chamber [9].**

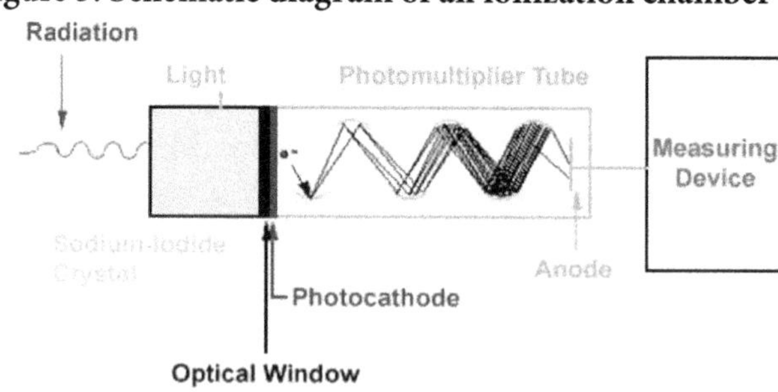


**Figure 6. A typical scintillation detector [10].**

Integrating technique: This technique provides the integrated concentration over a certain period of time. Such measurements are used to determine monthly or average 222 Rn. The passive detectors, which are expensive, are examples of integrating techniques [8].

Apart from measuring alpha particles during the decay of 222 Rn, radon concentrations are determined by measuring the beta activity during the decay of $^{214}$Pb and $^{214}$Bi by assuming secular equilibrium between 222 Rn and its progeny in the air. The beta activity is assayed with plastic scintillators mounted on photomultiplier tubes or the filter paper can be counted in a beta counter with the appropriate use of absorber film. Gamma spectrometry can also be used to determine radon concentrations by measuring the gamma activity during the decay of $^{214}$Pb and $^{214}$Bi.

## 5. PREDICTION TECHNIQUES

There are a few traditional approaches for predicting radon flux such as uninterrupted short-term monitoring to represent radon concentration over an extended period and laboratory investigations. These methods do not apply to all cases. Recently, Kayode et al. [11] developed an approach for predicting radon flux from fractured rocks, a discrete fracture network (DFN) model that can predict radon transport through fractures considering diffusion, advection, and radon generation with radon decay.

## 6. MITIGATION METHODS

Some of the important techniques to mitigate radon gas in underground mines are discussed below.

### 6.1 Sealant coating

The major sources of radon gas in non-uranium underground mines (with uranium mineralization) are the drift walls, floor, and roof. Shotcreting or applying radon sealants to the walls and roof effectively minimizes radon gas emissions into the mine atmosphere. The effectiveness of sealant coating in controlling the radon gas depends on the size of the capillary in which the acrylics (contained in the sealants) form barriers to prevent the escape of radon gas [12].

### 6.2 Bulkhead

Isolation of mined-out areas using bulkheads is one of the popular methods of controlling radon gas emissions into the active mine workings. Bulkheads prevent the contaminated air of mined-out regions containing high radon gas concentrations from mixing with the fresh air. Loring and others [13] reported that styrofoam and shotcrete/concrete bulkheads are used in a panel cave mine for a temporary and permanent sealing purpose, respectively. These bulkheads are installed at a 60-degree layback angle of the planned cave area to minimize damage to the bulkheads during the caving process. As the bulkheads are not leak proof, bleeder pipes creating a negative pressure inside the bulkhead area and connected to the main exhaust ventilation system can also be an effective measure [13]. Figure 7 shows the typical designs of bulkheads.

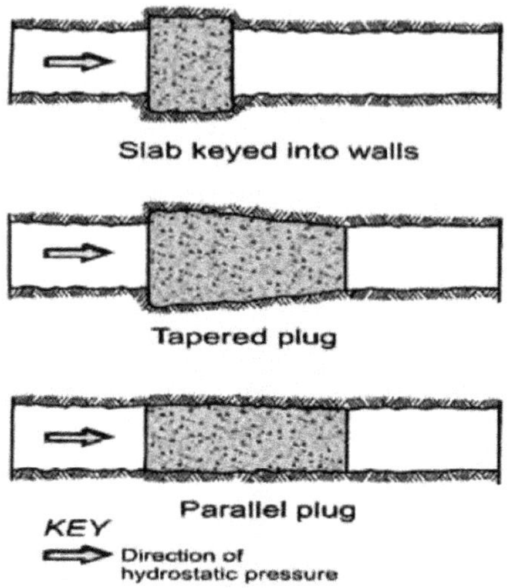


**Figure 7. Typical designs of bulkheads [14].**

## 6.3 Mine pressurization by mechanical ventilation

Mine pressurization can also play an important role in controlling radon gas emissions in underground workings, especially near-working faces. In a forced ventilation system, which is considered quite effective for control of radon gas in the mine environment, fresh air is pumped into underground workings with the help of fans; this follows the path of least resistance taking the contaminants along with it and out of the mine. In the forced ventilation system, the direction of seepage is toward the rock surface, causing less radon to be released.

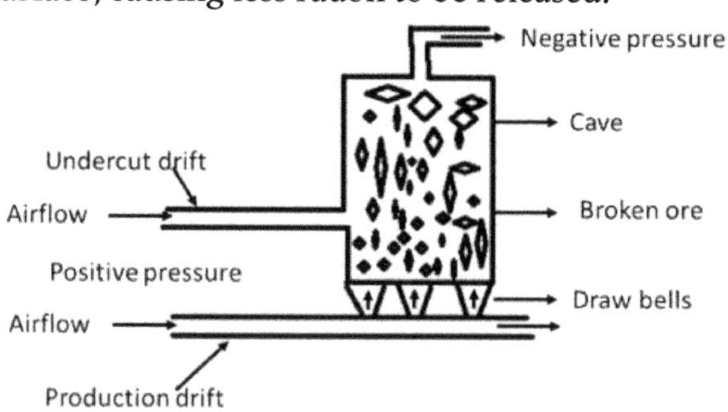


**Figure 8. A typical cave ventilation system in a panel/block cave mine.**

Studies [13] have shown that a successful blend of positive and negative pressure systems in a panel cave mine effectively reduces the radon gas concentrations at the production level. Negative pressure on the cave top minimizes the escape of radon gas from the broken ore to the production levels. Positive pressurization in the undercut levels also reduces the escape of radon gas into the working areas. Mine pressurization greatly depends on the porosity and permeability of the broken rock/ore for its effectiveness in controlling radon concentrations in the underground environment. Figure 8 shows a typical cave ventilation system in a block/panel cave mine.

Computational fluid dynamic (CFD) simulation studies by Kayode et al. [15] showed the effect of an undercut ventilation system on radon gas distribution in the production drift and cave. It was observed that the air flowing through the cave transports some of the radon generated within the cave into the production drift, increasing the production drift concentration. However, in the absence of undercut ventilation, radon concentration decreases significantly within the production drift but increases inside the cave. The radon growth through the production drifts is nonlinear due to differences in the source of radon. Maintaining a negative pressure on top of the cave and undercut pressurization significantly reduces radon concentration in the production drift. However, maintaining a negative pressure on top of the cave is not very effective without undercut pressurization. An increase in air volume flow rate reduces radon concentration through the production drifts; based on the drift configuration for radon source, different empirical relationships relate airflow and working level for each drift.

The knowledge of airflow behavior and system characteristics is vital in ventilating the block cave operations and reducing radon concentrations. Using field observations and laboratory experiments (scale model studies), Pan [16] investigated the effects of porosity, material size combinations, additional fan, ventilation devices, and undercut structure on cave airflow resistance. The study found that the cave airflow resistance increases with a decrease in porosity and particle size, additional fan operation, regulator installation, and air gap reduction in the undercut drifts. An additional fan operation can contribute extra total airflow through the system, but regulators will not increase the total airflow in the system; the air gap observed in the undercut drifts might lead to less airflow through the production drifts.

Rahul et al. [17] investigated the effect of changes in the bulk porosity of the broken rock on the cave airflow resistance using the computational fluid dynamics (CFD) approach. This study reveals that porosity plays a vital role in changing the resistance offered by the broken rock to the airflow leaking into the cave. The airflow resistance increases as the porosity of the broken rock pile decreases. The resistance of the block cave mine changes dynamically with the bulk porosity of the broken rock.

Jha et al. [18] studied the utility of different fans in reducing the radon concentration within the drifts using a physical scale model and CFD simulations. It was observed that the combination of main and cave fan is optimal in minimizing the gas concentration within the drifts. Observations of the scaled model also show that a fully operational cave fan significantly reduced the gas concentrations within the drifts. The study suggests using main fan in conjunction with a cave fan to minimize the gas concentration within the drift.

Erogul et al. [19] investigated the impact of air gap geometries on cave resistance and radon emissions using the CFD approach. This study reported an interesting airflow behavior within the air gap zone; initially, the airflow resistance increases up to a certain height and drops as the air gap height increases further.

## 6.4 Radon adsorption on activated carbon

Radon gas can be adsorbed by activated carbon, commonly known as a charcoal bed. The capacity of a charcoal bed to adsorb radon depends on the temperature and moisture content of the incoming air. Karunakara et al. [20] demonstrated that a coconut shell-based activated charcoal system can be used for designing effective and reliable radon mitigation systems. Degassing properties of the charcoal indicate its reusability potential. Adsorption of radon by activated carbon can also significantly reduce ventilation air requirements. Figure 9 shows the experimental setup for studying radon adsorption in a charcoal bed.

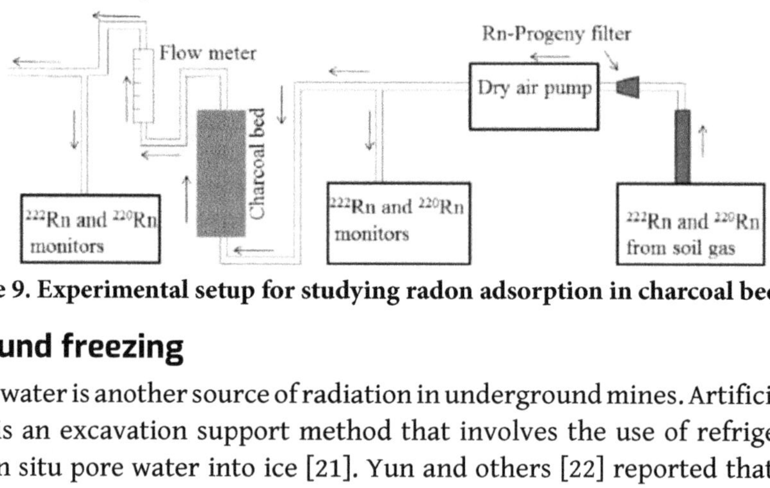


**Figure 9. Experimental setup for studying radon adsorption in charcoal bed** [20].

## 6.5 Ground freezing

Mine water is another source of radiation in underground mines. Artificial ground freezing is an excavation support method that involves the use of refrigeration to convert in situ pore water into ice [21]. Yun and others [22] reported that artificial ground freezing, to form a frozen curtain between the water-bearing sandstone and the ore body at McArthur River mining operation in Canada, helped prevent high-pressure, radon-bearing water from entering into the mine workings. Figure 10 shows a schematic of a typical ground freezing technique.

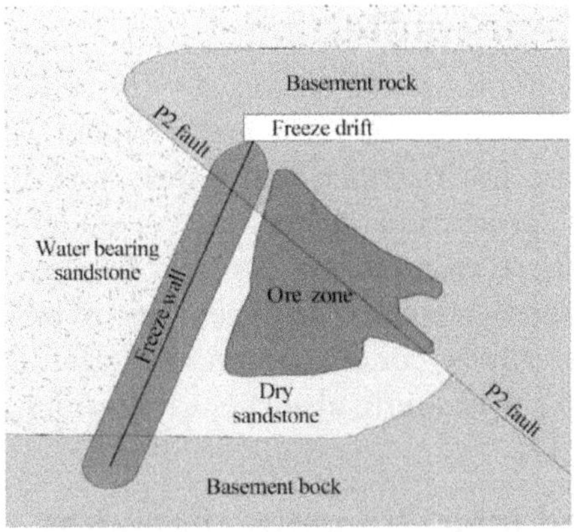


**Figure 10. Typical freeze wall insulation [22].**

## 6.6 Choice of mining method and ventilation system

The choice of mining method and the type of mechanical ventilation significantly impact the control of radon gas emissions into the underground mine atmosphere. Table 3 provides the type(s) of effective ventilation systems to be used for various mining methods for controlling radon emissions in underground mines.

**Table 3. Mining methods and ventilation types [4].**

| Mining methods | Mining types | Ventilation types |
|---|---|---|
| Cut and fill | Dry packing | Both forced and exhaust ventilation systems can be used. |
| | Hydraulic flushing | Both forced and exhaust ventilation systems can be used. Measures should be taken to control the release of radon from the seeping water. |
| Open stope | Shrinkage stoping | Downward forced ventilation can be used here to prohibit the release of radon. The air inlets are installed on the upper parts of the deposits. Local fans are installed where the amount of air introduced is inadequate. |
| | Breast stoping | Both forced, and exhaust ventilation systems can be used. However, the amount of air required at working faces increases as the number of mined-out areas increases. |
| Caving | Slicing | Forced ventilation and local fans should be used. |
| | Sublevel caving | Forced ventilation should be used. |
| | Block/panel caving | The combination of forced and exhaust ventilation systems. |

### 6.7 Personal respiratory protection

It is an indirect mitigation technique. In the environments where radon daughters' concentration exceeds 1.0 WL, miners should wear respirators approved by the National Institute for Occupational Safety and Health (NIOSH). The use of personal respiratory protection against radon daughters must be limited to temporary situations where engineering controls have not been developed or for maintenance and investigative work. For exposures up to 10 WL, proper filter-type respirators are available where concentrations of radon daughters exceed 10 WL, air devices, or face masks containing absorbent material capable of removing both radon and its daughters [7].

### 6.8 Dust control and miscellaneous measures

Airborne radon progeny (daughters) has an electrical charge associated with it; so, it can be attached to dust and other particles, which can be inhaled into the lungs of mineworkers who work in the dusty environment, particularly near the working faces. Some of the best practices that can help control radon levels in the mine atmosphere include implementing appropriate dust control measures by using air filters, measuring the performance of blasting practices at the end of the shift, and minimization of main/auxiliary fan shutdowns. Abd et al. [23] showed that the radon diffusion coefficient and diffusion length reduce significantly with increased water saturation of the material. This phenomenon can be used to reduce the rate of radon diffusion into the mine air.

## 7. SUMMARY

Several radon mitigation techniques, particularly bulkheads and sealant coating, are being successfully used in the underground mines in the United States. Activated charcoal bed and oxidizing agents are also viable options for treating the contaminated air locally, especially at the difficult mine working faces. The feasibility of the application of these agents in the challenging mine environment needs a greater in-depth study.

Even though sealant coatings and bulkheads effectively control radon gas concentrations in the active working areas, improvements to reduce the costs and design of application of sealants and bulkheads can be performed.

Activated charcoal beds present a viable option for radon mitigation, but a pilot study in the mine environment can be more helpful to understand their applicability and effectiveness.

The use of strong oxidizing agents to remove radon from the contaminated mine air can also be a possibility. However, high humidity and temperature conditions in the mine atmosphere might limit the applicability of a corrosive oxidizing agent inside the mine.

## REFERENCES

1. Daniels RD, Schubauer-Berigan MK. Radon in US workplaces: A review. Radiation Protection Dosimetry. 2017;176(3):278-286. DOI: 10.1093/rpd/ncx007

2. Dehnert J. Radon exposures of miners at small underground construction sites in old mining. Health Physics. 2020;118(1). DOI: 10.1097/HP.0000000000001117

3. Sahu P, Panigrahi DC, Mishra DP. Sources of radon and its measurement techniques in underground uranium mines – an overview. Journal of Sustainable Mining. 2014;13(3):11-18. DOI: 10.7424/jsm140303

4. Hu P, Li X. Analysis of radon reduction and ventilation systems in uranium mines in China. Journal of Radiological Protection. 2012;32(3):289-300. DOI: 10.1088/0952-4746/32/3/289

5. Miller KJ, Coffey MA. Radon and you: Promoting public awareness of radon in Montana's air and groundwater. Montana Bureau of Mines and Geology. 1998

6. Lubin JH et al. Lung cancer in radon-exposed miners and estimation of risk from indoor exposure. JNCI Journal of the National Cancer Institute. 1995;87(11):817-827. DOI: 10.1093/jnci/87.11.817

7. MSHA, "Radiation—Underground Only: 30 CFR §§ 57.5037 through 57.5047." Available from: https://www.ecfr.gov/cgi-bin/text-idx?SID=4d0ee9eb9bdc6f357eb5e74f99e7d7e1&pitd=20200722&node=sg30.1.57_15015.sg16&rgn=div7 [Accessed: October 23, 2020]

8. Baskaran M. Radon measurement techniques. In: Radon: A Tracer for Geological, Geophysical and Geochemical Studies. Cham: Springer International Publishing; 2016. pp. 15-35

9. Nagaraja K, Kumar KC, Pramodh B, Prasad TR, Rao TN, Ratnam MV. Temporal variation of radioactivity at NARL, Gadanki. International Journal of Advanced Research in Science and Technology. 2015;4(5):469-471

10. Equipco, "Introduction to Radiation Detectors." Availabe from: http://www.equipcoservices.com/support/tutorials/introduction-to-radiation-monitors/ [Accessed: October 23, 2020]

11. Ajayi KM, Shahbazi K, Tukkaraja P, Katzenstein K. A discrete model for prediction of radon flux from fractured rocks. Journal of Rock Mechanics and Geotechnical Engineering. 2018;10(5):879-892. DOI: 10.1016/j.jrmge.2018.02.009

12. Kown BT, Van der Mast VC and Ludwig KL, "Technical Assessment of Radon-222 Control Technology for Underground Uranium Mines. Technical Note." 1980. [Online]. Available from: https://inis.iaea.org/search/search.aspx?orig_q=RN:12611409 [Accessed: November 07, 2020]

13. Loring DM, Meisburger EP IV. A discussion of radon and the mitigation strategy at the Henderson Mine. In: 13th North American Mine Ventilation Symposium. 2010. pp. 73-78

14. Harteis SP, Dolinar DR. Water and slurry bulkheads in underground coal mines: Design, monitoring, and safety concerns. Mining and Engineering. 2006;58:41 Available from: https://me.smenet.org/abstract.cfm?articleID=1328&page=41

15. Ajayi K, Shahbazi K, Tukkaraja P, Katzenstein K. Numerical investigation of the effectiveness of radon control measures in cave mines. International Journal of Mining Science and Technology. 2019;29(3):469-475. DOI: 10.1016/j.ijmst.2018.07.006

16. Pan Y, Tukkaraja P. Experimental Investigation of Airflow Behavior in a Block Cave Mine. Journal of Mineral and Material Science. 2020;1(4). Available from: https://www.corpuspublishers.com/assets/articles/article-pdf-139.pdf

17. Bhargava R, Tukkaraja P, Adhikari A, Sridharan SJ, Vytla VVS. Airflow characteristic curves for a mature block cave mine. In: Mine Ventilation. London: CRC Press; 2021. pp. 56-64

18. Jha A, Pan Y, Tukkaraja P, Sridharan SJ. Scale model investigation of ventilation parameters in a block cave mine. In: Mine Ventilation. London: CRC Press; 2021. pp. 556-562

19. Erogul D, Ajayi K, Tukkaraja P, Shahbazi K, Katzenstein K and Loring D, Effect of Airgap Geometry on Immature Panel Cave Resistance. 2017

20. Karunakara N et al. Evaluation of radon adsorption characteristics of a coconut shell-based activated charcoal system for radon and thoron removal applications. Journal of Environmental Radioactivity. 2015;142:87-95. DOI: 10.1016/j.jenvrad.2014.12.017

21. Yun X, McNamara K, Murdock G. Geotechnical challenges and strategies at McArthur River operation. Procedia Engineering. 2011;26:1603-1613. DOI: 10.1016/j.proeng.2011.11.2344

22. Yun X, Tang B, Greg M, Brian M, Brian M. Radon bearing water protection in underground uranium mining – A case study. International Journal of Mining Science and Technology. 2017;27(4):599-603. DOI: 10.1016/j.ijmst.2017.05.013

23. Abd Ali FS, Mahdi KH, Jawad EA. Humidity effect on diffusion and length coefficient of radon in soil and building materials. Energy Procedia. 2019;157. DOI: 10.1016/j.egypro.2018.11.203

CHAPTER-3

# INTELLIGENT MINE PERIPHERY SURVEILLANCE USING MICROWAVE RADAR

## 1. INTRODUCTION

One of the crucial challenges of the mining sector is the prevention of financial loss due to illegal mining and mineral theft through an unauthorized path. This loss inflicts severe assault on the financial health of both the mining industry and government. Safety and security lapse is another worrisome aspect of this sector. Mining production highly depends on the safe interface between mining machinery and human being. Their proper and optimum utilization helps to maximize the production and productivity of a mine. Hence, protecting both these elements from safety and security hazards is a matter of immense importance. This calls for strict vigilance in the mine periphery to prevent unauthorized intrusion of any vehicle or person. Taking due cognizance of the stated situation, an intelligent mine periphery surveillance system (PSS) has been developed by CSIR-Central Institute of Mining and Fuel Research, Dhanbad, India, as a solution to these problems. Real-time detection of any suspected element or unwanted incidence by microwave radar and CCTV footage of the intruder is seen on the monitor, prompt alerting security personnel and thereby helps to avert untoward incidences by taking immediate action.

In recent years, microwave frequency modulated continuous wave (FMCW) radar has grown with demand in various domains. FMCW radars are found to realize the signals generated and processed in real-time for high-performance vehicle safety systems. The radar system has been employed in many safety applications, such as adaptive cruise control, crash mitigation and pre-crash sensing, to name a few. The FMCW radar can effectively detect moving and stationary target objects and are presently being marketed as safety systems for high-performance automotive applications as described by different authors [1, 2, 3, 4, 5]. This can also be applied in several other fields such as automotive applications, short-range radars for parking, traffic monitoring, anti-collision warning, adaptive cruise control, security, collision avoidance, defense, shipping, security, traffic, and medical imaging on under indoor and outdoor environments. The microwave FMCW radar security system is used for vehicle detection with a long detection range and high reliability, irrespective of environmental factors such as foggy weather, rain, dusty conditions etc. The range and velocity information of distinct targets may be measured concurrently in a short time for automotive safety applications. Various radar systems in use have been reported by several authors [6, 7, 8, 9, 10, 11, 12, 13, 14].

Unauthorized intrusion and illegal transportation of coal and minerals are significant issues about opencast mining industries. For example, in Tirap Opencast Mine, coal theft is widespread. The intrusion of illegal persons in this opencast mine is pervasive, leading to the unlawful transportation of coal and theft of mineral/coal and small mining equipment from the mine. Thus, there is a loss of revenue due to the above illegal activities, which is a grave concern and needs attention. Coal production of the mine largely depends on the safe interface between mining equipment and human beings. Protecting the assets and personnel against any possible hazards and optimizing their application by real-time location monitoring and control will improve mine safety and lead to increased productivity. The areas must be protected against unauthorized intrusion to manage the potential hazards in the sensitive areas inside the mining premises. Therefore, anintelligent mine periphery surveillance system has been developed and deployed in the mine for the first time. The developed system played a significant role in checking out these problems as this industrialized device could monitor the area efficiently.

Besides the above, the environmental conditions in opencast mining areas are dusty, full of smoke, foggy during the winter, and heavy rain during the rainy season. Thus, it raises a big challenge. These areas have different issues like soil erosion and dust coming from coal particles, leading to air and water pollution. These impact the environment and thus impact biodiversity as well. In recent years, the accumulation rate of waste dumps increased gradually, resulting in the great height of the waste dumps having a minimum ground cover area that created a danger to the environment. Illegal mining in the area marked with uneven slopes with an open pit is hazardous as it makes a warning bell for the human being and other animals living in the area. Open-pit slopes create disadvantages for mining industries as mining machinery cannot be used smoothly. There is always a chance of damage to machines due to land conditions created due to illegal mining as there is a lack of proper planning. Thus, there is a need for continuous monitoring and surveillance in that area which is a big challenge as the atmosphere in that area is full of dust and bad weather. Microwave FMCW radar is very suitable in these environmental conditions for surveillance and monitoring. It does not impact dust, vapor or waste particles suspended in the air, foggy weather, and rain. FMCW radar signals processing is good at different weather conditions such as humidity, snow, fog, rain, and dusty conditions. The microwave FMCW radar security system, is used for vehicle detection with a long detection range and high reliability. The objective of this experimental work is to showcase the impact of using our real-time monitoring and tracking, sensing and management system using surveillance microwave FMCW radar for controlling mineral overloading, coal theft and illicit mineral transportation from the mines, improving mine safety, security, and productivity management.

Mining activities form an essential part of the financial increase of any nation endowed with mineral resources. Unauthorized mining, vehicle overloading, adequate transparencies during mineral transportation, enhancement of equipment optimization and production scheduling, downtime of shovels and dumpers, etc., are some of the main concerns in opencast mines. As an obvious outcome of searching for proper solutions to these problems, recent decades have witnessed wide applications of communication, sensing, surveillance, and vehicle detection technologies.

In this field of research and investigation, the authors have put a pretty good step forward by developing a "microwave radar-based periphery surveillance system" using the advanced vehicle tracking and surveillance technologies.

In this chapter, the FMCW radar sensor is briefly discussed. The FMCW radar is the best for accurately measuring the distance of multiple targets and identifying the intruder using a pan-tilt-zoom (PTZ) camera. The principles of FMCW radar for measuring distance change and detection of a target is presented in this paper. Its application for monitoring of transportation of coal at the Tirap coal mine in Assam, India, has been discussed. In this system, a real-time object detection technique is used to provide a clear multilevel description of the environment around it for constant vigilance. The PSS has been developed using an FMCW radar sensor to maintain high accuracy with precise range information, which helps stop illicit coal transportation through the mine lease boundary. Based on this auto-generated information, the user is free to mark any suspicious object and raise the alarm. The experimental results show that the system can accurately measure the distance of 400 m approximately along the mine periphery. The objective of the field experiment is to showcase the impact of using real-time monitoring and tracking, sensing and management system in which a developed system is used for detecting mineral overloading, coal theft and illicit mineral transportation from the mines and to improve mine safety and security. A digital oscilloscope has been used to analyze the actual performance of the FMCW radar system, and the output waveform is the raw data received from radar.

## 2. RELATED WORKS

The development of a periphery surveillance system for detecting an unauthorized vehicle or target object has gained popularity in the mining industry in recent times. Choudhary and EI-Nasr [15] have developed an automatic target recognition system using a remote sensing system and radar sensor. The system detects the target by reflecting an electromagnetic signal between the radar sensor and the target object. Ibanez et al. and Ganapathi et al. [16, 17] have developed a sensor-based transportation system for traffic control and vehicle tracking. The system addresses the high level of traffic control issues and improves road safety by tracking a vehicle in the respected area. Mimbela and Klein [18] have developed a vehicular detection and surveillance system. The system enhances the speed of monitoring, vehicles classification and speed of vehicle tracking. Yulianto [19] has developed a vehicle actuated control (VAC) and adaptive traffic signal control (ATSC) system for decreasing traffic congestion, object detection time and air pollution. Santi et al. [20] have developed a GNSS based multi-static radar for the detection and localization of vessels at sea. This system detects the location of a vessel in seawater. Thiel et al. [21] have carried out a case study for a car periphery supervision system for the production line in the automobile industry. Chaulya and Prasad [22] have developed a sensor-based monitoring system for hazardous areas in mines. A wireless sensor network (WSN) has been used for monitoring mine hazard parameters. Kassim et al. [23] have evaluated the performance of an acceleration sensor of the vehicle security system for movement detection. The system determines acceleration for a car using the acceleration sensor and detects the location of a vehicle using the GPS receiver. However, the said periphery surveillance systems do not have the proper architecture for detecting an intruder in real-time for controlling illegal mineral transportation and intrusion through the vast opencast mine periphery. The existing solutions do not have appropriate identification facilities to recognize the intruder, such as integrated CCTV cameras and analysis software. Further, these systems have no provision for providing automatic audio-visual warning at the intrusion site and control room and storing intrusion events with video footage for taking necessary action against the intruders with the recorded proof of the intrusion.

Considering the above limitations of the existing surveillance systems, an intelligent periphery surveillance system has been developed by CSIR-Central Institute of Mining and Fuel Research, Dhanbad, India, by integrating radar, CCTV camera, WSN, display and warning devices with application software. The main advantage of the proposed periphery surveillance system is that it detects the exact location of an intruder at the mine periphery in real-time. The system also identifies the intruder by auto-focusing a PTZ camera to the intrusion location during the incident, which detects the intruders in real-time while observing the control room. If the system detects an intrusion, it automatically gives an audio-visual warning at the intrusion site where the radar is installed as well as in the control room. The system has the facility to record the intrusion data as well as video footage with timestamp events in the form of a log for taking necessary legal action against the intruder with the proof of the intrusion. Further, the system has a long-range detection capability covering around 400 m distance with integration facility using a dynamic WSN for deploying multiple numbers of sub-systems to protect the long periphery of an opencast mine for controlling illegal mineral transportation from the mine as well as preventing the unauthorized entry into the mine. The system has suitable integrated software that adequately handles the radar and wireless devices, display unit, and warning devices.

## 3. PERIPHERY SURVEILLANCE SYSTEM

The main components of the developed periphery surveillance system (PSS) are an FMCW radar, a PTZ CCTV camera, a wireless sensor network (WSN), a fast graphical processing unit (GPU) and a display unit.

### 3.1 FMCW radar

The microwave radar sensor operates in FMCW mode in the industrial, scientific and medical (ISM) K band of the transmit frequencies of 24.00 to 24.25 GHz. For short and long-range applications, the radar sensor measures the distance and displacement of a static or slow-moving target object [9, 10, 11, 12, 13, 14]. The radar system consists of transmitting and receiving antenna; receiver consists of allowing noise amplifier (LNA) and in-phase/quadrature (I/Q) mixer, amplifier, a band-pass filter (BPF), two analog-to-digital (A/D) converters, a digital-to-analog (D/A) converter, and a digital signal processor (DSP). The output power of the radar front end is 16 dBm.

### 3.2 PTZ camera

The FMCW radar is combined with the commercial PTZ camera. This high-resolution network camera is powered over the Ethernet and provides PTZ capability.

The PTZ camera has been installed at mines at about 12 m height, with the radar front end covering the observation area. When operating in tracking mode, the PTZ camera observes the complete area and looks for sudden changes in the data stream. As soon as an intruder is detected, the camera switches to auto-focus mode. The camera zooms into the scene (the zoom factor depends on the target distance) and follows the intruder across the monitored area. During this time, high-resolution images of the target are produced, which can be used for assortment and recognition reasons. Therefore, a background image is intended and continuously updated by the system, similar to radar detection. The investigation of visual data was performed using the application software developed.

## 3.3 Wireless sensor network

Using radio signals, communication can be done in a self-configuring network of tiny sensor nodes called a wireless sensor network. To sense, monitor and understand the physical world around us, a wireless sensor network (WSN) is needed to be deployed in large quantities. It is a subject of high prospective technology, which has been successfully implemented and tested in a real-time scenario and is practically deployed for many applications in different areas. Its real-time application is capable of monitoring, responding immediately to user input or controlling an external environment. Sensors play an essential role in connecting the external environment to the computer system.

## 3.4 Graphics processing unit

The graphic processing unit (GPU) is preferred over the central processing unit (CPU) as it has unique features of computational display operations, which are faster than the CPU. Thus, the graphical presentation of the data can be easily understood through it. The GPU devices have more active threads than existing computer resources. Radar signal processing (RSP) represents a complex task that involves advanced signal processing techniques and intense computational efforts. The computational load of modern radar signal processors is more complex. In most applications, real-time radar data processing is required with the constraints of space ever haunting. The gamut of radar signal processor hardware ranges from general-purpose hardware like PC, workstations or mainframes, and application-specific hardware such as multi-core processors to reconfigurable computing platforms such as field-programmable gate arrays (FPGA). Radar signal processing is a data-parallel operation that also benefits from parallel processing architectures. The most promising of all high-performance computational architectures is the GPU, which can leverage hardware multithreading capabilities and single instruction multiple data (SIMD) or single instruction multiple threads (SIMT) execution schemes leading to incredible levels of performance on data-parallel based applications.

### 3.5 Advantages of periphery surveillance system

This developed PSS has many advantages and capabilities in the mining environment. These include the ability to filter on distance, direction, angle, and velocity measurement of object target up to 150° horizontal detection and up to 400 m (depending upon the object's size). It provides accurate incident notifications at night and in all weather conditions like foggy weather, dusty environment, rainy weather etc. The system working has been for 24 hours in seven days (24 × 7) and detects moving objects in the periphery for intruder detection at remote locations. It receives all the radar measurement data and converts it into meaningful information/ reports through TCP/IP, integrated display and storing of intrusion data and video for reports and records. Audio-visual warning at the site and in the control room is received and recorded.

## 4. FUNDAMENTALS OF RADAR OVERVIEW

This part discusses the FMCW radar working principle, radar sensor hardware overview, signal processing, and radar signal waveform raw data measurement through a digital oscilloscope.

### 4.1 Principle for FMCW radar

The principle of operation of FMCW radar is simple. This radar sensor sends continuous waves with increasing frequency and receives them back after reflecting by an object or target. It is used to find the range and other information from a target using a frequency modulation technique on a continuous signal. The radar transmitter continuously transmits this modulated signal as a continuous wave (CW). The frequency modulation used by the radar can take many forms, such as triangular, saw-tooth, sinusoidal, or some other shape. The characteristic of a radar sensor is low transmitting power, ease of modulation, simple processing and ability to measure both range and velocity (Doppler) simultaneously. The radar signal processing can be used for real-time object recognition, target tracking, parameter deduction, and sometimes even signal classification of multi-target positions under all weather situations like foggy weather, dusty environment, rainy weather, etc. The advantages of FMCW radar against the other types of radar are low peak power, less sensitivity to clutter and accurate short-range measurement, which means that it is easier to integrate, a simpler algorithm for digital signal processing and cheaper to manufacture [24, 25, 26]. A continuous carrier modulated periodic function like a saw-tooth wave is transmitted to provide range data as shown in Figure 1, a frequency-time relation in the FMCW radar where the red line denotes the transmitted signal, the blue line indicates the received signal, $\upsilon_0$ denotes the central frequency, $\upsilon_w$ denotes frequency bandwidth for sweep and tw denotes period for the sweep. The modulation waveform has a linear saw-tooth sample, as shown in Figure 1. A signal obtained is having some delay time.

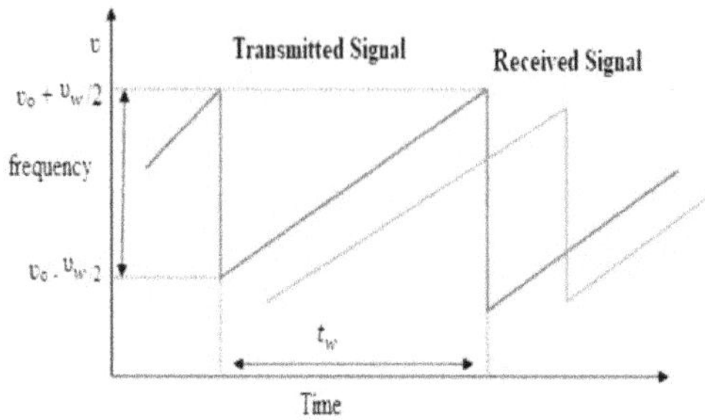


**Figure 1. Saw-tooth frequency modulation.**

In the FMCW radar system, the frequency modulated signal received at a voltage-controlled oscillator (VCO) is transmitted from the transmitter TX terminal and the reflected signals from the targets are received at the receiver $R_X$. These TX and RX signals are multiplied in a mixer, and thus beat signals are generated. The beat signals are then passed through a low pass filter, and an output signal is thus obtained. In this method, the frequency of the input signal varies with time at the VCO.

Figure 2 shows the block diagram of the FMCW radar system. Here, D/A denotes the digital to analog converter, VCO denotes the voltage controlled oscillator, BPF indicates the band-pass filter, and A/D means analog to the digital conversion, FFT means fast Fourier theorem, TX denotes the transmitter unit, and RX denotes the receiver unit [26].

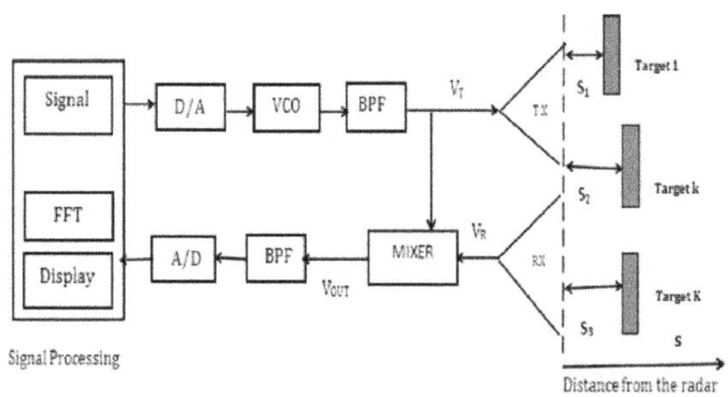


**Figure 2. Block diagram of the FMCW radar system.**

The frequency of the transmitted signal VT (υ; s) at TX, the transmitter unit is represented as:

$$V_T(\upsilon, s) = Ae^{j\frac{2\pi\upsilon}{c}s} \quad (1)$$

Where υ indicates the frequency at a particular time, s indicates the target's distance from the transmitter where s = 0, A denotes amplitude of the transmitted signal, and c represents the speed of light. The frequency reflected signal VR (υ, s) at the receiver unit RX is expressed as:

$$(V_R(\upsilon, s) = \sum_{k=1}^{K} A\alpha_k\gamma_k e^{j\varphi_k} e^{j\frac{2\pi\upsilon}{c}(2d_k - s)} \tag{2}$$

Where φk and γk are reflective coefficients for the phase and amplitude of the k[th] target, respectively. The αk denotes the amplitude coefficient for transmission loss from the target and dk denotes the distance between the transmitter and the k[th] target.

At the receiver where, s = 0, Eq. (2) can be rewritten as:

$$V_R(\upsilon, 0) = \sum_{k=1}^{K} A\alpha_k\gamma_k e^{j\varphi_k} e^{j\frac{2\pi\upsilon}{c}(2d_k)} \tag{3}$$

To get the frequency of a beat signal, the transmitted signal's frequency in Eq. (1) is multiplied by the frequency of the received signal in Eq. (3) at the position s = 0.

Thus, the frequency of beat signal = VT(υ,s) ××VR (υ, 0).

$$= A\, e^{j\frac{2\pi\upsilon s}{c}} \sum_{k=1}^{K} A\alpha_k\gamma_k e^{j\varphi_k} e^{j\frac{2\pi\upsilon}{c}(2d_k)}. \tag{4}$$

The output signal Vout (υ, 0) is generated by passing through a BPF is presented as:

$$V_{out}(\upsilon, 0) = \sum_{k=1}^{K} A^2\alpha_k\gamma_k e^{j\varphi_k} e^{j\frac{4\pi\upsilon d_k}{c}} \tag{5}$$

The distance and displacement of the target are assumed from the generated output signal in Eq. (5) by the use of signal processing.

The distance spectrum of the output signal P(x) is calculated by using Fourier transform:

$$\begin{aligned} P(x) &= \int_{\upsilon_0 - \frac{\upsilon_w}{2}}^{\upsilon_0 + \frac{\upsilon_w}{2}} V_{out} e^{-j\frac{4\pi\upsilon}{c}} dv \\ &= \int_{\upsilon_0 - \frac{\upsilon_w}{2}}^{\upsilon_0 + \frac{\upsilon_w}{2}} \sum_{k=1}^{K} A^2\alpha_k\gamma_k e^{j\frac{4\pi\upsilon d_k}{c}} e^{-j\frac{4\pi\upsilon s}{c}} dv \\ &= A^2 \sum_{k=1}^{K} \alpha_k\gamma_k e^{j\varphi_k} \int_{\upsilon_0 - \frac{\upsilon_w}{2}}^{\upsilon_0 + \frac{\upsilon_w}{2}} e^{j\frac{4\pi\upsilon(d_k - s)}{c}} dv \\ &= A^2 \sum_{k=1}^{K} \left[ \alpha_k\gamma_k e^{j\varphi_k} e^{j\frac{4\pi\upsilon_0(d_k - s)}{c}} \upsilon_w sinc\left\{ \frac{2\pi\upsilon_w(d_k - s)}{c} \right\} \right] \end{aligned} \tag{6}$$

In this equation, the function of Sin c(s) denotes:

$$Sin\ (cs) = \frac{Sins}{s} \tag{7}$$

The amplitude value of the distance spectrum |P(x)| in Eq. (6) is given as:

$$\begin{aligned}|P(s)| &= A^2\left|\sum_{k=1}^{K}\alpha_k\gamma_k e^{j\varphi_k} e^{j\frac{4\pi\upsilon_0(d_k-x)}{c}}\upsilon_w sinc\left\{\frac{2\pi\upsilon_w(d_k-s)}{c}\right\}\right| \\ &\le A^2\upsilon_w\sum_{k=1}^{K}\left[|\alpha_k\gamma_k|\left|sinc\left\{\frac{2\pi\upsilon_w(d_k-s)}{c}\right\}\right|\right]\end{aligned} \tag{8}$$

This is possible when the phase components $\phi_\kappa + \frac{4\pi\upsilon_o(d_k-s)}{c}$ for all of κ are equal.

$$|P(s)| = A^2\upsilon_w\sum_{k=1}^{K}\left[|\alpha_k\gamma_k|\left|sinc\left\{\frac{2\pi\upsilon_w(d_k-s)}{c}\right\}\right|\right] \tag{9}$$

When the number of a target to be 1, the distance spectrum in Eq. (6) becomes:

$$|P(s)| = \left[A^2\alpha_1\gamma_1 e^{j\varphi_1} e^{j\frac{4\pi\upsilon_0(d_1-s)}{c}}\upsilon_w sinc\left\{\frac{2\pi\upsilon_o(d_1-s)}{c}\right\}\right] \tag{10}$$

Its amplitude value of the distance spectrum is given as:

$$|P(s)| = A^2\upsilon_w\alpha_1\gamma_1\left|sinc\left\{\frac{2\pi\upsilon_w(d_1-s)}{c}\right\}\right| \tag{11}$$

This Equation indicates the distance of the target is specified by the amplitude value of the distance spectrum.

The phase value of the distance spectrum, P(s), is represented as:

$$<\mathrm{P(s)} = \phi_1 + \frac{4\pi\upsilon_o(d_1-s)}{c} = \theta_1(s) \tag{12}$$

Here, because θ1(s) satisfies - π≤θ1(s)≤π

The displacement of the target is:

$$\frac{c(-\pi-\varphi_1)}{4\pi\upsilon_o} \le d_1 \le \frac{c(\ \pi-\varphi_1)}{4\pi\upsilon_o} \tag{13}$$

If the phase value satisfies $\varphi_1 = \frac{\pi}{6}$, and υo=24.15 GHz in Eq. (13). Thus, it can be rewritten as -0.0036 [m] ≤≤$d_1$≤≤ 0.0026 [m] with υo=24.15 GHz. This means a slight displacement of the target within −0.0036 [m] ≤≤$d_1$≤≤0.0026 [m] is generated by the phase value of the distance spectrum.

On the other hand, the maximum distance for measuring dmax can be calculated using the following equation:

$$d_{\max} = \frac{c}{4\Delta\upsilon}[\mathrm{m}] \tag{14}$$

Where c denotes the speed of light and Δυ denotes the frequency resolution of the distance spectrum and expressed in hertz (Hz), which can be calculated using the following equation:

$$\Delta\upsilon = \frac{\upsilon_w}{t_w/t_s}[\mathrm{Hz}] \tag{15}$$

Where tw denotes the sweep time, ts denotes the interval time for sampling and υw denotes the bandwidth of sweep frequency, dmax denotes the maximum distance is expressed in metre (m).

Now, when sweep time, tw = 1024 μμs. Interval time for sampling, ts = 1μμs, the bandwidth of sweep frequency, υw = 200 MHz.

Then,

$$\begin{aligned} \Delta\upsilon &= \frac{\upsilon_w}{t_w/t_s} = \frac{200 \times 10^6 Hz}{1024\times10^{-6}s/1\times10^{-6}s} \\ \Delta\upsilon &= 1.95 \times 10^5[\mathrm{Hz}] \end{aligned} \tag{16}$$

Using value of Δυ, dmax can be calculated as follows:

$$d_{max} = \frac{c}{4\Delta\upsilon} = \frac{3 \times 10^8}{4 \times 1.95 \times 10^5} = 384[\mathrm{m}] \tag{17}$$

## 4.2 Radar hardware overview

In the transmitter unit of the radar system, a 'saw-tooth' voltage sequence is generated by the 'saw-tooth' generator. It is used to control a VCO to generate a frequency modulated radio frequency (RF) signal. The receiver channel, with the help of the beam forming array, receives the signal reflected by obstructions. The fundamental frequency output from VCO is connected to the transmit antenna array and halved frequency output. Signals received from the antenna array are mixed with the transmitted signal in the sub-harmonic mixer. The intermediate frequency (IF) signal obtained from the mixer is then amplified by the variable gain amplifier (VGA) and filtered by a band-pass filter (BPF). These two components are controlled by the radars electronic control unit (ECU) unit, which also communicates with the PC host via the USB interface [27, 28, 29, 30]. The photograph of the manufactured FMCW radar unit is shown in Figure 3.

**Figure 3. View of the FMCW radar.**

## 4.3 Signal processing overview

The algorithm for signal evaluation is implemented on a field-programmable gate array (FPGA) to facilitate real-time processing. A parallel signal processing and control of all peripheral units such as ADC, DAC, radar, data transmission interface (USB), etc., are set up. The signal processing starts with the FMCW ramp generation inside the FPGA using very high description language (VHDL) software. This ramp is converted from digital data to analog with a DAC and is amplified. Finally, it reaches the radar interface FMCW transceiver. The transceiver, using the ramp, generates a modulated signal to transmit it. Then the signal is reflected by some targets and is received by each receiver antenna, and then the calculation of beat signals is done. Thus, the beat signal is amplified and converted from analog to digital data with an ADC to adapt measured signals to the FPGA. This block contains digital to analog (or vice versa) conversions, amplification, and FPGA processing. The ramp generated in the FPGA is then sent to a 16 bit digital to analog converter (DAC). The FMCW radar uses the ramp information to emit a transmitted signal, which is used to obtain the beat signal by mixing with the received one. Fast Fourier transform (FFT) is primarily used for signal processing.

The presence and distance of targets are identified by identifying the peaks. The signal processing is achieved on-board entirely by the microcontroller with ARM Cortex-M4F core, a group of 32-bit reduced instruction set computer (RISC) based ARM processor cores. The cores, when intended for micro-controller use, consist of the Cortex-M4F core features SIMD type instructions (single instruction, multiple data) and the floating-point unit, which, combined with high operating frequency, 32-bit hardware multiplies with the 64-bit result, 12 cycles interrupt latency results in very efficient data handling. The FFT composed of 1024 samples of single-precision (32 bit) floating-point type is calculated slightly less than 5 ms. The ARM Cortex-M4F processor is very well appropriated for mainly deterministic real-time applications, even for low-cost platforms [30, 31, 32, 33]. Microprocessor algorithms provide powerful digital signal processing to identify the digital signature of intruders walking, automotive, etc., through the detection range. Intruders entering the detection zone are monitored in real-time. Signal processing using application software in the periphery surveillance system is mainly consists of software design, pre-processing, computation, FFT, graphical interface, and control module [33, 34, 35, 36].

## 4.4 Digital oscilloscope measurement

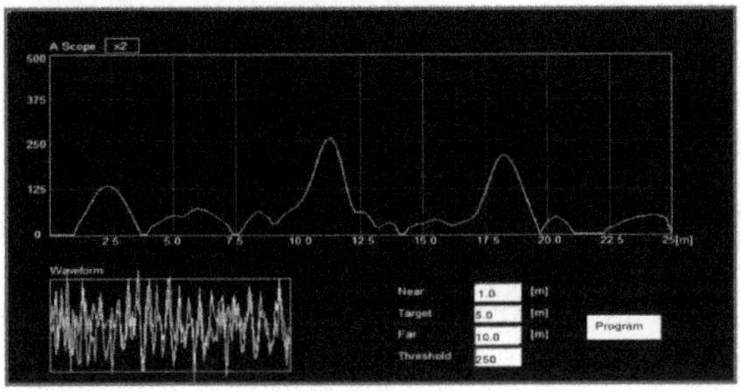


**Figure 4. Output radar signal graph from the oscilloscope.**

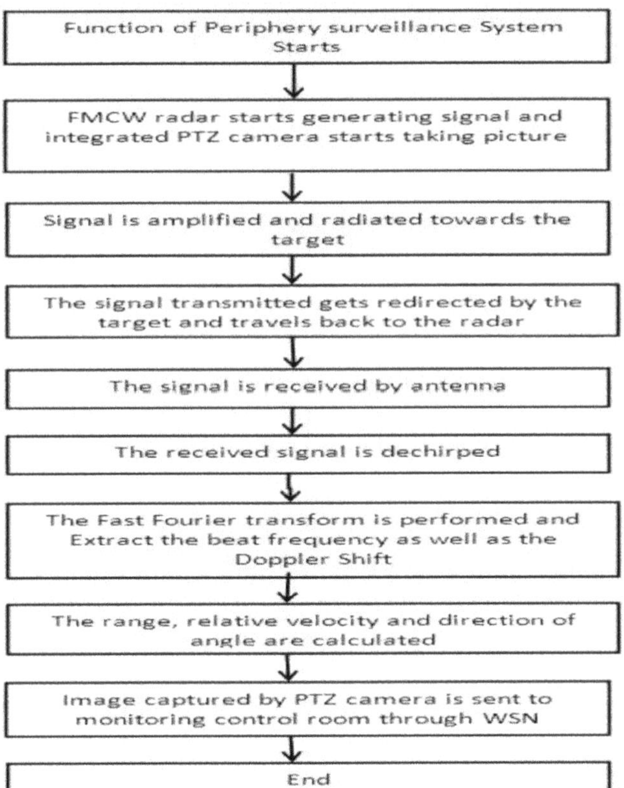


**Figure 5. Flow chart of intelligent mine periphery surveillance system implementation process used in the FMCW radar.**

Figure 4 shows the radar waveform received from the digital oscilloscope. These are raw data received from the FMCW radar. There are two different lines in the A-scope graph, viz. the yellow line and the red line. The yellow line represents the data after DSP signal processing in the distance domain. Red line is the user configured threshold to cancel out noise detection. Based on the above, the radar application gives alarm for the distance domain. The signal program the user-configured threshold set value 250 to cancel out noise detection, and object target 5 m and distant object 10 m. The flow chart of the function of the periphery surveillance system implementation process used in the FMCW radar, PTZ camera, and wireless sensor network has been shown in Figure 5.

## 5. FIELD STUDIES

The study area is Tirap Opencast Coal Mine, owned by North Eastern Coalfields (NEC) of Coal India Limited (CIL), located at the north-western end of the Makum Coalfield, Assam in India. The nearest township, Ledo, is about 3 km to the eastof Margherita. The headquarters of NEC is located at a distance of about 10 km. The national highway, NH38, forms the northern boundary of this colliery. The nearby railheads for the coalfield are Margherita, Ledo, and Baragolai on a broad-gauge line of the North-East Railway.

### 5.1 Field installation

Generally, mine lease covers a wide area with a long lease boundary, and most of the boundaries are not fenced. Each mine has separate entry and exit gates which are the authorized routes for vehicle transportation and mine personnel. Entry through these authorized routes is usually controlled by installing an access control system comprising radio frequency identification (RFID) tags, RFID reader, Internet protocol (IP) based motorized boom barrier, signal lights, computer and integration software. The boom barrier opens the gate for entry or exit of the authorized vehicle or person only when the access control system reads the valid RFID tag assigned to the respective vehicle or person. Entry or exit through the rest of the significant mine lease boundary is unauthorized and prohibited. However, illegal mineral transportations are found from some mines through these unauthorized routes of mine boundaries. Hence, a periphery surveillance system has been developed by integrating radar, CCTV camera, wireless network, server and software for day and night surveillance of the mine lease boundary from a remote control room.

The system detects any vehicle or person entering through the particular unauthorized routes or boundary with simultaneous CCTV footage of the intrusion location. Further, it provides a real-time warning to the system's operator in the control room regarding the intrusion along with CCTV footage of the incidence. It saves the intrusion location and video footage with a time stamp, and these records of the log can be retrieved any time for further analysis. Thus, the system detects all intrusions. The control room operator verifies each intrusion through the respective CCTV footage whether the intruder is an authorized or unauthorized vehicle or person.

Field installation of the periphery surveillance system has been conducted at Tirap Opencast Coal Mine of North Eastern Coalfields (NEC), having latitude 27°17′35.09″ N and longitude 95°46′10.29″ E. The microwave FMCW radar sensor and PTZ surveillance camera installed in the mine periphery of Tirap Opencast Coal Mine has shown in Figure 6.

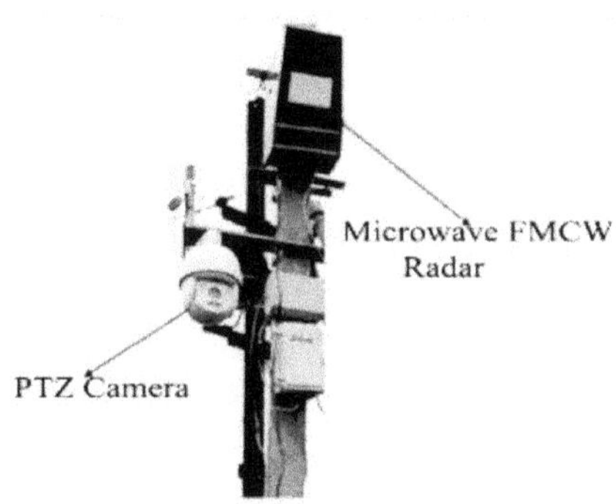


**Figure 6. The microwave FMCW radar sensor and integrated PTZ surveillance camera were installed in the mine periphery of Tirap Opencast Coal Mine.**

An FMCW radar sensor, an integrated PTZ camera, and a wireless sensor network have been installed on few electric poles along with railway siding of the mine roadside. After the installation of the periphery surveillance system, the selected area has been kept under rigorous vigilance. There is multi-radar connectivity with a wireless network for real-time detection. Any intruding object can be detected through the sensor. The virtual framework of an integrated periphery surveillance system for opencast mine has been shown in Figure 7.

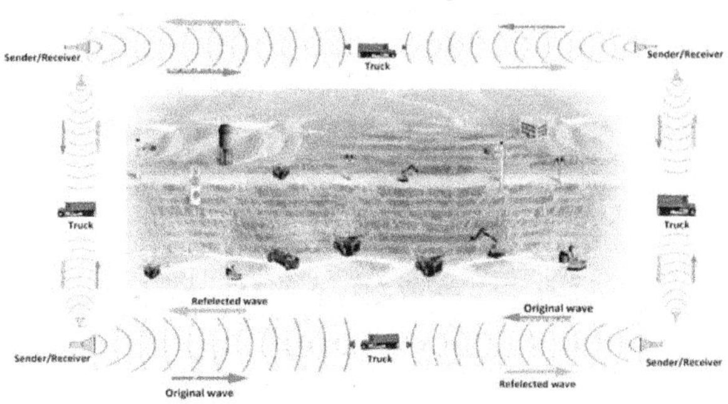


**Figure 7. Virtual framework of an integrated periphery surveillance system for an opencast mine.**

Suppose any unauthorized vehicle or any object is sensed to be entering into the boundary, in that case, wireless sensor nodes trigger an alarm and also send intrusion notifications to the central monitoring computer. The vehicle's position or a target is traced by the transmitting sensor node. Furthermore, long-distance PTZ cameras installed along with the radar sensor provide actual pictures of the intruders. A centralized observation station consists of a large digital display, computer, server, GPS antenna, walkie-talkie, alarm, centralized continuous power supply, etc. The arrangement of an integrated periphery surveillance system deployment has been shown in Figure 8. It is also equipped with software modules to track and perform real-time assignments and operations. The radar sensor node is also attached to a central monitoring station via a wireless sensor network. This station performs various tasks such as initiation of geo-fencing for each truck, tracking vehicle movement throughout its transportation route, assigning trucks in real-time, etc. It is also responsible for monitoring operating threshold values for equipment and maintaining the database. The watching administrator also can communicate with the authorized supervisors about moving vehicles in the area. The central observing operator also generates an audible alarming signal in case of accidents, mineral theft, or illegal activities in the mine's excavation area. Performance of the system was also evaluated during severe weather conditions like foggy weather, heavy rain and dusty environment. It has been found that the version of the radar is not significantly affected during the said severe weather conditions.

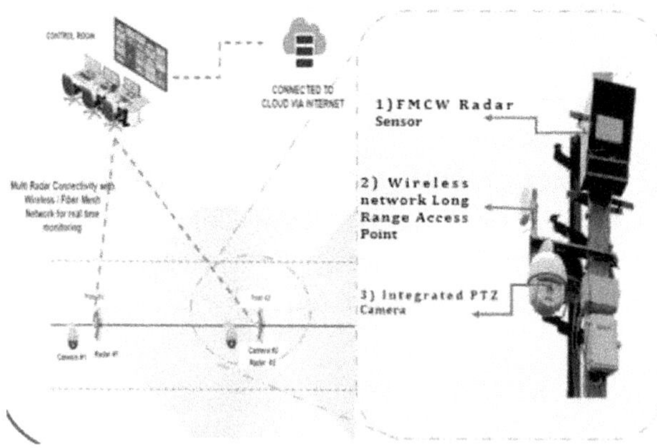


**Figure 8. Architecture of mine periphery surveillance system deployment.**

## 5.2 Observations and discussions

Figure 9 shows a snapshot for the distance-direction graph generated by using application software and a photograph taken by PTZ camera during these detections of incidences. The actual pictures are taken from the PTZ camera, real-time radar detection and distance graphs of different objects obtained during field experiments.

Photographs show the presence of trucks and many persons. The interaction between the user and the high language software system has taken place in the application layer. It is implemented through a visual system simulator for front end simulation. The radar distance graph plots the continuous detection of intrusion along the mine periphery up to 400 m. The lines in different colors in the graphs correspond to the velocity and direction of varying mining vehicles or persons concerning the radar sensor's location. The other color lines represent different moving and stationary objects. The radar sensor generates an integrated volumetric perimeter detection zone. The developed application software is set to trigger an alarm if the thing crosses the boundary lines or attempts to cross the detection zone.

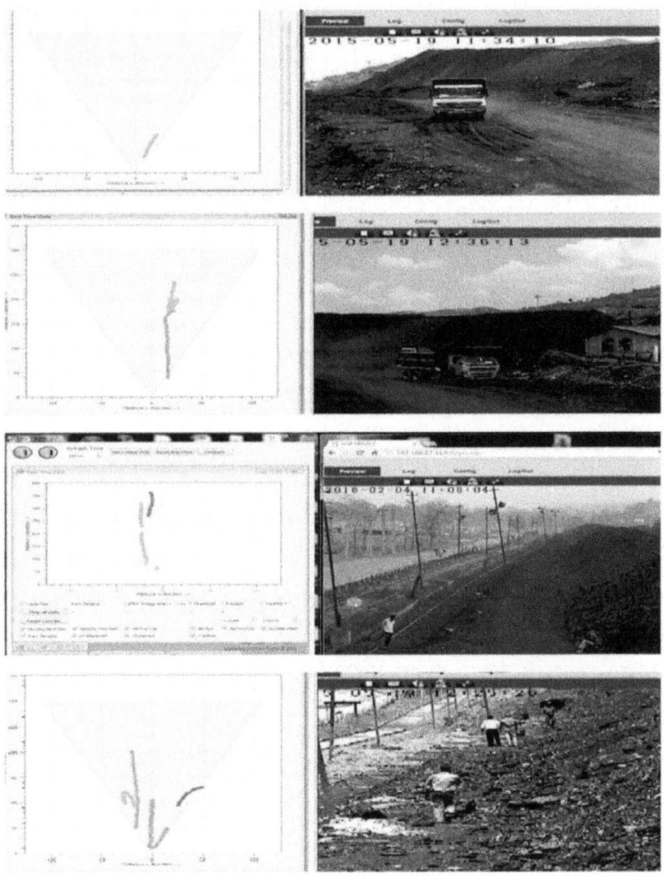

**Figure 9. View of real-time monitoring of the diverse position of periphery surveillance system at an opencast mine.**

Figure 9 represents screenshots of continuous radar view and CCTV video surveillance of a control room screen installed in an opencast coal mine site. Each line shows the radar detection location for a particular vehicle or person. The movement of each intruder is shown in the form of the path in the graph, i.e., X and Y coordinate concerning the location of radar and its center line, as shown in the left side graph of Figure 9. When an intruder is in stationery position, there will be no variation of the intrusion detection path displayed in the control room screen. Further, the respective detection line vanishes automatically from the display screen when an intruder crosses beyond the length and width of the radar detection range.

Table 1 presents various data gathered by radar regarding trucks and different objects. This experimental fieldwork showcases the impact of real-time monitoring, tracking and sensing management systems using the developed application software. The developed method can capture single, double and multiple targets placed at various locations in the different test areas of a mine. Thus, it can detect the intruders and intruding objects like trucks and other vehicles to control illegal mining-related activities in the mining area.

**Table 1. The periphery surveillance system monitors parameters.**

| Object ID | Quality | Distance in X-direction (m) | Distance in Y-direction (m) | Velocity of the object in X-direction (km $h^{-1}$) | Velocity oftheobjectin Y-direction (km $h^{-1}$) | Object type | Distance polar (m) | Speed polar (km $h^{-1}$) | Angleof direction (°) |
|---|---|---|---|---|---|---|---|---|---|
| 15038 | 1 | -50.5419 | 240.648 | -23.397 | 10.6527 | 0 | 245.898 | 0 | 11.8611 |
| 150183 | 8 | -55.6701 | 248.83 | -2.65974 | 8.75161 | 0 | 254.982 | 0 | 12.611 |
| 149785 | 9 | 3.01645 | 58.5682 | -0.167479 | -6.04272 | 0 | 58.6458 | 0 | -2.94831 |

Real-time data from the FMCW radar information are saved in the database by the application software and are extracted as given in Table 1. This object target information includes the following:

- ☆ Object ID is the identifier for a valid object, and it does not change during a lifetime.
- ☆ Quality is the indicator for the track quality that equals 10 for best quality.
- ☆ Distance X and distance Y denote the distance of the traced object from a reference point in X and Y-directions, respectively.
- ☆ Velocity X and velocity Y represent the velocity of the tracked objects in X and Y-directions, respectively.
- ☆ Polar distance denotes the distance from a reference point to the tracked object in polar coordinates.
- ☆ Polar speed denotes the speed of the tracked object in polar coordinates.
- ☆ The angle of direction indicates the angle of the tracked object to the reference point in degree (polar coordinates).

## 6. CONCLUSIONS

The developed intelligent mine periphery surveillance system is an effective and economical device that can keep constant vigilance over a selected area or a place even in adverse weather conditions like foggy weather, rainy season, dusty environment, etc. As the system is quite capable of detecting the position and movement of an object from a long distance, it would bebeneficial for preventing (i) unauthorized intrusion of a vehicle or person into the mining area and thereby avoiding many safety and security problems, (ii) illegal transportation of coal and other minerals from the mining area especially where there is no boundary wall, (iii) detection of several other incidences such as surface mine fire due to burning of coal, etc. Thus, this surveillance system would undoubtedly go a long way in preventing financial loss of the mining industry due to mineral theft, and ensuring the safety and security of the mines.

## REFERENCES

1. Komarov IV, Smolskiy SM. Fundamentals of short-range FM radar. New York (NY): Artech House; 2003.
2. Russell ME, Crain A, Curran A. et al. Millimeter-wave radar sensor for automotive intelligent cruise control (ICC).IEEE Trans. Microw. Theory Tech. 1997; 45(12):2444–2453.
3. Skolnik MI. Radar Handbook. New York: McGraw-Hill; 2008.
4. Skolnik MI. Introduction to Radar Systems. New York: McGraw-Hill; 2003.
5. Ozturk H, Yegin K. Predistorter based K-Band FMCW radar for vehicle speed detection. Proceedings of the 17th IEEE International Radar Symposium Conference, Krakow, Poland; 2016:1–4.
6. Gale RAN, Hong L. Automated traffic surveillance using fusion of Doppler radar and video information. Math. Computer. Model. 2011; 54(1):53–43.
7. Siversima. FMCW radar sensors. App. Notes. 2011.
8. Giubbolini L. A multistatic microwave radar sensor for short range anti-collision warning. IEEE Trans. Veh. Technol. 2000; 49(6):2270–2275.
9. Steinhauer M, Ruo H, Irion H, Menzel W, et al. Millimeter-wave-radar sensor based on a transceiver array for automotive applications. IEEE Trans. Microw. Theory Tech. 2008; 56(2):261–269.
10. Fujimori S, Uebo T, Iritani T. Short-range high-resolution radar utilizing standing wave for measuring of distance and velocity of a moving target. Electron. Com. Japan. 2006; 89(5):52–60.

11. Lin JJ, Li YP, Hsu WC, et al. Design of an FMCW radar baseband signal processing system for automotive application. Springer Plus. 2016; 5(1):42.https://doi.org/10.1186/s40064-015-1583-5

12. Villeval S, Bilik I, and Gurbuz S. Application of a 24 GHz FMCW Automotive radar for urban target classification. Proceedings of the IEEE Radar Conference, Rome, Italy; 2014:1237–1240. DOI: 10.1109/RADAR.2014.6875787

13. Lee TY, Jeon SY, Han J, et al. A Simplified technique for distance and velocity measurements of multiple moving objects using a linear frequency modulated signal. IEEE Sens. J. 2006; 16(15):5912–5920.

14. Ash M, Ritchie M, Chetty K. On the application of digital moving target indication techniques to short-range FMCW radar data. IEEE Sens. J. 2018; 18(10):4167–4175.

15. Choudhary PK, EI-Nasr MA. Insight into remote monitoring systems. J. Electromagn. Waves Appl. 2019; 33(7):795–798.

16. Ibanez JG, Zeadally S, Castillo CJ. Sensor technologies for intelligent transportation systems. Sens. 2018; 18(4):1212.https://doi.org/10.3390/s18041212

17. Ganapathi P, Shanmugapriya D, Kalaivani M. A study on vehicle detection and tracking using wireless sensor networks. Wirel. Sens. Netw. 2010; 2(02):173–185.

18. Mimbela LEY, Klein LA. Summary of vehicle detection and surveillance technologies used in intelligent transportation systems. https://www.fhwa.dot.gov/policyinformation/pubs/ vdstits2007/vdstits2007.pdf. 2007

19. Yulianto B. Detector technology for demand responsive traffic signal control under mixed traffic conditions. Proceedings of the AIP Conference; 2008:040021. DOI: 10.1063/1.5042991

20. Santi F, Pieralice F, Pastina D. Joint detection and localization of vessels at sea with a GNSS-based multistatic radar. IEEE Trans. Geosci. Remote Sens. 2019; 57(8):5894–5913.

21. Thiel S, Ferber S, Fischer T, et al. A case study in applying a product line approach for car periphery supervision systems. SAE Trans. 2001; 50–62.

22. Chaulya SK, Prasad GM. Sensing and monitoring technologies for mines and hazardous areas. USA: Elsevier; 2006.

23. Kassim AM, Jaya AKRA, Azahar AH, et al. Performance Analysis of Acceleration Sensor for Movement Detection in Vehicle Security System. Int. J. Adv. Comput. Sci. Appl. 2019; 10(10):395–401.

24. Fan Y, Xiang K, An J, et al. A new method of multi-target detection for FMCW automotive radar. Proceedings of the IET International Conference, Xi'an, China; 2013:1–4.DOI: 10.1049/cp.2013.0119

25. Kazuhiro YM, Saito M, Miyasaka K, et al. Design and performance of a 24 GHz Band FM-CW radar system and its application. Proceedings of the IEEE Asia Pacific Conference on Wireless and Mobile, Bali, Indonesia; 2014:28–30.DOI: 10.1109/APWiMob.2014.6920270

26. Yamaguchi K, Mitumasa S, Takuya A, et al. A 24 GHz FM-CW radar system for detecting closed multiple targets and its applications in actual scenes. Open J. Internet Things. 2016; 2(1):1–15.

27. Ayhan S, Pauli M, Kayser T, et al. FMCW radar system with additional phase evaluation for high accuracy range detection. Proceedings of the 8th European Radar Conference; 2011:117–120.

28. Peng Z, Ran L, Li C. A K-Band Portable FMCW radar with beam forming array for short-range localization and vital-Doppler targets discrimination. IEEE Trans. Microw. Theory Tech. 2017; 65(9):3443–3452.

29. Kurniawan D, Wael C, Miftahushudur T, et al. Implementation of automatic I/Q imbalance correction for FMCW radar system. Proceedings of the 2nd IEEE International Conference on Information Systems and Electrical Engineering, Yogyakarta, Indonesia, 2017:100–105. DOI: 10.1109/ICITISEE.2017.8285464.

30. Kaminski P, Slomin I, Wincza K, et al. Fully integrated, multipurpose low-cost K-band FMCW radar module with sub-milimeter measurement precision. Int. J. Info. Electr. Eng. 2015; 5(2):74. DOI: 10.7763/IJIEE.2015.V5.505

31. Hyun E, Kim S, Ju Y, et al. FPGA based signal processing module design and implementation for FMCW vehicle radar systems. Proceedings of the IEEE CIE International Radar Conference, Chengdu, China, 2011:273–275.DOI: 10.1109/Radar17764.2011

32. Peng Z, Li C. A portable 24-GHz FMCW radar based on six-port for short range human tracking. Proceedings of the IEEEInternational Microwave Workshop Series on RF and Wireless Technologies for Biomedical and Healthcare Applications (IMWS-BIO), Taipei, Taiwan; 2015:81–82. DOI: 10.1109/IMWS-BIO.2015.7303787

33. Sediono W, Lestari A. Software design to Simulate FMCW radar signal: a case study of INDERA. Proceedings of Indonesia-Malaysia Microwave Antenna Conference (IMMAC); 2010. http://www.ee.ui.ac.id/immac2010/

34. Sediono W. Method of measuring Doppler shift of moving targets using FMCW maritime radar. Proceedings of the IEEE International Conference on Teaching, Assessment and Learning in Engineering (TALE), Bali, Indonesia; 2013:78–381. DOI: 10.1109/TALE.2013.6654465

35. Ayhan S, Scherr S, Pahl P, et al. Radar-based high-accuracy angle measurement sensor operating in the K-band. IEEE Sens. J. 2015; 15(2):937–945.

36. Hyun E, Jin Y, Lee J. Design and implementation of 24 GHz multichannel FMCW surveillance radar with a software-reconfigurable baseband. J. Sens. 2017; 2017, 1–11, Article ID 3148237, https://doi.org/10.1155/2017/3148237

CHAPTER-4

# QUALITY ASSESSMENT OF INSTALLED ROCK BOLTS

## 1. INTRODUCTION

The role of a rock bolt support system is to secure and reinforce the rock zone in the near field of an underground opening and to fasten it to deeper rock strata [1, 2]. Mostly steel rock bolts are used for that purpose [3, 4]. The rock bolt consists of a steel bar grouted in an oversize hole. A portable installation machine is used to spin the bolt into the hole filled with fast setting epoxy resin cartridges. After hardening of the resin layer a plate and nut are driven up the bolt. Although robust resin cartridges are used, in mining practice the rock bolt may not be fully encapsulated as a consequence of various geotechnical conditions [5, 6, 7]: rock divergence, escape of grout into crevices, rock strata movement and improper grouting. The lack of proper grouting may be very hazardous and should be monitored [8]. Current publications in the field of rock bolt diagnosis, indicate that much effort is being taken to estimate the rock bolt integrity and grout quality in the most precise way. Different approaches have been proposed e.g. Granit, Boltometer, RBT and other inventions or methods [9, 10, 11, 12, 13, 14]. These methods rely on excitation of a tested rock bolt to vibration along its axis of symmetry and the analysis of output signals. Depending on the proposed method, both acoustic and ultrasonic waves are generated. Correspondingly, different analytical approaches are used as wavelet transform analysis, Fast Fourier Transform (FFT) and neural network algorithms [5, 14, 15, 16, 17, 18]. Also smart sensors techniques are introduced for observation of behavior of grouted rock bolts [19], in particular load measurements at the head of them [20], but the problem is not yet fully resolved.

Accordingly, the method for non-destructive identification of grouting discontinuity of rock bolts is proposed to extend the diagnose scope in rock bolting. Thus the diagnosis of void spaces—regions of lack of bonding is seen as crucial here. In the method a transverse excitation is applied which is seen as more adequate for that purpose. At present a diagnose is completed after the analytical phase has been performed in laboratory conditions, so results are not accessible in situ. Its usage is restricted to steel rock bolts up to 2.5 m long, though not only in mining but also in building engineering. It is worth noticing that the same approach to test the integrity of installed rock bolts was described by Godfrey [21]. Though not known to the author at the experimental and analytical stage of the current work, it is very encouraging that similar methodology was presented over forty years ago.

The chapter starts with a theoretical description of the main rules and relationships between investigated modal parameters and measured data. Then the method and structure of a reference base of FE models are presented. Subsequently it is shown how the method was validated in an experimental coal mine. Finally the results of the research realized in working coal mines are discussed.

## 2. MATERIALS AND METHODS

### 2.1 Method and critical parameters

Unlike previously mentioned approaches, the proposed method uses modal analysis procedures and excitation forces are generated by an impact hammer. To perform such a quality assessment of grouting rock bolts several conditions must be fulfilled. One of the primary conditions of realization of the method is identification of a modal model of a tested structure. The modal model of a mechanical system basically consists of two matrices [22, 23, 24, 25]:

- ☆ Fundamental matrix with natural frequencies and damping factors of the modes (eigenvectors),
- ☆ Modal matrix which consists of eigenvectors [Φ].

The modal model may be constructed starting from identification of a single modal eigenvector, and a more sophisticated model (not necessarily complete) would be a set of modal eigenvectors coordinates together with their natural frequencies and damping factors. From an individual characteristic of frequency response function $H_{jk}(\omega)$, where j, k stand for excitation and response points, evaluation of a natural frequency, a damping factor and a residue for an r-mode is possible, Eq. (1).

$$H_{jk}(\omega) \rightarrow \omega_r, \eta_r, {}_rA_{jk}; \quad r = 1, m \tag{1}$$

In order to calculate foregoing elements of the modal matrix [Φ], as coordinates of modal vectors $\varphi_{jr,}$ it is necessary to conduct a series of measurements of frequency response functions in different points of a tested mechanical system. The measurement of a frequency response function at excitation point is very important. The coordinates of an r-mode may be calculated knowing a residue ${}_rA_{kk}$ at this point using formula (2):

$$\phi_{kr}{}^2 = {}_rA_{kk} \tag{2}$$

The rest of modal vector coordinates may be calculated using Eq. (3):

$$\phi_{jr} = \frac{{}_rA_{jk}}{\phi_{kr}} \tag{3}$$

where: φkr,φjr - vector coordinates after the process of normalization.

So, for complete presentation of vibration motion of the tested structure with n degree of freedom, it is necessary to measure frequency response function at n different points of the structure, including a measurement at the excitation point [23, 24, 26, 27]. That is equivalent to the measurement of frequency response functions for a column or vector of a matrix [H]. In practice however, it is quite often appropriate to increase the number of measurement points and perform measurements of additional matrix elements, additional column or row of the matrix, for example hitting the rock bolt in an additional perpendicular direction to an axis of symmetry.

The measurement setup is shown in Figure 1. For realization of the method a response transducer was localized at a visible part of the rock bolt, attached using steel ring and stud [26] and a force transducer was localized at an impact hammer head. The direction of excitation was perpendicular to the symmetry axis of the rock bolt as well as is the main axis of the response transducer. After excitation of the rock bolt to transverse vibration, the signals from both the force transducer and the accelerometer (response transducer) were recorded and frequency response function (FRF) was calculated. The excitation was repeated at several points positioned along the outer part of the bar when the accelerometer remained at the same place. The subsequent frequency response functions were stored in universal file format in the computer memory. In the next step data were exported to a workstation where modal parameter extraction methods were realized. Since the installed rock bolt acts as an oscillator, its modal parameters are changed by different lengths and positions of grouting discontinuity. By proper extraction of those parameters, the intended identification was possible.

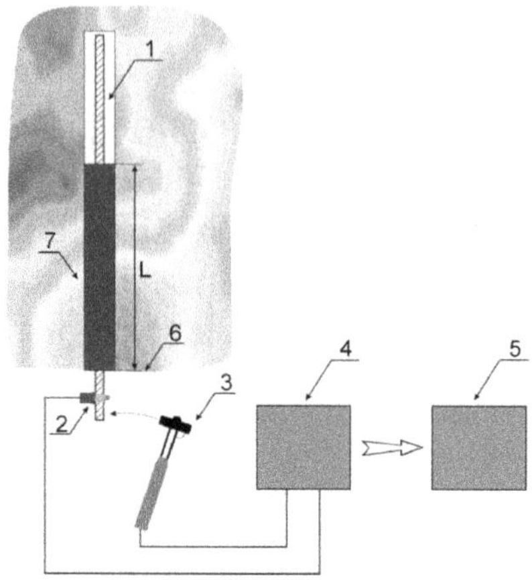


**Figure 1. Measurement setup: (1) rock bolt, typical length 1.5 m-2.5 m; (2) the accelerometer; (3) the impact hammer; (4) portable measurement system; (5) workstation for modal analysis; (6) the surface of the upper roof section; (7) the grout. L is a grouted length.**

In this research the natural (resonant) frequency was the main modal parameter taken into account to differentiate foregoing cases of grouting discontinuity. To increase the accuracy of the method frequency response measurements were performed at 5-7 points positioned on the outer part of a rock bolt. It enabled calculating natural frequencies with the use of a larger number of equations and averaging obtained results in the least square sense. Additionally, it was possible to avoid a casual excitation at a nod point of a mode shape [27]. Mode shapes, which is self-understandable, could not be measured on the whole length of a rock bolt (the grouted part of a bar inaccessible). It is only possible in laboratory conditions. Figures 2 and 3 present the example results of research on known cases of grouting discontinuities in real working conditions where a rock bolt support system was used. The amplitude of FRF function depends on the location of measured points and may differ for each pair of response and reference points, shown on Figure 3.

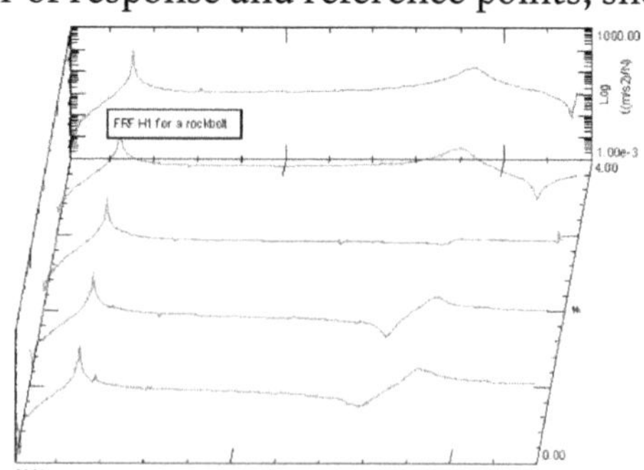


**Figure 2. An example of FRF functions (waterfall curve) for a known case of grouting discontinuities in real working conditions.**

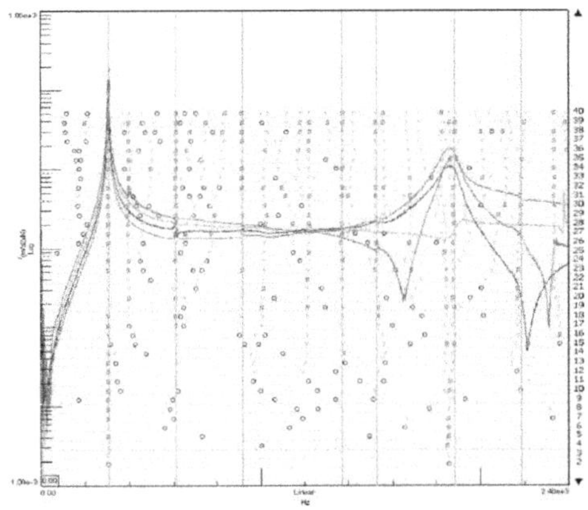

**Figure 3. An example of stabilization diagram for a known case of grouting discontinuities in real working conditions, the FRF curves for all measured points are shown (the order number of the model was set as 40).**

It was also necessary to have a reference point to compare our results with. With this aim the theoretical modal analysis was introduced [23, 24, 25, 26] and a base of Finite Element (FE) models were built, encompassing different types of discontinuities (different boundary conditions).

## 2.2 Reference model

The lengths on which a rock bolt (a steel bar) is grouted into a roof section form defined border conditions. Different cases of grouting discontinuity can be modeled in theoretical models. To be used as a reference the theoretical model had to be reconciled to the experimental one taking into account a wide range of cases with controlled, known discontinuities of grouting.

In the presented research ANSYS program was used to build the finite element model of a grouted rock bolt, shown in Figure 4. The program enables modeling of finite elements with the help of advanced programming tools, so even very complicated geometry shapes can be developed. In the first phase geometry of the examined structure was involved. Then meshing process was realized and particular physical properties of materials were introduced including density, Young Modulus, Poisson Ratio etc., shown in Table 1. These parameters are crucial since mass and stiffness matrices are built in relation to them. Except steel these parameters were evaluated experimentally. Afterwards adequate physical parameters as well as loads and boundary conditions were attributed to groups of elements. The rock component was ascribed fixed support at the side and back faces and frictional support was attributed to connections between a nut, a plate and roof strata surface. Also, for modeling of torsion force applied to screw the nut and plate to a rock bolt, a bolt pretension feature was utilized (results for different torsion forces were calculated, but that value is controlled by an operator of a bolter and is given). After the process of reconciliation, which comprised all the above mentioned parameters, the validated FE model could be used as a reference base for unknown experimental cases. An example of an analyzed case study and a specific mode of natural frequency is presented in Figure 5. The influence of rock strata in which rock bolts are installed was also taken into account but the results obtained both in the experimental and working coal mines (sand stone and mud stone rock strata) showed that the type of rock strata has only a slight impact in comparison with grout discontinuity. As an example, for the particular case, lack of grout at the half length of a rock bolt, the difference ranged from 0.7% to 2.4% for 8 calculated natural frequencies.

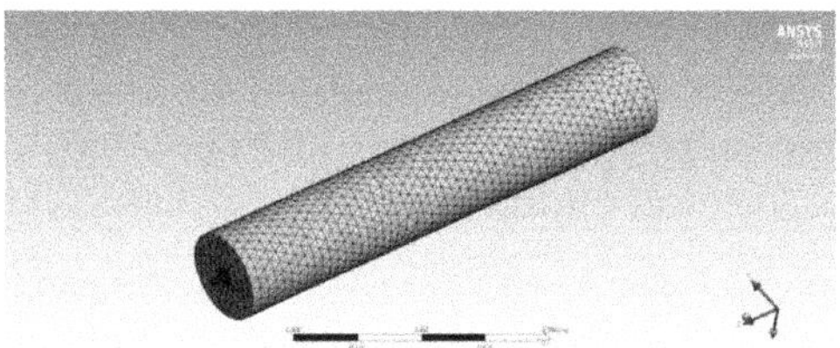

**Figure 4. An example of a finite element model for an analyzed case study.**

**Table 1. The properties of components for FE modeling of the investigated rock bolt.**

| **Property** | **Component material** | | | | |
|---|---|---|---|---|---|
| | **Steel (bar, nut)** | **Grout** | **Cement (optional)** | **Rock (mudstone)** | **Rock (sandstone)** |
| Density, kgm$^{-3}$ | 7850 | 1990 | 2300 | 2560 | 2160 |
| Young's Modulus, Pa | 2.00E+11 | | 3.00E+10 | 6.388E+09 | 3.722E+09 |
| Poisson's Ratio | 0.30 | 0.10 | 0.18 | 0.16 | 0.09 |

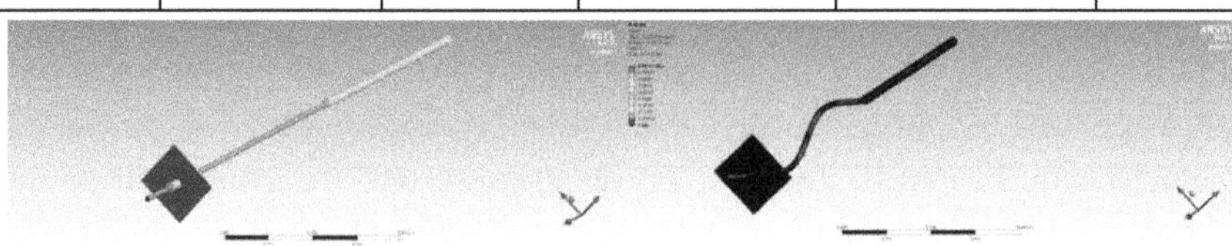

**Figure 5. An example of an analyzed case study and a specific mode of natural frequency 232,5 Hz (the amplitude of the mode is scaled for presentation purposes).**

As a result of theoretical modal analysis frequency response functions and natural frequencies were calculated (for excitation at the outer part of a rock bolt). Then sets of natural frequencies characteristic of different types of grouting discontinuities were collected and a large data base was set up. Table 2 presents the sample of data sheets for the carried out calculations and obtained convergence charts of the analyzed cases.

**Table 2. The calculated natural frequencies of the finite element models of investigated rock bolts.**

| Lack of grout, cm | f1 | f2 | f3 | f4 | f5 | f6 | f7 | f8 | f9 | F10 | F11 | F12 |
|---|---|---|---|---|---|---|---|---|---|---|---|---|
| 5 | 2325.6 | 0 | 0.0 | 0.0 | 0.0 | 0.0 | 0.0 | 0.0 | 0.0 | 0.0 | 0.0 | 0.0 |
| 10 | 917.5 | | 0.0 | 0.0 | 0.0 | 0.0 | 0.0 | 0.0 | 0.0 | 0.0 | 0.0 | 0.0 |
| 15 | 470.3 | 2487.3 | 0.0 | 0.0 | 0.0 | 0.0 | 0.0 | 0.0 | 0.0 | 0.0 | 0.0 | 0.0 |
| 20 | 284.1 | 1686.5 | 0.0 | 0.0 | 0.0 | 0.0 | 0.0 | 0.0 | 0.0 | 0.0 | 0.0 | 0.0 |
| 25 | 192.6 | 1175.4 | 0.0 | 0.0 | 0.0 | 0.0 | 0.0 | 0.0 | 0.0 | 0.0 | 0.0 | 0.0 |
| 30 | 137.1 | 843.8 | 2280.2 | 0.0 | 0.0 | 0.0 | 0.0 | 0.0 | 0.0 | 0.0 | 0.0 | 0.0 |
| 35 | 102.7 | 635.2 | 1739.9 | 0.0 | 0.0 | 0.0 | 0.0 | 0.0 | 0.0 | 0.0 | 0.0 | 0.0 |
| 40 | 80.0 | 496.5 | 1368.4 | 2552.1 | 0.0 | 0.0 | 0.0 | 0.0 | 0.0 | 0.0 | 0.0 | 0.0 |
| ⋮ | ⋮ | ⋮ | ⋮ | ⋮ | ⋮ | ⋮ | ⋮ | ⋮ | ⋮ | ⋮ | ⋮ | ⋮ |
| 175 | 4.5 | 28.2 | 79.0 | 154.6 | 255.3 | 380.7 | 530.6 | 704.8 | 902.9 | 1124.5 | 1369.2 | 1636.5 |
| 180 | 4.3 | 26.7 | 74.7 | 146.2 | 241.4 | 360.0 | 501.8 | 666.6 | 854.1 | 1063.9 | 1295.7 | 1549.0 |
| 185 | 4.0 | 25.3 | 70.8 | 138.6 | 228.8 | 341.2 | 475.7 | 632.0 | 809.9 | 1009.0 | 1229.0 | 1470.6 |
| 190 | 3.8 | 24.0 | 67.1 | 131.4 | 217.0 | 323.7 | 451.4 | 599.8 | 768.6 | 957.7 | 1166.7 | 1396.2 |
| 195 | 3.6 | 22.8 | 63.8 | 124.8 | 206.1 | 307.5 | 428.8 | 569.8 | 730.3 | 910.1 | 1108.9 | 1327.3 |

## 2.3 Utilizing of regression methods

In order to enable fast and effective comparison of theoretical (FE) and experimental models regression methods were reviewed. Cluster analysis seemed to be adequate for that purpose. It is one of the statistical methods to adjust parameters (in the presented research: natural frequencies) measured experimentally with calculated data. The concept of cluster analysis, a term introduced in the work of Tryon [28] actually includes several different classification algorithms. For researchers of many disciplines it poses a major problem to organize the observed data in a sensible structure, or data grouping. In other words, cluster analysis is a tool for exploratory data analysis, whose aim is to arrange objects in a group, in such a way that the degree of binding properties of objects belonging to the same group is the largest, and with objects from other groups is as small as possible. Analysis of the cluster can be used to detect data structures without deriving interpretation/explanation. In short: cluster analysis only detects structure in the data without explaining why it occurs. The general types of methods of cluster analysis are: agglomeration, grouping of objects and characteristics, and k-means clustering. Analysis of the cluster is not a statistical test, but a collection of different algorithms that group objects with specific features. Unlike many other statistical procedures, methods of cluster analysis are used mostly when we do not have any a priori hypotheses, while we are still in the exploratory phase of our research. Therefore, testing the statistical significance in the traditional sense of the term actually is not applicable. Instead measurement discrepancies or the distances between objects are used. The most direct way to calculate the distance between objects in multidimensional space is Euclidean distance calculation. If we have a two-or three-dimensional space, this measure is the actual geometric distance between objects in space. From the point of view of a matching algorithm the actual distances or other derivatives of the distance may be used. The following are the types used.

The first is Euclidean distance. This is a geometric distance in multidimensional space. It should be calculated as follows: distance $(x,y) = \{\Sigma_i (x_i - y_i)^2\}^{½}$.

Euclidean distance (and squared Euclidean distance) are calculated based on the raw data, and not on the basis of the standardized data. This method has some advantages (for example, the distance between any two objects is not affected by adding new objects that can be dispersed). However, the differences of units of dimensions may have a big impact on the way distances are calculated. In general, it is appropriate to standardize them in order to have a comparable data scale.

For squared Euclidean distance the distance is raised to a square, to assign more weight to objects that are more remote. It should be calculated as follows: distance $(x,y) = \{\Sigma_i (x_i - y_i)^2\}^{½}$.

Another type of distance is City distance (Manhattan, City block). This distance is simply the sum of the differences measured along the dimensions. In most cases, this distance measure yields similar results to the ordinary Euclidean distance. In the case of this measure, the impact of single large differences (outliers) is suppressed (because they are not raised to the square). City distance is calculated as follows: distance $(x,y) = \Sigma_i |x_i - y_i|$.

We use the distance power when we want to increase or decrease the importance that is assigned to the dimensions for which the relevant properties are quite / completely different. This can be achieved using just the power. It is counted as follows: distance $(x,y) = (\Sigma_i |x_i - y_i|^p)^{1/r}$, where r and p are parameters defined by the user. The parameter p increases / decreases the weight that is assigned to the differences in the individual dimensions, the parameter r increases / decreases the weight that is assigned to differences between objects. If r and p are equal to 2, then the distance is equal to the Euclidean distance.

In the realized research the application was developed to assign experimentally measured natural frequencies to the appropriate corresponding classes of cases of discontinuity calculated on the base of finite element models. The algorithm uses

City distance (x,y) = $\Sigma_i |x_i - y_i|$. The match procedure was realized in STATISTICA environment. So, for unknown cases we seek for the lowest value of that distance which represents the best fit to the theoretical model (an estimated grout length and position). Figure 6 presents the characteristics of the transfer function for the analyzed case, Table 3 the identified natural frequencies and Figure 7 the scatter plot of the differences between FE model and data evaluated experimentally.

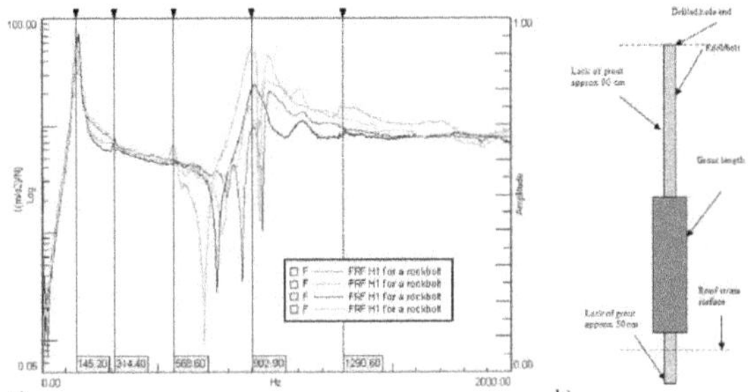

a) b)

**Figure 6. The characteristics of the transfer function for the analyzed case (a), and the estimated grout length (b), the length of the rock bolt is equal to 1.8 m, the chart axis are: the vertical axis—inertance, in (m/s$^2$)/N, the horizontal axis the frequency, in Hz.**

**Table 3. The identified natural frequencies of the investigated rock bolt.**

| No | Frequency, Hz | | Difference, % |
|---|---|---|---|
| | Experiment | FE model | |
| 1 | 145.2 | 137.1 | -5.6 |
| 2* | 314.4 | 291.4 | -7.3 |
| 3* | 568.1 | 568.6 | 0.1 |
| 4 | 902.9 | 843.8 | -6.5 |
| 5* | 1290.6 | 1387.2 | 7.5 |

* The frequency characteristic for the hidden end part of a rock bolt.

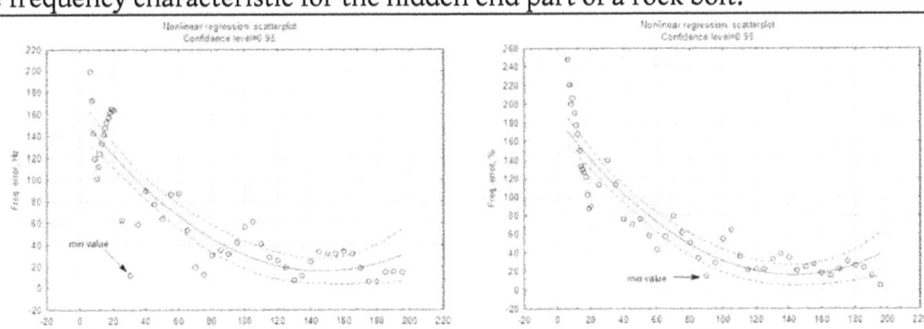

a) b)

**Figure 7. Scatter plot of the differences between FE model and data evaluated experimentally. The values of the lengths of discontinuity are: (a) 30 cm and (b) 90 cm. These values are specified for the first minimum differences of models and are clearly outside the values of the random scatter.**

# 3. RESULTS AND DISCUSSION

## 3.1 Measurements in the experimental coal mine Barbara GIG

The research work on the rock bolts grouted in a controlled way in real coal mine conditions yielded much information about the possibility of identification of grouting discontinuities and the influence of their changes on modal parameters. The measurements were performed in an experimental coal mine Barbara GIG. At the first stage the measurements were performed with previously developed working prototype assembled with National Instruments components, and at the second one, after large modification with the new measurement unit fulfilling ATEX requirements, shown in Figure 8 (ATEX directives consists of two EU directives describing the minimum safety requirements of the workplace and equipment used in explosive atmosphere. ATEX derives its name from Equipment intended for use in EXplosive ATmospheres).

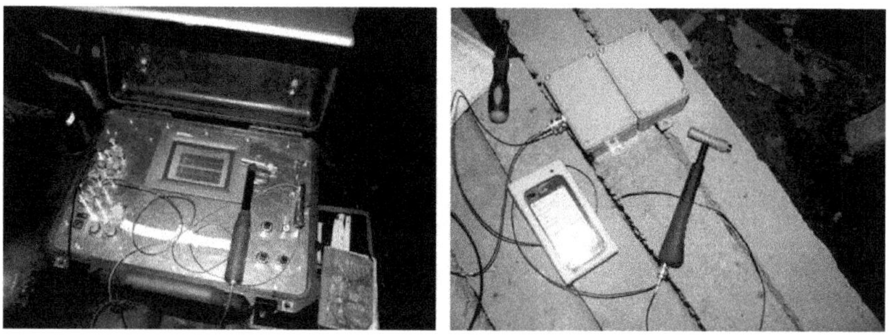

**Figure 8. The portable measurement system for quality control of installed rock bolts, working prototype (left) and final version fulfilling ATEX requirements (right).**

The total amount of investigated rockbolts in the experimental coal mine was 30. Initially, as it was not known how a supporting plate and a nut may influence the proper identification of grouting discontinuity the diagnose was realized on cases where supporting plate and nut were unscrewed and removed. Later on the experiments were performed with a complete assembly (a plate and a nut fixed), as shown in Figure 9 and the results were compared (discussed in the second part of this paragraph). The characteristics of transfer functions for the analyzed cases were utilized for evaluation of natural frequencies, which were crucial parameters for proper matching with finite element modal models base and diagnosis of related discontinuity length. Basing on in situ measurements and the analysis, we concluded that damping did not convey satisfactory information on the subject and might vary to a certain degree from sample to sample overshadowing its proper usefulness. Since tests in real conditions were performed on a relatively short length of a rock bolt, a mode shape usage was also constrained.

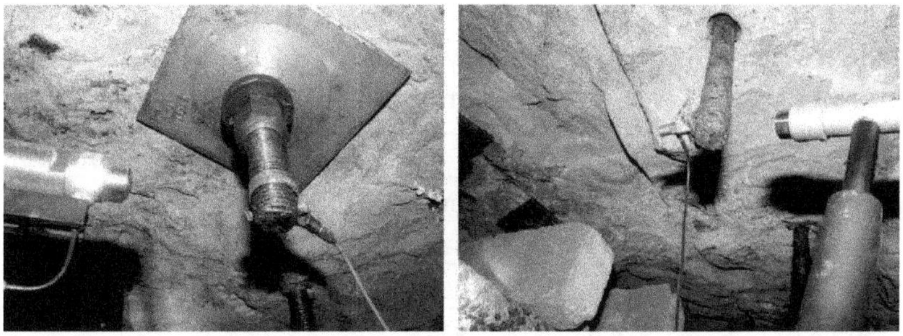

**Figure 9. Impact excitation of installed rock bolts, with the working prototype (left) and the unit fulfilling ATEX requirements (right).**

The example results of the undertaken investigations are presented below. The comparison is made for measurements realized with the working prototype and the unit fulfilling ATEX requirements. The analyzed example case corresponds to the discontinuity length shown in Figure 10, the lack of grout from the drilled hole end and in the outer part of a rock bolt (supporting plate and nut unscrewed and removed). The differences in upper and lower plots may be attributed to different accelerometer orientation and consequently different impact direction. The identified natural frequencies are shown in Table 4 and the scatter plots of the differences between FE model and data estimated experimentally for that case are presented in Figure 11.

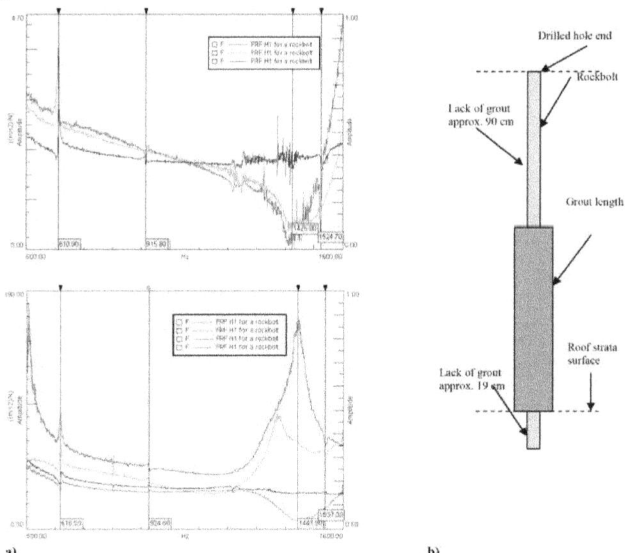


**Figure 10. The characteristics of the transfer functions for the analyzed case (measurements realized with the working prototype (a-upper chart) and the unit fulfilling ATEX requirements (a-lower chart)) and the estimated grout length (b), the length of the rock bolt is equal to 2.0 m. The chart axes are: the vertical axis—inertance, in (m/s$^2$)/N, the horizontal axis the frequency, in Hz.**

**Table 4. The identified natural frequencies of the investigated rock bolt, measurement with the working prototype (a), and the unit fulfilling the ATEX requirements (b).**

| No | Frequency, Hz | | | Difference (a), % | Difference (b), % |
|---|---|---|---|---|---|
| | Experiment (a) | Experiment (b) | FE model | | |
| 1 | 305.7 | 308.9 | 311.3 | 1.8 | 0.8 |
| 2* | 610.9 | 616.5 | 568.6 | -6.9 | -7.8 |
| 3* | 915.8 | 924.6 | 934.9 | 2.1 | 1.1 |
| 4* | 1425.0 | 1441.0 | 1387.2 | -2.7 | -3.7 |
| 5* | 1524.7 | 1537.3 | 1387.2 | 9.0 | 9.8 |
| 6 | 1707.0 | 1739.2 | 1832.9 | 7.4 | 5.4 |
| The frequency characteristic for the hidden end part of a rock bolt. | | | | | |

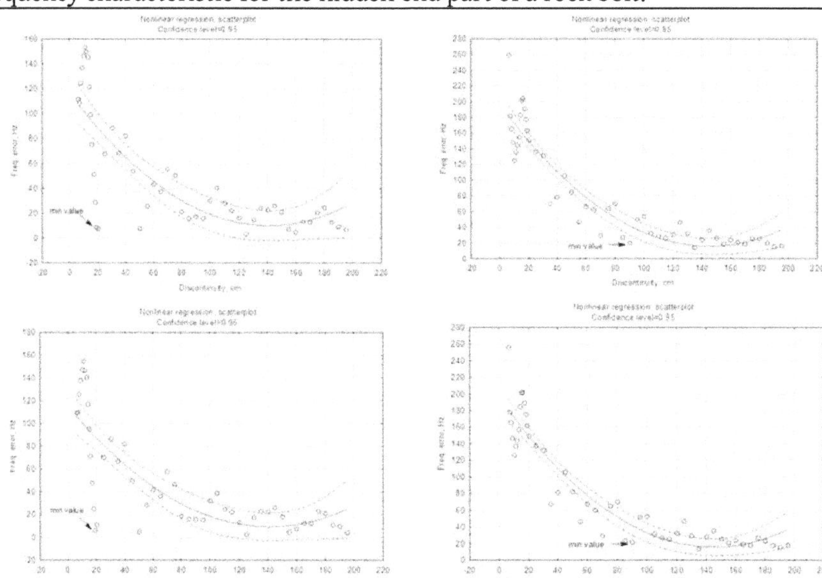

a) b)

**Figure 11. Scatter plot of the differences between FE model and data evaluated experimentally. The values of the lengths of discontinuity are: (a) 19 cm and (b) 90 cm. These values are specified for the first minimum differences of models and are clearly outside the values of the random scatter. The upper plots are for measurements with the working prototype, the lower ones for measurements with the unit fulfilling the ATEX requirements.**

In order to validate this method experiments were continued on the same cases of discontinuity deliberately prepared with the complete assembly of elements, so after screwing plate and nut to the rock bolt. Below the comparison of the measurements performed without the supporting plate and nut, and after screwing them to the rock bolt is discussed. A typical torsion force applied in the real working conditions is 250

Nm, so such a value was used in the finite element model (FE). Of course it is not a constraint and other torsion forces may be used according to real situations; a thorough discussion on that topic is accessible in technical literature [20, 29]. The example cases (at first without a nut and a plate) are shown in Figures 12 and 13. Utilizing the characteristics of the transfer function for the analyzed cases (a), the scatter plots of the differences between FE model and data evaluated experimentally were used and the designated sections of the length of discontinuity were obtained (c). For the rock bolt grouted from a rear, hidden end, shown in Figure 12, the discontinuity length is approximately equal to 1.15 m. That value is specified for the first minimum difference of models and is clearly outside the values of the random scatter.

a)

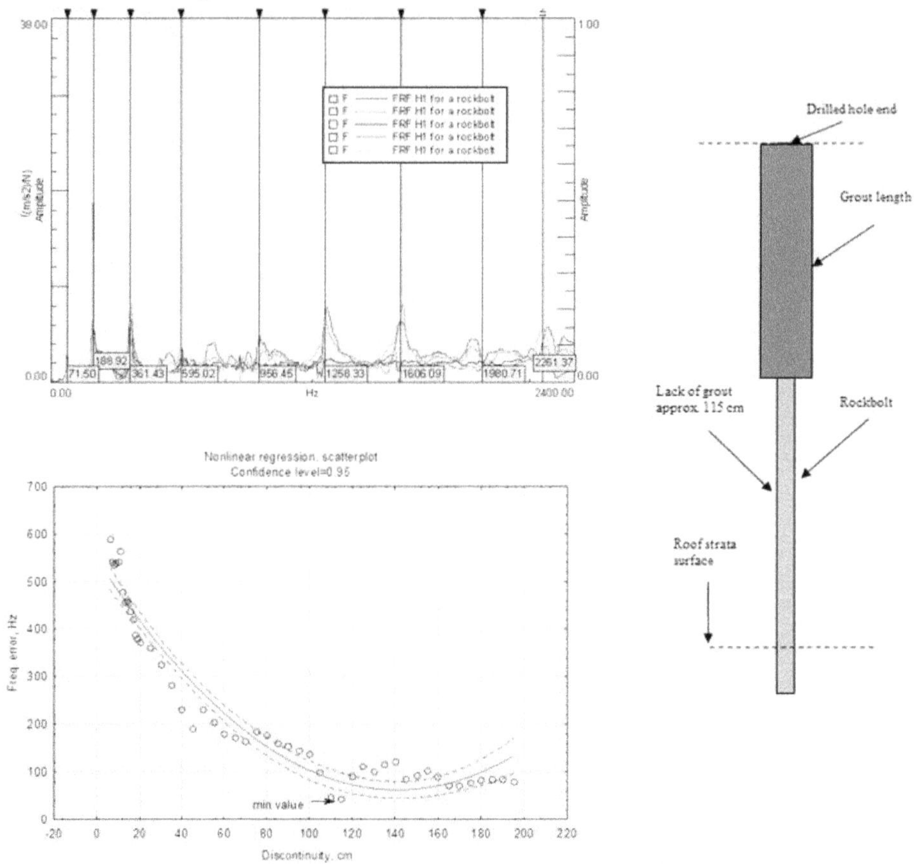


b) c)

**Figure 12. The results of estimation of the grout length: (a) the characteristics of the transfer function for the analyzed case, the vertical axis of the chart—inertance, in (m/s²)/N, the horizontal axis—frequency, in Hz, (b) the scatter plot of the differences between FE model and data evaluated experimentally, (c) the estimated grout length, the length of the rock bolt is equal to 2.0 m.**

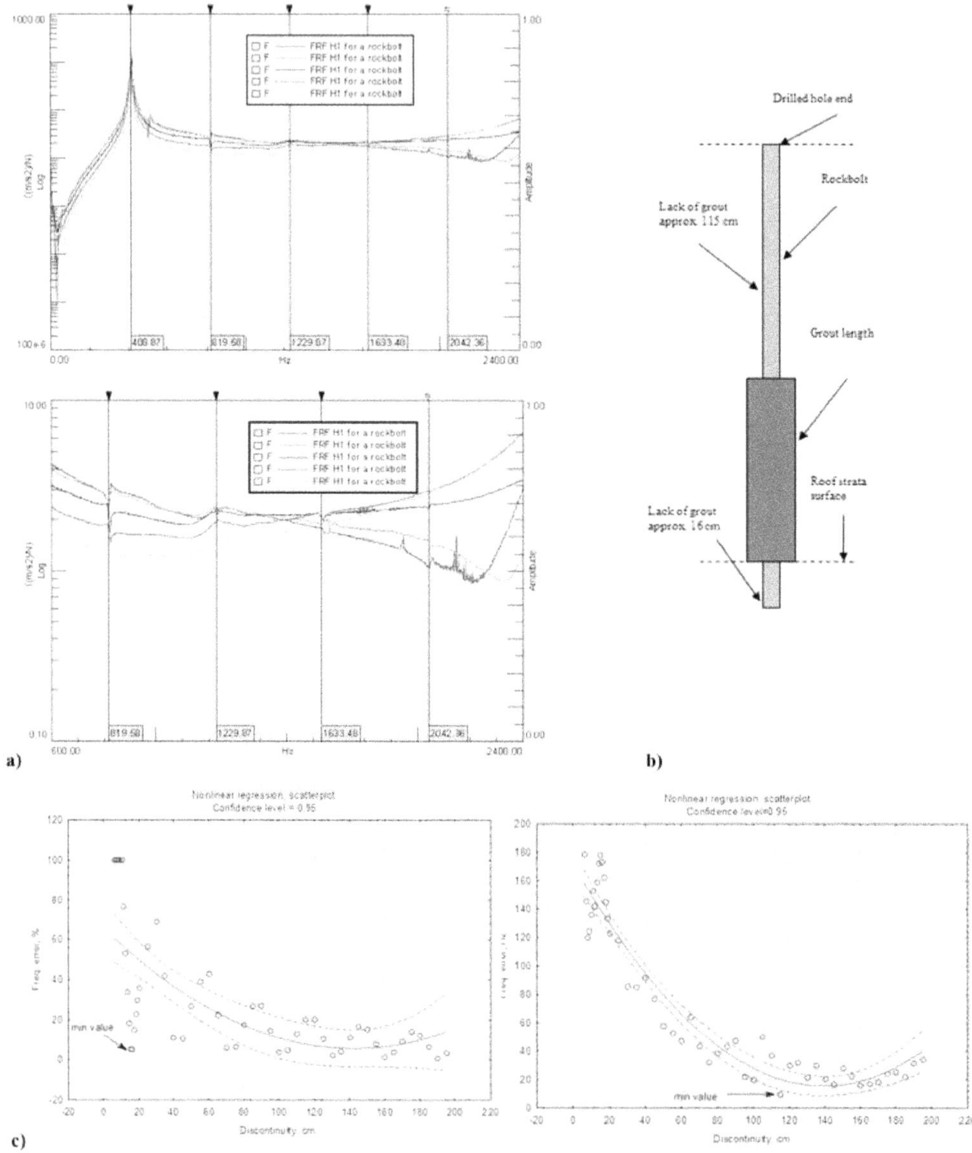


**Figure 13. The results of estimation of the grout length: (a) the characteristics of the transfer function for the analyzed case, the vertical axis of the chart—inertance, in (m/ s²)/N, the horizontal axis—frequency, in Hz, (b) the estimated grout length, the length of the rock bolt is equal to 2.0 m, (c) the scatter plot of the differences between FE model and data evaluated experimentally.**

The experimentally identified and numerically calculated (FE model) natural frequencies are presented in Table 5.

**Table 5. Comparison of identified natural frequencies for a rock bolt grouted from a rear, hidden end, the measurement using working prototype.**

| No | Frequency, Hz | | Difference, % |
|---|---|---|---|
| | Experiment | FE model | |
| 1 | 71.50 | 64.78 | -9.40 |
| 2 | 188.92 | 181.09 | -4.14 |
| 3 | 361.43 | 354.0 | -2.05 |
| 4 | 595.02 | 583.34 | -1.96 |
| 5 | 956.45 | 868.02 | -9.25 |
| 6 | 1258.33 | 1206.7 | -4.10 |
| 7 | 1606.09 | 1597.9 | -0.51 |
| 8 | 1980.71 | 2039.3 | 2.96 |
| 9 | 2261.37 | 2520.6 | 11.46 |

For the rock bolt grouted from a roof strata surface, shown in Figure 13, the discontinuity length is approximately equal to 1.15 m and the length of the outer part is approximately equal to 0.16 m. These values are specified for the first minimum differences of models and are clearly outside the values of the random scatter.

The identified experimentally and calculated numerically (FE model) natural frequencies are presented in Table 6.

**Table 6. The identified natural frequencies of the investigated rock bolt grouted from a roof strata surface, the measurement using unit using working prototype.**

| No | Frequency, Hz | | Difference, % |
|---|---|---|---|
| | Experiment | FE model | |
| 1 | 408.873 | 420.71 | -2.81 |
| 2* | 819.581 | 868.02 | -5.58 |
| 3* | 1229.866 | 1206.7 | 1.92 |
| 4* | 1633.481 | 1597.9 | 2.23 |
| 5* | 2042.362 | 2039.3 | 0.15 |

* The frequency characteristic for the hidden end part of a rock bolt.

The results of measurements performed with the supporting plate and nut, after screwing them to the rock bolt are shown in Figures 14 and 15. For the rock bolt grouted from a rear, hidden end, shown in Figure 14, the discontinuity length is approximately equal to 0.95 m. Though there are two minimum values outside the random scatter, the first one may be chosen as valid, the second may be attributed to aliasing phenomena observed in frequency analysis as well.

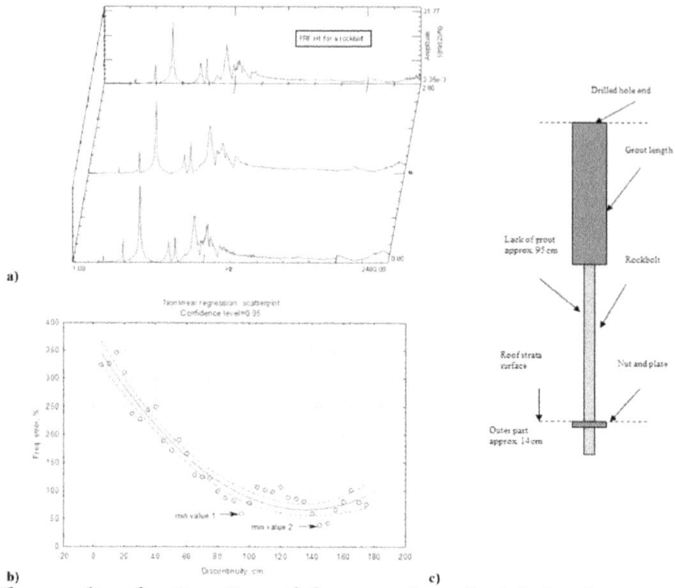


**Figure 14. The results of estimation of the grout length: (a) the characteristics of the transfer function for the analyzed case, the vertical axis of the chart—inertance, in $(m/s^2)/N$, the horizontal axis—frequency, in Hz, (b) the scatter plot of the differences between FE model and data evaluated experimentally, (c) the estimated grout length, the length of the rock bolt is equal to 2.0 m.**

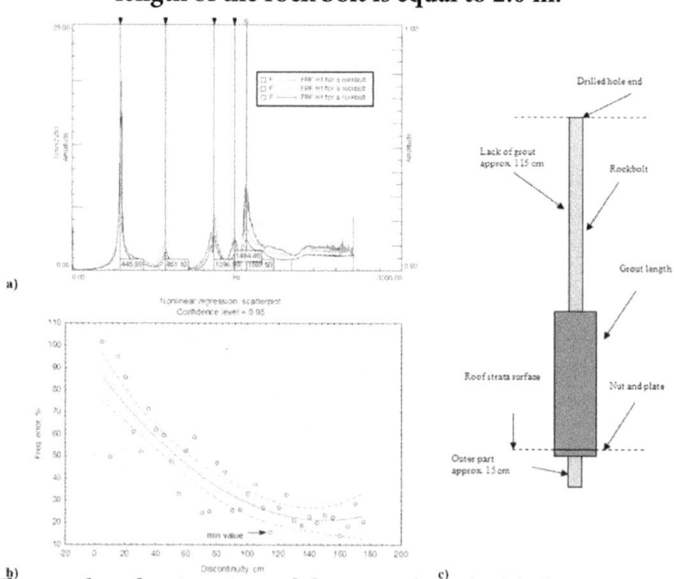


**Figure 15. The results of estimation of the grout length: (a) the characteristics of the transfer function for the analyzed case, the vertical axis of the chart—inertance, in $(m/s^2)/N$, the horizontal axis—frequency, in Hz, (b) the scatter plot of the differences between FE model and data evaluated experimentally, (c) the estimated grout length, the length of the rock bolt is equal to 2.0 m.**

The experimentally identified and numerically calculated (FE model) natural frequencies are presented in Table 7.

**Table 7. Comparison of identified natural frequencies for a rock bolt grouted from a rear, hidden end for measurement units—the working prototype based on National Instrument's components and the new one fulfilling the ATEX requirements.**

| No | Frequency, Hz | | | Difference 1, % | Difference 2, % |
|---|---|---|---|---|---|
| | Experiment 1 | Experiment 2 | FE model | | |
| 1* | 123.2 | 123.4 | 101.43 | -17.7 | -17.8 |
| 2* | 238.7 | 238.9 | 251.25 | 5.3 | 5.2 |
| 3* | 390.6 | 391.0 | 346.06 | -11.4 | -11.5 |
| 4 | 518.7 | 521.4 | 528,86 | 2.0 | 1.4 |
| 5* | 783.2 | 782.9 | 814.46 | 4.0 | 4.0 |
| 6* | 932.4 | 935.1 | 814.46 | -12.7 | -12.9 |
| 7* | 1616.5 | 1609.0 | 1624.9 | 0.5 | 1.0 |
| 8* | 2017.4 | 2008.9 | 1874.9 | -7.1 | -6.7 |
| * The frequency characteristic for the hidden end part of a rock bolt. | | | | | |

The grout length assessment is quite consistent with that obtained at the first stage, when a plate and a nut were unscrewed.

For the rock bolt grouted from a roof strata surface, shown in Figure 15, the discontinuity length is approximately equal to 1.15 m.

The experimentally identified and numerically calculated (FE model) natural frequencies are presented in Table 8.

**Table 8. The identified natural frequencies of the investigated rock bolt, measurement unit—working prototype.**

| No | Frequency, Hz | | Difference, % |
|---|---|---|---|
| | Experiment | FE model | |
| 1 | 445.8 | 470.3 | -5.5 |
| 2* | 851.1 | 850.7 | 0.1 |
| 3* | 1296.9 | 1182.2 | 8.8 |
| 4* | 1484.4 | 1564.8 | -5.4 |
| 5* | 1589.5 | 1667.4 | -4.9 |
| * The frequency characteristic for the hidden end part of a rock bolt. | | | |

The grout length assessment is also quite consistent with that obtained at the first stage, when a plate and a nut were unscrewed.

## 3.2 Measurements in working coal mines

Further experiments were realized in working coal and copper mines and around 50 rock bolts were tested. The aim of one of these experimental studies was connected with rock mass characterization [30] and examination of the strength of rock bolts mounted in the rock strata [3, 4] at different depths. The study took place in a chosen corridor of the working coalmine. The rock bolts were grouted in the roof of the roadway. There were 12 rock bolts mounted in 4 rows and the lengths of the rock bolts were: 2.4 m, 1.85 m, 1.25 m and 0.85 m. Localization of the research and distribution of investigated rock bolts are presented in Figure 16. All rock bolts were grouted using the resin material type Lokset. The grout length was 30 cm from the bottom of the hole.

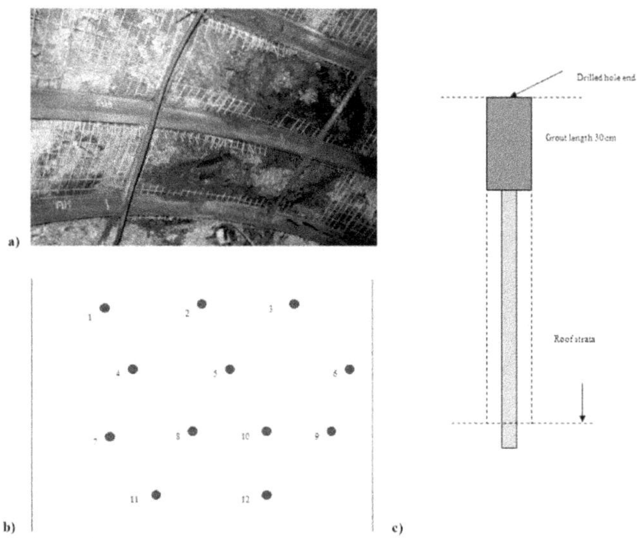


**Figure 16. The exploited seam with investigated rockbolts and hydraulic jack for pull out test (a), distribution of measured rock bolts no 1–12 (b) and the example geometry of the identified discontinuity case (c). The lengths of rock bolts: no 1, 2, 3—2.4 m, no 4, 5, 6—1.85 m, no 7, 8, 9—1.25 m, no 10, 11, 12—0.85 m.**

Then a pull out test was conducted by technical staff, who made a thorough analysis of obtained characteristics of pulling (put forward) of the rock bolts taking into account not only pulling of the rock bolt from the grout but also extending of the rock bolt as a result of applied force.

The quality assessment of grouting of rock bolts was performed as complementary to these tests. Although localization and length of the grout were known, the research was undertaken assuming that the result of the grouting process does not necessarily coincide with the intended one. Following are the results of the identification studies of quality assessment of grouted rock bolts. The reference models (FE models), with a specific location of grout, corresponding to experimental cases were matched. The research was conducted for 7 cases and for 4 cases studies were performed before and after pull out tests. For the shortest rock bolts, length 85 cm, lack of sufficient grout strength was also observed (rocks were too weak at that lengths).

The examples of the analysis results in ANSYS environment are shown in Figures 17 and 18 (visible parts are: a rock bolt and a resin layer). Correct matching cases with calculated mismatch errors are shown in Tables 9–11. The diagnosed grout lengths were localized at the end, bottom part of the rock bolts and were very close to the intended grout length of 30 cm. In order to check the accuracy of the assessment the FE calculations were performed also for smaller and larger grout lengths. For example, for the rock bolt with a length of 1.25 m, the smallest difference was obtained for the grout length 31 cm, and by increasing the length of the modeled grout by 1 cm the error changed from positive to negative values, which meant that the correct value was somewhere between 31 cm and 32 cm.

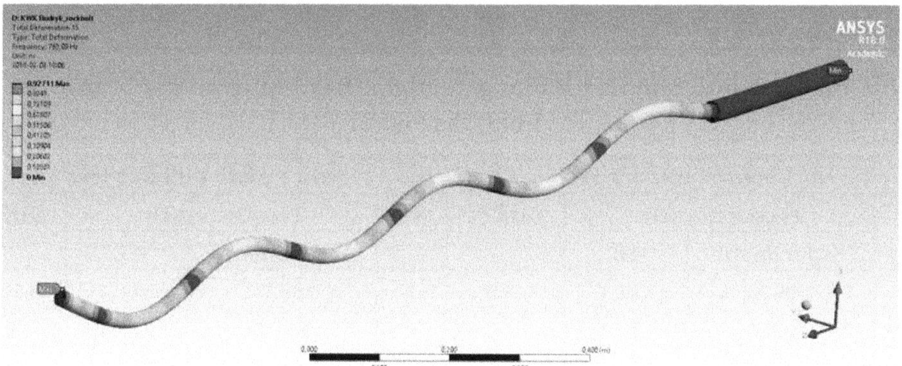


**Figure 17. The example of analysis results in ANSYS environment for a rock bolt length of 1.85 m.**

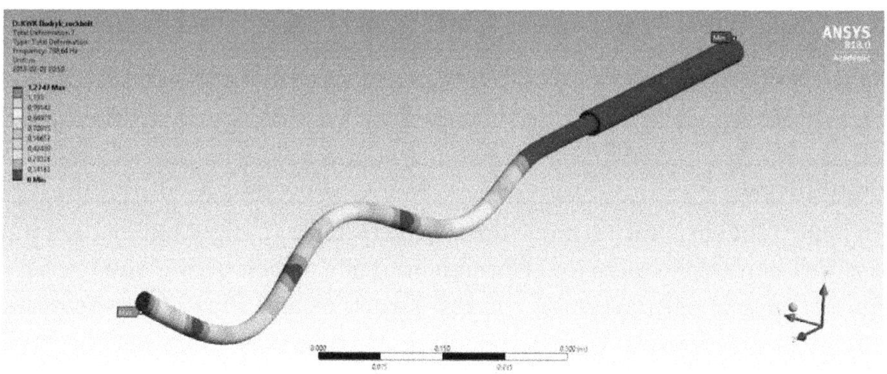


**Figure 18. The example of analysis results in ANSYS environment for a rock bolt length of 1.25 m.**

**Table 9. Rock bolt length 2.4 m, grout length 0.3 m from the bottom of the hole, case no 1.**

| No 1 before pull out test | | | | No 1 after pull out test | | | |
|---|---|---|---|---|---|---|---|
| No | Frequency. Hz | | Diff. % | No | Frequency. Hz | | Diff. % |
| | Experiment | FE | | | Experiment | FE | |
| 1 | 204.4 | 198.0 | 3.2 | 1 | 208.4 | 198.0 | 5.2 |
| 2 | 303.9 | 295.4 | 2.9 | 2 | 308.3 | 295.4 | 4.4 |
| 3 | 424.1 | 411.8 | 3.0 | 3 | 430.3 | 411.8 | 4.5 |
| 4 | 565.3 | 547.1 | 3.3 | 4 | 565.8 | 547.1 | 3.4 |
| 5 | 717.8 | 701.1 | 2.4 | 5 | 741.1 | 701.1 | 5.7 |
| 6 | 892.3 | 873.5 | 2.2 | 6 | 910.2 | 873.5 | 4.2 |
| 7 | 1091.1 | 1064.0 | 2.5 | 7 | 1091.4 | 1064.0 | 2.6 |
| 8 | 1307.5 | 1272.4 | 2.8 | 8 | 1355.9 | 1272.4 | 6.6 |
| 9 | 1540.7 | 1498.2 | 2.8 | 9 | 1589.2 | 1498.2 | 6.1 |
| Average difference. % | | | 2.8 | Average difference. % | | | 4.9 |

**Table 10. Rock bolt length 1.85 m, grout length 0.3 m from the bottom of the hole, case no 5.**

| No 5 before pull out test | | | | No 5 after pull out test | | | |
|---|---|---|---|---|---|---|---|
| No | Frequency. Hz | | Diff. % | No | Frequency. Hz | | Diff. % |
| | Experiment | FE | | | Experiment | FE | |
| 1 | 104.5 | 111.1 | -5.9 | 1 | 88.7 | 111.1 | -20.1 |
| 2 | 207.6 | 217.3 | -4.4 | 2 | 211.7 | 217.3 | -2.6 |
| 3 | 349.1 | 358.3 | -2.6 | 3 | 347.4 | 358.3 | -3.0 |
| 4 | 513.4 | 533.7 | -3.8 | 4 | 516.6 | 533.7 | -3.2 |
| 5 | 714.5 | 743.0 | -3.8 | 5 | 733.2 | 743.0 | -1.3 |
| 6 | 948.1 | 985.4 | -3.8 | 6 | 960.4 | 985.4 | -2.5 |
| 7 | 1206.1 | 1260.2 | -4.3 | 7 | 1231.9 | 1260.2 | -2.2 |
| 8 | 1495.4 | 1566.5 | -4.5 | 8 | 1581.3 | 1566.5 | 0.9 |
| 9 | 1819.8 | 1902.8 | -4.4 | 9 | — | — | — |
| Average difference. % | | | -4.3 | Average difference. % | | | -7.5 |

An important observation made during the tests was a slight but distinct increase of identified natural frequencies after pull out tests, which proves the impact of the test on mechanical parameters of the test structure and shows a stress hysteresis. Because of the elongation, that is, a slight increase of the length of the rock bolt, this change should go in the opposite direction, namely a decrease of the natural frequencies. In analyzed cases it appears that the first factor is dominant—stress hysteresis. During a normal quality assessment of grouted rock bolts this effect will not take place. It should also be noted that in investigated cases not all natural frequencies were identified, however, their number was sufficient to match the experimental and theoretical (FE) models. The results were quite satisfactory and proved the usefulness of the method.

**Table 11. Rock bolt length 1.25 m, grout length 0.3 m from the bottom of the hole, case no 8.**

| No 8 after pull out test | | | | No 8 after pull out test | | | |
|---|---|---|---|---|---|---|---|
| No | Frequency. Hz | | Diff. % | No | Frequency. Hz | | Diff. % |
| | Experiment | FE | | | Experiment | FE | |
| 1 | — | — | — | 1 | 103.9 | 102.8 | 1.1 |
| 2 | 292.4 | 286.7 | 2.0 | 2 | 295.2 | 286.7 | 3.0 |
| 3 | 568.0 | 559.0 | 1.6 | 3 | 571.0 | 559.0 | 2.1 |
| 4 | 932.8 | 918.0 | 1.6 | 4 | 927.8 | 918.0 | 1.1 |
| 5 | 1382.2 | 1360.3 | 1.6 | 5 | 1376.3 | 1360.3 | 1.2 |
| 6 | 1945.7 | 1880.8 | 3.4 | 6 | 1900.7 | 1880.8 | 1.1 |
| Average difference. % | | | 2.2 | Average difference. % | | | 1.7 |

Based on obtained knowledge and experience research was continued for quality assessment of rock bolt support system realized as a project of above 2 km length corridor drilled for excavation purposes to enable access to large coal deposits. The research was performed in several sessions and it seems to be relevant to perform such a control on a periodic basis.

The diagnosed natural frequencies with calculated mismatch errors for the example case are presented in Table 12.

**Table 12. The identified natural frequencies of the investigated rock bolt.**

| No | Frequency, Hz | | Difference, % |
|---|---|---|---|
| | Experiment | FE model | |
| 1 | 363.8 | 362.0 | -0.5 |
| 2 | 676.3 | 689.2 | 1.9 |
| 3 | 1023.0 | 1061.8 | 3.8 |
| 4 | 1296.9 | 1336.3 | 3.0 |
| 5 | 1468.3 | 1336.3 | -9.0 |
| 6 | 1778.7 | 1785.2 | 0.4 |
| 7 | 2135.0 | 2398.9 | 12.4 |

The FRF functions (waterfall curve) for an investigated rock bolt, a placement of the response transducer, and the identified discontinuity length are presented in Figure 19. The discontinuity length is about 80 cm from the outer part. What was observed in that particular session that in the adjacent area several similar cases of discontinuity were diagnosed.

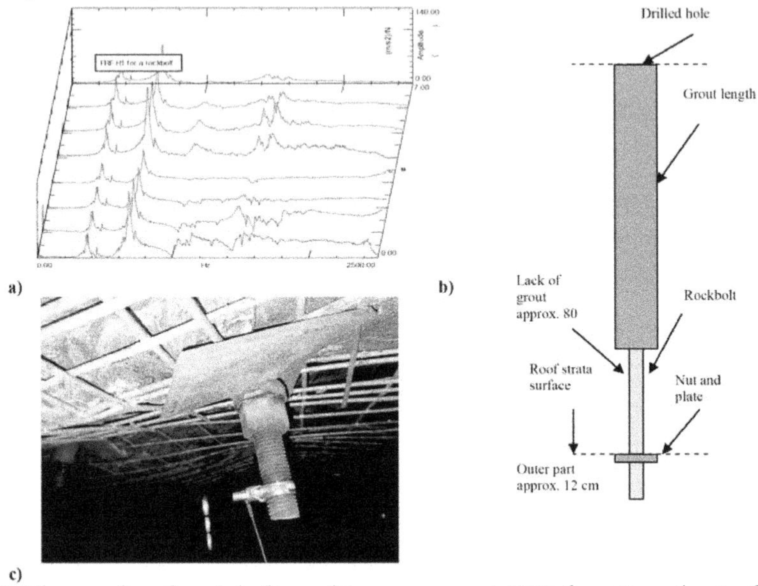


**Figure 19. The results of rock bolt quality assessment, FRF functions (waterfall curve) for an investigated rock bolt (a), the identified discontinuity case (b), a placement of the response transducer (c), the length of the rock bolt is equal to 2.5 m.**

While explaining possible reasons of improper grouting it is worth considering the technology of installation of rock bolts. There are mainly three phases of fixing the rock bolt into rock strata: a placement of grout cartridges into a drilled hole using a rockbolt (a rock bolt is inserted up to it half length), turning phase with continued insertion of a rock bolt up to the end of the hole (depending on the environmental conditions a time period is about 10 s), spinning phase (about 4-5 s) and hold phase (about 15 s). It is very crucial to control these phases especially the turning and spinning ones. Otherwise lack of grouting connection may occur. Too fast insertion of a rock bolt may lead to leakage of grout from the hole and lack of grout in the back part. Too long spinning phase may cause damage of contact between a rock bolt and grout in the inner part (close to the end of the hole). It is because the hardening time in that part is shorter than that in the outer part (specific preparation of grout cartridges). Too slow insertion may result in not full mixing of grout, especially at the end of a rock bolt (one of the consequences might be a rock bolt sticking out more than it is supposed to). If there are crevices in rock strata some amount of grout may leak into that area with the result of local discontinuity of grout layer. Another case might be a larger diameter of the hole then projected, mainly in the outer part of a hole (quite often when rock strata is hard). Then the amount of grout inserted is not enough for proper connection of a rock bolt to rock strata and it also may lead to lack of grout in the outer part of the hole. Inspection of camera records of holes in the investigated area revealed that it could be the reason for not proper grouting for the case shown in Figure 19.

## 4. CONCLUSIONS

The increasing interest in the use of rock bolt support systems has its economic background. This system of prevention is less time and material consuming as well as technically more feasible. In strong rocks the use of rock bolt systems is prevailing. In Polish coal mines where rock strata are weaker, the interest in the usage of rock bolt support system is much lower but recently marked changes may be observed in this area. At the same time there is no satisfactory non-destructive method for testing rock bolt installation [6]. It was the reason for undertaking the research on the method for identification of grouting discontinuity for rock bolts. The invented method uses modal analysis procedures and is based on an impact excitation and reconciliation of experimental and theoretical modal models.

In laboratory conditions a cause-effect relation was found between excitation of a rock bolt to transverse vibration and response characteristic of the examined structure. To enable in situ measurement a portable measurement system was invented and constructed. The LabVIEW environment was used as a programming tool. Simultaneously, import of recorded data and derivation of modal parameters were performed utilizing modal analysis software LMS TestLab.

Dynamic parameters of a tested structure (installed rock bolt) are determined by its border conditions, which are directly connected with a grouting discontinuity length. That fact enabled us to diagnose the discontinuity length.

It was necessary to build a theoretical modal model of an installed rock bolt where different cases of grouting discontinuity were encountered. The results of theoretical modal analysis performed on validated FE model constituted a reference base for unknown cases (correlation and comparison techniques were used to validate the model). The reference to the base of validated theoretical models was found reasonable (the discontinuities of verification tests were determined a priori). The reference base may be used for different types of rocks.

Based on the prototype construction the final version fulfilling ATEX requirements was constructed.

The transverse excitation was found as more adequate to identify the discontinuity length of the resin layer of the installed rock bolts.

A mass of a response transducer has influence on the results [26], hence it is desired to minimize it.

The measurement system was verified in real coal mine conditions.

On the basis of the carried out research and calculations of finite element models of the system under test, rock bolt - resin - rock mass, it can be concluded that the developed method and analytical application actually classifies the measured natural frequencies group and enables to identify cases of discontinuity (regions of lack of bonding, which is seen as crucial here).

At present a diagnosis is completed after analytical phase performed in laboratory conditions, so results are not accessible in situ. Its usage is restricted to steel rock bolts up to 2.5 m long (longer rock bolts were not investigated), though not only in mining but also in building engineering.

## REFERENCES


1. Li Charlie C. Principles of rock bolting in high stress rock masses, Mining & Environment, Vol. 2/1:133-143. Central Mining Institute, Poland (2010).
2. Li Charlie C. Principles of rock bolting design. Journal of Rock Mechanics and Geotechnical Engineering, Vol.9, Issue 3: 396-414, 2017. https://doi.org/10.1016/j.jrmge.2017.04.002.
3. Tadollini S.C. Current roof bolting applications, technologies and theories in US mines", Mining & Environment, Vol. 2/1:305-314. Central Mining Institute, Poland (2010).
4. Ulusay R., Hudson J.A. The Complete ISRM Suggested methods for rock characterization, Testing and Monitoring: 1974-2006. Ankara, Turkey (2007).
5. Beard M.D., Lowe M.J.S. Non-destructive testing of rock bolts using ultrasonic waves. International Journal of Rock Mechanics and Mining Sciences 40: 527-536 (2003).
6. Hebblewhite B., Fabjanczyk M., Gray P. Investigations into premature rock bolt failures in the Australian coal mining industry. Underground Coal Operators' Conference, 167 (2003).
7. Kidybiński A, Nierobisz A, Masny W Maintenance of an opening affected by tremor enforced within nether roof strata. Proceedings of the Rockbursts 2005 Conference: 41-52. Central Mining Institute, Poland (2005).
8. Hartman W., Esterhuizen H. A geotechnical risk assessment tool for underground mine drives – The Fourth Australasian Ground Control in Mining Conference, 48 (2018).
9. Bačić M., Gavin K., Kovačević S. Trends in non-destructive testing of rock bolts. Journal of the Croatian Association of Civil Engineers GRAĐEVINAR, 71(2019) 10: 823-831, https://doi.org/10.14256/JCE.2727.20.

10. Bergman SGA, Krauland N, Martna J, Paganus T. Non-Destructive Field Test of Cement-Grouted Bolts With the Boltometer, 5th ISRM Congress. Melbourne, Australia (1983).

11. Hartman W., Lecinq B., Higgs J., Tongue D. Non destructive integrity testing of rock reinforcement elements in Australian mines. Underground Coal Operators' Conference (2010).

12. Knape P. Boltometer testing of reference bolt in the final repository for reactor waste (SFR), Forsmark. INIS:SV-UB--1988-15. Sweden (1988).

13. Starkey A., Ivanovic A., Neilson R.D., Rodger A.A. The integrity testing of ground anchorages using Granit. 20-th International Conference on Ground Control in Mining. USA (2001).

14. Starkey A., Ivanovic A., Neilson R.D., Rodger A.A. Using a lumped dynamic model of rock bolt to produce training data for neural network for diagnosis of real data. Meccanica 38:131-142. Kluwer Academic Publishers (2003).

15. Hao Y., Wu Y., Li P., Tao J., Teng Y., Hao G. Non-destructive inspection on anchorage defect of hollow grouted rock bolt using wavelet transform analysis. Journal on Image and Video Processing 146 (2018).

16. Patil D.P., Maiti S.K. Experimental verification of a method of detection of multiple cracks in beams based on frequency measurements, Journal of Sound and Vibration: 439-451 (2005).

17. Sadettin O. Analysis of free and forced vibration of a cracked cantilever beam. NDT&E International Vol.40, Issue 6: 443-450 (2007).

18. Sinha J.K., Friswell M.I. Simulation of the dynamic response of a cracked beam. Computers & Structures, Vol. 80, Issues 18-19: 1473-1476 (2002).

19. Gangbing S., Weijie Li, Bo Wang, Siu Chun M. H. A Review of Rock Bolt Monitoring Using Smart Sensors. Sensors 2017, 17, 776; doi:10.3390/s17040776.

20. Hyett, A., Mitri, H., Spearing, A. Validation of two new technologies for monitoring the in situ performance of rock bolts. Proceedings of the 7th International Symposium on Rockbolting and Rock Mechanics in Mining. AIMS 2012, Aachen: 177-190.

21. Godfrey DE, Kuchar NR Method of testing the integrity of installed rock bolts. United States Patent US4062229A (1977).

22. Ewins D.J. Modal Testing: theory, practice and application. Research Studies Press Ltd., England (2000).

23. Maia N.M.M., Silva J.M.M. Theoretical and Experimental Modal Analysis. Research Studies Press Ltd., England (1997).

24. Remington P. J., Experimental and theoretical Studies of Vibrating Systems, Encyclopedia of Acoustics, Vol. 2, Ch. 63, pp. 715-734, John Wiley & Sons, New York (1997).

25. Uhl T. Computer Aided Identification of Mechanical Models. WNT, Poland (1997).

26. Randall R. B. Mechanical Vibration and Shock Measurements, Bruel & Kjaer handbook: 122-129, Naerum (1982).

27. Dossing O. Structural Testing, Part II: Modal analysis and Simulation. Bruel & Kjaer, Denmark (1988).

28. Tryon R.C. Cluster Analysis. Ann Arbor, MI: Edwards Brothers (1939).

29. Cała M., Flisiak J., Tajduś A. The mechanism of interaction between rockbolt support system and rock strata of inconsistent layers positioning. Polish Academy of Science, Cracow (2001).

30. Haneol K., Hafeezur R., Wahid A., Abdul Muntaqim N., Jung-Joo K., Jonguk K., Hankyu Y. Classification of Factors Affecting the Performance of Fully Grouted Rock Bolts with Empirical Classification Systems. Applied Sciences, 9, 4781 (2019).

CHAPTER-5

# SONIC DRILLING WITH USE OF A CAVITATION HYDRAULIC VIBRATOR

## 1. INTRODUCTION

Sonic drilling is an effective method for sampling soft soils without disturbance, which can also be used for rapid drilling of bedrocks using vibration shock technology with rotary drilling [1]. Hydraulic hammers are of a dynamic type, operate on the energy of the flushing mud. Their operation principle is based on the effect of a water hammer as a result of interrupting the flow of fluid [2]. The main disadvantages of submersible hydraulic hammers are still:

- ☆ their low efficiency, not exceeding 10%;
- ☆ increased flow rate of the working fluid, which in some cases contradicts the drilling conditions, for example, leads to erosion of the borehole walls in zones of weak rocks;
- ☆ an acceptable operating mode at a liquid pressure drop of less than 6 MPa;
- ☆ the presence in their design of rapidly wearing moving parts, springs and rubber cuffs, which significantly reduce the period between inspection and service life;

☆ negative impact of pressure oscillations to the mud pump, causing increased wear of its parts and deteriorating drilling efficiency due to the unambiguous dependence of the bottomhole power on the pump characteristics [3].

At present, researchers from various countries continue to work on improving the characteristics of hydraulic hammers. For example, in the last decade in the Russian Federation, research has carried out on volumetric hydropercussion machines [3]. The foundations of the theory have been developed and original hydraulic shock and distribution devices have been created. Their peculiarity lies in the presence of a hydraulic accumulator, which complicates the design, especially for significant depth drilling.

Analysis of recent studies and publications indicates the trend of using hydrodynamic cavitation as a source of vibration loading on the drilling tool to increase the drilling speed in hard and super hard formations. Such studies are presented by authors from different countries at conferences on geomechanics and well drilling. So, for example, in the works [4, 5, 6] in the process of experimental studies it was found to improve the operational characteristics of the drill bit. This was achieved by intensifying the removal of crushed material from the contact zone between the surfaces of the bit cutters and the rock during drilling due to cavitation effects in the high-pressure flow of the drilling fluid in the bit nozzle. It was found that for drilling with a cavitation impulse tool more efficient cutting of the rock and transportation of drill cuttings occurs, and friction in the drill string is also reduced.

Possibilities of increasing the profitability of well construction using pulsating jet technologies in future designs of the drill string with the optimization of the frequency and amplitude effects of the bit, taking into account the lithology of drilled rocks, are given in [7]. It was shown, "this could lead to faster and more efficient drilling, which will reduce drilling costs and make more oil and gas wells profitable".

In the last decade, researchers from China have been intensively engaged in the creation of a new cavitating drill bit [8]. This was due to the need to overcome a number of problems in its western region during exploration and construction of superdeep wells with the depth ranging from 2000 m to 6000 m. In particular, the rate of penetration (ROP) of wells and the rate of development of new fields in these difficult geological conditions decreased significantly, and the cost of drilling increased dramatically.

To overcome the above problems, a new drilling tool was developed with the installation of a hydraulic impulse generator of a cavitation jet. Tests of such a generator have shown that at a flow rate of flushing fluid from 32 l/s, it implements fluid pressure oscillations with amplitude range $\Delta P$ from 2.1 to 2.2 MPa and a fundamental frequency up to 10 Hz. Field experiments conducted in oil fields throughout China on more than 100 wells with the maximum depth of 6162 m have shown that drilling with this tool increases the ROP by 16 ÷ 104%. This is due to the pulsation of the jet, cavitating erosion and the effect of local negative pressure, as well as an improvement in the cleaning efficiency of the bottomhole [9, 10].

At the same time, studies to assess the effect of the vibration frequency of a drill bit on rock fragmentation in experimental and theoretical works on drilling various rocks by the sonic method showed that vibration frequencies of 1.4 kHz [11] are the most beneficial for ensuring the maximum drilling speed in hard rocks.

At the end of the last century (in the 80 s) the Institute of Technical Mechanics of the National Academy of Sciences of Ukraine (ITM NASU) together with the 'Geotechnika' special design bureau (Russia) created a new scientific direction in the development of submersible percussion machines using the effects of hydrodynamic cavitation [12]. The main goal of this direction was the creation of a new method of dynamic loads on the drill bit, allowing to eliminate the disadvantages of existing hydropercussion machines. This method was implemented in the development of a drill string with a cavitation hydraulic vibrator.

Analysis of the latest publications on the study of promising devices that intensify the technological process of drilling exploration and production wells shows that the drilling technology using the cavitation hydraulic vibrator has a number of advantages. It lacks the main disadvantages of submersible hydraulic hammers [3] and impulse devices [10]. Cavitation hydraulic vibrator does not require additional energy sources and does not contain moving parts, it is easy to manufacture and fits organically into existing equipment without affecting the pump, since drill mud pressure oscillations are not transmitted above the place of the vibrator installation.

## 2. DRILLING RIG WITH A CAVITATION HYDRAULIC VIBRATOR FOR INTENSIFYING THE TECHNOLOGICAL PROCESS OF WELL CONSTRUCTION

The cavitation hydraulic vibrator (Figure 1) is a part of a drill pipe 1 of drilling rig with drill bit 6. The hydraulic vibrator 5 is mounted in the pipe using tapered threads, the structure of the vibrator contains the cavitation generator 2 of flushing fluid pressure oscillations.

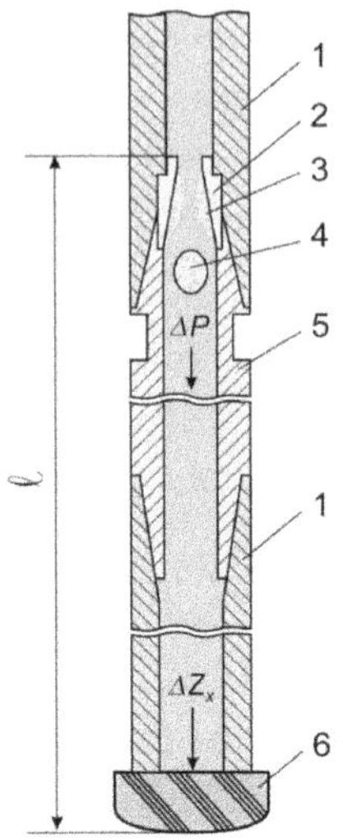

**Figure 1. Layout of a drill string with a cavitation hydraulic vibrator. 1 is drill pipe; 2 is cavitation generator; 3, 4 are the cavity is sedentary and its cavity part that has come off; 5 is hydraulic vibrator; 6 is drill bit.**

## 2.1 Cavitation generator of fluid pressure oscillations and its characteristics

The cavitation generator of pressure oscillations is the Venturi tube of special geometry that converts a stationary fluid flow into a periodically stalling cavitation flow [12]. In this case, high-frequency shock self-oscillations of the liquid pressure are realized, exceeding the pressure at the generator inlet, transforming into axial vibration accelerations of the drill string [13].

A diagram of the cavitation flow in generators of this type with the distribution of pressure and flow velocity along the flow axis and the designation of its dimensions are shown in Figure 2.

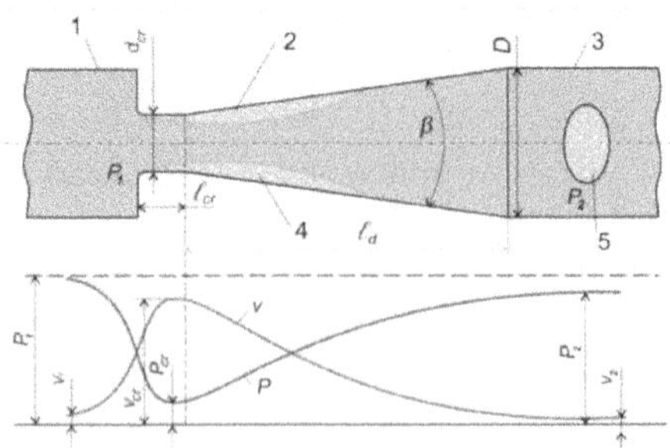

**Figure 2. Scheme of the cavitation flow in the generator with pressure and flow velocity distribution along the generator length. 1 is inlet pipeline; 2 is generator; 3 is outlet pipeline; 4 is cavitation zone with cavity volume V; 5 is detached part of the cavity $V_2$; $P_1$ is total pressure at the cavitation generator inlet; $P_2$ is full back pressure.**

Cavitation occurs when the local static pressure drops to a critical one, equal to or close to the saturated vapor pressure of the liquid, caused by an increase in the liquid velocity in the cavitation generator throat. In this case, discontinuities of the liquid appear and cavities filled with vapors and gases are formed. It has been established that the most developed cavitation oscillations are observed in the hydraulic system behind a local constriction of the Venturi tube type when the diffuser opening angle $\beta \geq 16°$ [12]. The frequency and amplitude of oscillations in a wide range of their values can be easily controlled by changing the operating parameters of the generator.

The cavitation generator is characterized by the following parameters:

☆ geometric parameters:

dcr and $\lambda_{cr}$ are the diameter and length of the throat; β is the diffuser opening angle; D and $\lambda_d$ are the outlet diffuser diameter and the diffuser length;

☆ regime parameters:

$P_1$, $P_2$ and Q are total inlet and back pressure and liquid flow rate through the generator; τ is parameter of the mode of the liquid cavitation flow;

☆ dynamic parameters:

f is self-oscillation frequency; $\Delta P = P_{2max}-P_{2min}$ is the range (peak to peak value) of pressure self-oscillations due to the nonharmonic shapes of oscillations; P2max is the maximum value of the pressure in the pulse behind the generator; P2min is the minimum value of the pressure in the pulse); ΔQ is the range (peak to peak value) of self-oscillations of the volumetric liquid flow rate.

The cavitation parameter τ is a dimensionless number used in flow calculations. It expresses the relationship between the difference of a local absolute pressure P2 (at the generator outlet) from the vapor pressure Pcr and the velocity head, which is determined by the velocity in the generator throat:

$$\tau = \frac{P_2 - P_{cr}}{\rho \frac{v_{cr}^2}{2}} \quad (1)$$

where vcr is the velocity of the liquid through the generator throat; ρ is the liquid density; Pcr is the liquid pressure in the generator throat.

The numerator of this parameter includes the total pressure or head, under the cavity collapses, and the denominator is the flow velocity head, determined by the pressure difference P2-Pcr. The change in pressure on the surface of the body or on the walls of any channel limiting the flow is mainly associated with a change in the flow velocity. Therefore, the velocity head can be considered as a value that determines the pressure drop, as a result of which a cavity can form and expand.

From this point of view, the cavitation number is the ratio of the pressure under which the cavity collapses to the pressure under which the cavity appears and grows.

Abnormally high values of liquid pressure in the pulse are observed at the generator diffuser angle of the 16 < β ≤ 45° in the range of values of the cavitation parameter τ from 0.02 to 0.4. As an example, in Figure 3 shows a fragment of an oscillogram of the time dependence of the pressure p2(t) and a filmogram of the process of growth and detachment of the cavity volume V. This results were obtained during testing of the hydraulic system with the cavitation generator (the Venturi tube throat diameter of dcr = 6 mm, the diffuser opening angle of β = 20° and outlet diameter of D = 24 mm). In this case, the inlet pressure P1 and the outlet pressure P2 were of 20 MPa and of 2.0 MPa (i.e. τ ≈ 0.1). In the event of cavitation oscillations in the hydraulic system after the cavitation generator, the pressure P1 at the inlet to the cavitation generator practically did not contain a dynamic component.

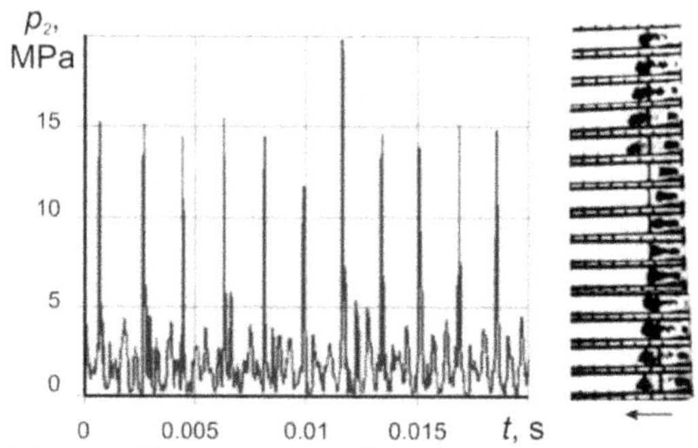


**Figure 3. Fragment of the oscillogram recording the pressure $p_2$ in time at the cavitation generator output with the critical section diameter $d_{cr}$ = 6 mm at τ ≈ 0.1 and a filmogram of the growth and separation of the cavitation cavity in the generator tube (the direction of fluid flow is indicated by an arrow).**

The figure shows that when cavitation occurs, the cavity begins at the entrance to the cylindrical section with dcr. The cavity volume V grows over the entire length of the critical section at the fixed pressure value at the outlet of the generator P2. Then the cavity enters the diffuser and spreads along the walls. When the cavity, at a certain mode, reaches its maximum length, reverse flows along the diffuser wall are observed, which tear off the part of the cavity located in the diffuser. The separation section of the cavity becomes constant and corresponds to the transition of the cylindrical section of the tube into the diffuser [12]. The process of detachment and collapse of a part of the cavity in a certain mode occurs strictly periodically, that is, with a constant frequency of several hundred Hz.

The frequencies of pressure oscillations in the hydraulic system, calculated from the pressure recording oscillograms, and the frequencies of the part of the detachment cavity located in the diffuser, determined from the time marks on the films obtained during the tests of the generator at different values of the cavitation parameter τ, are in satisfactory agreement. This allows us to conclude that the anomalously high periodic pressure impulses of a shock nature behind a local constriction of the Venturi type (see Figure 3, curve p2(t)) are caused by the collapse of large-volume cavities in the fluid flow.

The pressure wave from the collapse center propagates along the flow over rather long distances (practically not attenuating in experiments up to 2.0 meters). The pressure wave propagates against the flow, is damped by a new cavity that has grown by this time, as evidenced by the absence of oscillations at the generator inlet, but it takes part in the formation of reverse flows and creates conditions for the separation of the next cavity. Thus, a self-synchronized process of separation and collapse of cavitation cavities is established.

Figure 4 shows the calculated dependences of the swing of pressure oscillations ΔP on the cavitation parameter τ and the experimental data obtained during bench tests. Calculated and experimental data are given for generators with dcr, equal to 8 mm, 6 mm, and 2.5 mm. The inlet pressure values were P1 = 1 MPa, 10 MPa, 20 MPa, and 30 MPa.

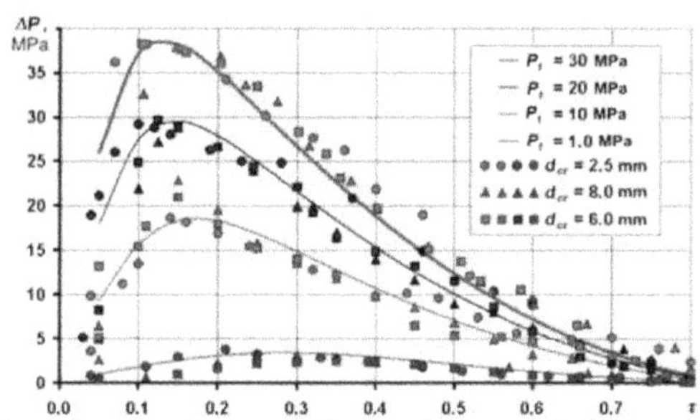


**Figure 4. Theoretical and experimental dependences of the amplitude ΔP of pressure oscillations on the cavitation parameterτ realized by the cavitation generator for case of the inlet pressure $P_1$ changes from 1 MPa to 30 MPa.**

The location of the experimental points relative to the theoretical dependences of the swing ΔP of the pressure oscillations at the generator output on the cavitation parameter τ shows their satisfactory convergence. The relative error of the given results does not exceed 15%. It was found that the regime of periodically stalling cavitation flow is realized in the range of variation of the cavitation parameter τ from 0.01 to 0.8. At a fixed value of τ, an increase in liquid pressure P1 at the inlet to the experimental sample of the cavitation generator leads to an increase in the magnitude of the pressure oscillation range ΔP. The nature of the established dependences ΔP(τ) shows that for all values of pressure P1, the value ΔP of the oscillatory pressure with increasing τ first sharply increases, reaches its maximum value, and, further, at a certain value of τ decreases.

The dependences of $\Delta P(\tau)$ have the maximums in the range cavitation parameter $\tau$ from 0.1 to 0.3 for different values of steady-state pressure P1. By the increase in the pressure P1, the maximum $\Delta P$ shifts towards lower values of the cavitation parameter $\tau$.

The maximum value of the swing $\Delta P$ of the oscillatory pressure value is approximately in 1.2-3.5 times higher than the steady-state pressure P1 at the generator inlet. In this case, with an increase in the pressure P1, the ratio $\Delta P/P1$ decreases. So, at P1 = 1 MPa $\Delta P/P1 \approx 3.5$, and at P1 = 30 MPa the value of is $\Delta P/P1 \approx 1.2$.

Analysis of the dependencies, presented in Figure 4, shows clearly that the amplitude of the oscillatory pressure $\Delta P$ is determined by the input pressure P1 and the cavitation parameter $\tau$. There is no influence of the diameter of the critical section of the generator, and, consequently, of the fluid volumetric flow rate on the values $\Delta P$ of the oscillation peaks. So, for example, at P1 = 30 MPa with a change in dcr from 2.5 mm to 6.0 mm, the value of the fluid volumetric flow rate increased in proportion to the increase in the flow area of the generator by 5.76 times (from 1.12 to 6.46 l/s,), and the swing level $\Delta P$ did not change. At first glance, this paradox is associated with the fact that an increase in the volumetric flow rate of liquid through the generator Q leads to an increase in the volume of the detached part of the cavitation cavity. This was recorded by visual studies [12] and by theoretical determination of the amplitude $\Delta Vc$ of oscillations of the volume of the detached part of the cavity. It would seem that the collapse of a larger volume of the cavity, with an increase in the flow section of the generator, should lead to an increase in the amplitude of oscillations $\Delta P$. However, as follows from Figure 4, this does not happen.

According to the results of the study carried out in [14], it was found that from the physical point of view and from the position of the existing linear mathematical model, the pressure that arises when the cavitation cavity collapses does not depend on its size, but is determined by the speed of its wall movement, which is determined by the difference pressure and discharge pressure.

However, we note that the energy of the discrete-pulse action of a liquid in any technological process is determined not only by the range of pressure fluctuations, but also by the oscillatory component of the volumetric flow rate, which increases with an increase in the generator flow area.

Figure 5 shows the dependences of the theoretical cavitation oscillation frequency f on the cavitation parameter $\tau$ for generators with dcr = 2.5 mm, 6 mm, and 8 mm (solid line) and experimental data at fixed values of pressure at the generator inlet P1 = 1 MPa, 10 MPa, 20 MPa, and 30 MPa.

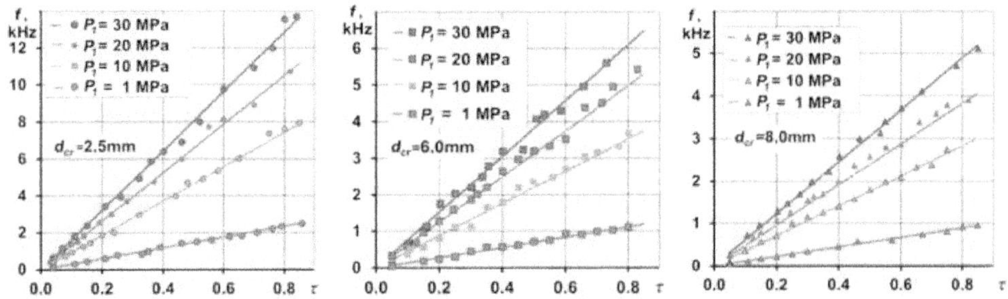


**Figure 5. Theoretical and experimental dependences of the frequency f vs. the cavitation parameter τ for the steady-state inlet pressure $P_1$ changes from 1 MPa to 30 MPa.**

It can be seen from the figure that for all the generators presented, the theoretical dependences f(τ) obtained by calculations are in satisfactory agreement with the experimental data in almost the entire range of variation of the cavitation parameter τ and are linear. The relative error of the given results does not exceed 10%.

It was found that, at fixed values of the cavitation parameter τ and pressure at the generator inlet, an increase in the diameter of the critical section of the cavitation generator (and, consequently, the volumetric flow rate of the liquid) leads to a decrease in the frequency of cavitation oscillations. So, at the values $P_1 = 30$ MPa and τ =0.6 increase in the value of the cavitation generator throat diameter from 2.5 mm to 8.0 mm leads to decrease in the frequency of cavitation self-oscillations by about 2.63 times (from 9.74 kHz to 3.71 kHz). An increase in the liquid injection pressure P1 leads to an increase in the frequency of cavitation self-oscillations. So, with the values of the throat diameter of the cavitation generator 6 mm and the cavitation parameter 0.6, an increase in the fluid inlet pressure P1 from 1 MPa to 30 MPa leads to an increase in the cavitation self-oscillations frequency from 0.93 kHz to 4.57 kHz.

Thus, it has been established that in a drilling rig with a hydraulic vibrator, that includes the cavitation generator of fluid pressure oscillations, the stationary flow of the process fluid turns into a discrete-pulse flow of increased power. It is realized in the form of high-frequency (from 200 Hz to 20000 Hz) drill bit vibration accelerations [15]. In case of repeated exposure to power impulses from drill bit, the rock destruction takes on fatigue nature. Due to resonance processes in the 'drill string with a hydraulic vibrator – rock' dynamic system and the development of a network of microcracks in the rock, the discontinuity of the rock mass, as a rule, occurs at stresses lower than the ultimate strength of the rock. This leads to an improvement in the removal of the destroyed motive from the zone of its contact with the tool, an increase in the drilling speed, wear resistance of the drilling tool, and an improvement in the stabilization and stability of the operation of the drill string.

It was also found that the magnitude of the pressure pulses and their repetition rate can be controlled by setting the regime parameters of the cavitation flow.

## 2.2 Dependences of the drill string dynamic parameters on the operating mode of the cavitation hydraulic vibrator

The correctness of the choice of the proposed method of dynamic loading to the drill bit is confirmed by studies of the influence of the operating and design parameters of the cavitation hydrovibrator on the dynamic parameters of the drill string at the drill bit section. Such work was carried out at the ITM NASU hydraulic stand and drilling stands at the 'Geotechnika' special design bureau (Russia).

The most interesting are the results of an experimental study of the dynamic parameters of a drill string in the process of drilling a well. These results and their comparison with the calculated data are given in [15]. The general scheme of testing a drill string in a borehole 87 m deep is shown in Figure 6 (on the left of the Figure is a photograph of the hydraulic cavitation vibrator of this drill).

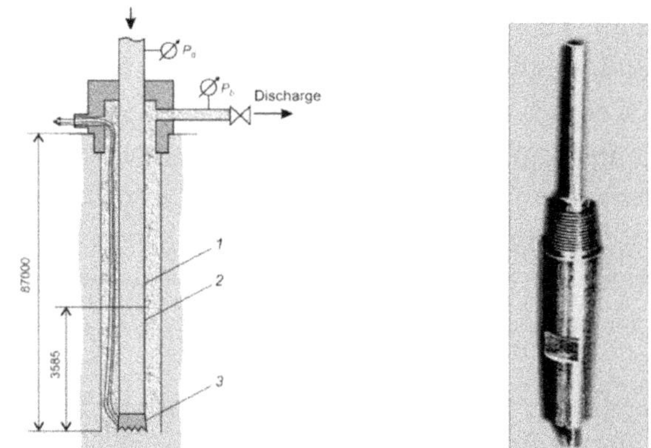


**Figure 6. The schematic of the testing drill string in the well (1 is drill pipe; 2 is drilling rig; 3 is drill bit) and the photographic image of the cavitation hydrovibrator.**

The static pressures values at the inlet of the drill string P1 and at its exit P2 were calculated using the formulas: P1 = (Pd + 0.83) MPa and P2 = (Pb – 0.87) MPa, where Pb is the backpressure (Pd is the pressure of the drilling fluid created by the pump). When carrying out these drill string tests, the I-24.2141 piezoelectric sensors were used to measure fluid pressure pulsations and their frequency. In the same place, vibration accelerations were measured by two ABC-034 sensors. The three tests were carried out for this drill string structure design at differing in pressure of Pd = 3 MPa, 4 MPa and 5 MPa.

Table 1 shows the main geometrical parameters of the drill string and the results of its tests at the pressure of Pd = 4 MPa and the contact of the drill bit with the rock (granite) at the axial static load F of 9.8 kN.

**Table 1. The basic geometrical parameters of the drill string with and cavitation generator and the results of the drill string dynamic tests at the pump discharge pressure of Pd = 4 MPa and axial static load of F = 9.8 kN.**

| Basic geometrical parameters of the drill string τ | | Test results | | | |
|---|---|---|---|---|---|
| | | ΔP, MPa | ΔZx, g | f, Hz | |
| throat diameter, dcr | 6.0 mm | 0.100 | 4.80 | 1960 | 196 |
| length of the throat,λ cr | 8.2 mm | 0.137 | 6.00 | 2793 | 326 |
| outlet diffuser diameter, D | 24 mm | 0.161 | 5.90 | 3201 | 374 |
| diffuser length,$\lambda_d$ | 51 mm | 0.184 | 5.15 | 2564 | 423 |
| diffuser opening angle, β | 20° | 0.200 | 4.30 | 1570 | 508 |
| outlet channel diameter, dh | 24 mm | 0.340 | 3.20 | 928 | 793 |
| output channel length,λ h | 240 mm | 0.415 | 2.78 | 1401 | 995 |
| drill string length, λ | 3585 mm | 0.475 | 2.55 | 1027 | 1188 |

Considering that the oscillation modes of the parameters of the dynamic process in the hydrovibrator differ significantly from the shapes of harmonic oscillations, the analysis of the experimental and theoretical studies was carried out using not the amplitudes, but the peak to peak values ΔP of the fluid pressure and vibration accelerations ΔZx in the axial direction. The values of the ranges of these parameters were determined as the difference between their maximum and minimum values. The frequency was calculated based on the analysis of the time dependence of the fluid pressure in the hydrovibrator (the fundamental mode of the fluid oscillations).

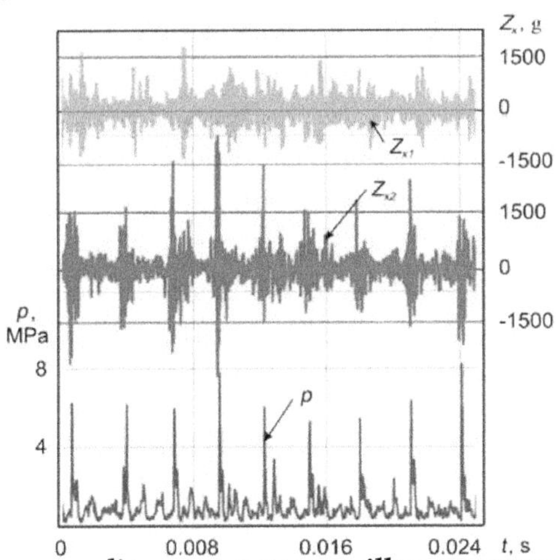


**Figure 7. Waveform recording parameters oscillatory process of the drill string experimental sample: Discharge pressure of $P_2$, longitudinal vibration accelerations $Z_{x1}$ and $Z_{x2}$ of the drill string structural elements.**

As an example, Figure 7 shows an oscillogram with a real-time recording of the dynamic parameters of the drill string experimental sample: the fluid pressure p oscillations and vibration accelerations Zx1 and Zx2 in the drill bit section for the pump pressure, equal to the Pd = 4 MPa, and the cavitation parameter of $\tau = 0.161$. The results of this test presented in the Figure describe the dynamic process determined by the development in the generator of the regime of periodically stall cavitation, characterized by the shock shape of pressure oscillations in the hydrovibrator flow channel.

These vibrations propagate along the drill string length and are converted into the drill bit vibration accelerations with average values of $\Delta Zx \approx 3200$ g and the dominant frequency of cavitation pressure oscillations in the hydraulic vibrator flow path of 374 Hz. The longitudinal vibration accelerations of the drill string structural elements indicated in Figure 7 by Zx1 and Zx2).

As a result of the tests, carried out for different inlet pressure, it was found that an increase in the steady-state pressure p1 at the hydraulic vibrator inlet leads to the increase in the values of vibration accelerations in the drill bit section from 2280 g (at Pd = 3 MPa) to 4580 g (at Pd = 5 MPa).

## 2.3 Comparative analysis of the results of theoretical and experimental research of the drill string vibrations by hydraulic vibrator excitation

Mathematical modeling of the oscillatory motion of the drill string with the high-frequency hydraulic vibrator was carried out on the assumption that the drill string structure carries out vibration motion along the flow path longitudinal axis of the fluid flow. This limitation is also due to the axial symmetry of the drill string structure itself and the direction of the total components of the forces acting on the drill string structure [13]. The mathematical model of the 'drill string with a hydraulic vibrator' dynamic system as the coupled hydrodynamic system was proposed in [15]. For various structural elements of the drill string, the model describes the time variation of such system parameters as vibration displacement, vibration velocity, vibration acceleration, as well as pressure and fluid mass flow rate in the flow path of the corresponding drill string structural elements.

Modeling of axial vibrations of the drill string structure was carried out on the basis of its finite element scheme, in which the elements are characterized not only by elasticities and masses, but also by dissipative losses, the magnitudes of which depend on the vibration amplitudes of the structural elements. Thus, the damping coefficients in the equation of motion of the center of mass of the i-th finite element of the drill string

$$(m_i + m_i^p)\frac{d^2x_i}{dt^2} + c_i(x_i - x_{i-1}) + b_i\left(\frac{dx_i}{dt} - \frac{dx_{i-1}}{dt}\right) + c_{i+1}(x_i - x_{i+1})$$
$$+ b_{i+1}\left(\frac{dx_i}{dt} - \frac{dx_{i+1}}{dt}\right) = \sum_n F_i^n, \quad (2)$$

were calculated based on the dependences and experimental data [16].

$$b_i = \left(b_i^0 + b_i^a(a_i)\right)\cdot\frac{\sqrt{c_i \cdot m_i}}{2\pi} \quad (3)$$

where xi is the displacement of the center of mass of the i-th finite element from the position of dynamic equilibrium; mi and mpi are the distributed mass and concentrated mass of the i-th finite element of the drill string; ci=Ei Ai Δli-1 is the stiffness coefficient of the i-th finite element; Ai is cross-sectional area of the i-th structural element; Δli is longitudinal length of the i-th structural element; Ei is Young's modulus of elasticity of the material of the i-th structural element; b0i is the damping coefficient of the i-th finite element at small structural vibrations; Fni is deviation of the force acting on the i-th structural element of the drill string from its steady-state value; bai(ai) is the component of the damping coefficient of the mechanical elements, taking into account the damping coefficient increase at 'considerable' nonlinear amplitudes ai of the drill string structure vibrations.

The time dependences of the displacement, vibration velocity and vibration acceleration of structural elements, fluid pressure and flow rate, the volume of the cavity attached and collapsing in the hydrovibrator flowing part was gotten by numerical integration by the Runge–Kutta method of the system of differential equations describing the drill string longitudinal vibrations for the hydrovibrator steady-state operating mode (at $\tau$ = const). These dependences were obtained at the discharge pressure Pd = 4 MPa, the axial static load F = 9.8 kN, and values of the criterion parameter of cavitation $\tau$ = 0.12, 0.16, 0.184, 0.2, 0.34, 0.415, 0.475. This data corresponds to experimental studies of the drill sample, the geometric parameters and test results of which are given in Table 1.

The calculated time dependences of pressure p, volumetric flow rate Q, vibration acceleration Z, vibration velocity v, vibration displacement x and vibration force Fm in the drill bit section for the value of the cavitation parameter $\tau$ = 0.16 are presented in Figure 8.

As follows from the given dependences, the oscillatory process is impulsive in nature. For the indicated value of the cavitation parameter the fundamental harmonic frequency of cavitation oscillations is 323 Hz, the range of pressure oscillations is ΔP ≈ 6.19 MPa, the volumetric flow rate is ΔQ ≈ 3.17 l/s, the vibration acceleration is ΔZ ≈ 3139 g, the range of vibration velocity is Δv ≈ 28 m/s, the range of vibration displacement is Δx ≈ 3.1 mm and the vibration force is ΔFm ≈ 4.5 kN. It is seen from the results of the calculations that the frequency of drill string structure vibration (equal to about 970 Hz) is superimposed on the fundamental harmonic of the frequency of cavitation oscillations. This phenomenon occurs due to the dynamic interaction of the drill string structure and the mass of fluid flowing inside the drill pipe.

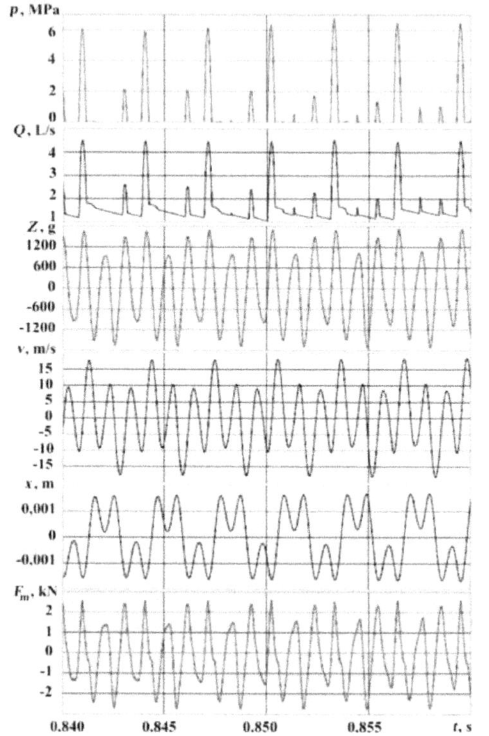


**Figure 8. Calculated drilling parameters vs. time: Pressure p, volumetric flow rate Q, vibration acceleration $Z_x$, vibration velocity v, vibration displacement x and vibration force $F_m$ at the drill bit section of drill string.**

The calculated and experimental dependences on the cavitation parameter τ of frequency of the cavitation oscillations of the fluid pressure ΔP, as well as the frequencies of hydraulic oscillations fcav in the flow channel of the hydraulic vibrator and the drill string second mode frequency fm2 mechanical oscillations are presented in Figure 9. It also shows the calculated dependence volume flow rate ΔQ on the cavitation parameter τ.

The nature of the dependences ΔP and ΔQ on τ is nonlinear. The ranges of pressure oscillations ΔP and volumetric flow rate ΔQ increase with an increase in the value of the parameter τ from 0.1 (with an increase in the pump head pressure Pb at Pd = const), reaching the maximum values of 6.19 MPa and 3.17 l/s at τ = 0.16, and then decreases. The maximum value of the oscillatory pressure in the cross section of the sensor installation is approximately in 1.5 times higher than the discharge pressure Pd. Despite the complexity of the processes occurring in the flow channel of the cavitation hydrovibrator, in the entire range of variation of the value of τ, not only a more qualitative, but also a quantitative (in comparison with work [15]) agreement was obtained for the calculated pressure oscillation ranges with experimental data, including on dynamic system resonant modes.

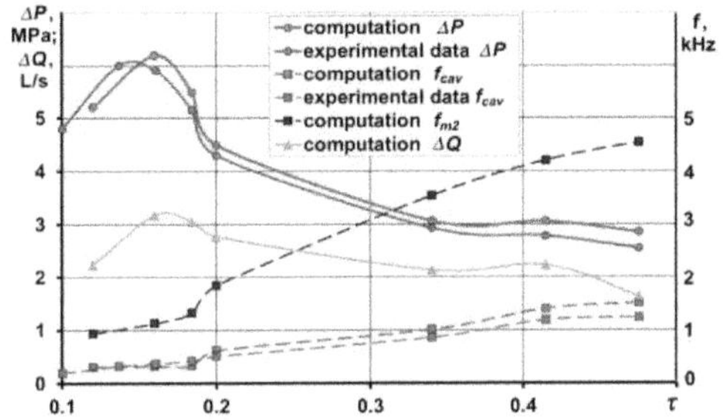


**Figure 9. Calculated and experimental pressure oscillations range ΔP, volumetric flow rate ΔQ and hydraulic oscillations frequency f in the drill bit section vs. the cavitation parameter τ .**

The experimental and calculated dependences of the frequency fcav of cavitation self-oscillations on the cavitation parameter τ have a character close to linear. Satisfactory agreement is observed between the calculated and experimental frequencies of cavitation vibrations in the investigated range of variation of the cavitation parameter τ. The frequency of the first mode of the forced drill string structure vibrations corresponds to the oscillation frequency of the fluid in the hydraulic vibrator flow channel. This is clearly illustrated in Figure 8. As it follows from the figure that the frequency of cavitation self-oscillations of pressure and volumetric flow rate of liquid in the cavitation hydrovibrator flow channel and the first mode of the frequency of forced vibrations of the drill string structure (vibration acceleration, vibration velocity, vibration displacement and vibration force) are equal to 323 Hz. The frequency of the second mode of drill string mechanical vibrations is approximately in three times higher than the first mode frequencies.

The dominant frequency of cavitation oscillations is 1230 Hz at the value of the cavitation parameter $\tau = 0.415$, the second mode of the drill bit mechanical vibrations is approximately in 3.4 times higher and is equal 4202 Hz (see Figure 9). This mode caused by repeated collapse of the cavitation cavity and the interaction of the drill bit structure with drill mud in hydrovibrator channel. The swing of pressure oscillations of $\Delta P \approx 3.06$ MPa, the swing volumetric flow rates $\Delta Q \approx 1.83$ l/s and vibration acceleration $\Delta Z \approx 1247$ g. It should be noted that with an increase in the value of the parameter τ from 0.12 to 0.475, the duty cycle of the shock process of changing the parameters of pressure and volumetric flow rate (see Figure 9) decreases.

Oscillatory parameters of pressure and volumetric flow rate of the liquid determine the hydraulic power of the cavitation hydraulic vibrator, which characterizes the quality of the removal of the drilled rock from under the drill bit.

Vibration acceleration and vibration force refer to the parameters that determine the ROF. The theoretical dependences of the swing of vibration accelerations ΔZ and the swing vibration force ΔF on the cavitation parameter τ and experimental data on vibration accelerations ΔZ at the drill bit are shown in Figure 10.

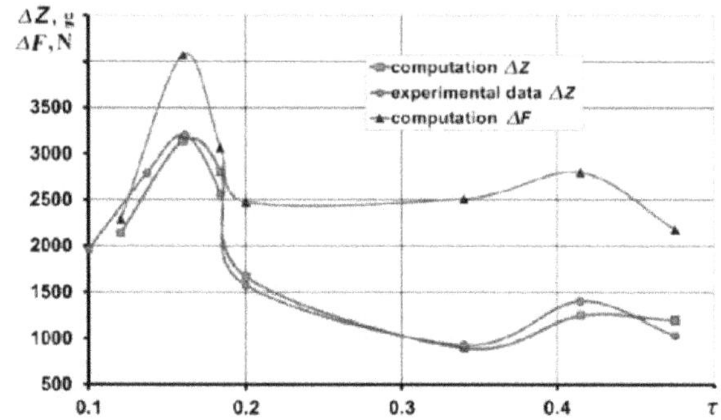


**Figure 10. Calculated dependences of the vibration acceleration peak to peak values ΔZ and the peak to peak values of vibration force ΔF vs. the cavitation parameter τ and experimental data on vibration accelerations ΔZ at the drill bit.**

Analysis of the data in this figure shows that an increase in the amplitudes of forced oscillations in the drill fluid pressure at cavitation numbers from 0.1 to 0.16 (see Figure 9), leads to an increase in the drill string vibration acceleration and vibration force. The maximum values of the amplitude of vibration acceleration and vibration force on the drill bit for this hydraulic vibrator design are realized at τ = 0.16 and are approximately 3200 g and 4100 N. At the same time, in the research range of the cavitation parameter τ from 0.1 to 0.475, there are two resonant modes of drill string operation. The first resonant mode corresponds to the value of the cavitation parameter τ ≈ 0.16, which coincides with the maximum values of the pressure oscillations swing (see Figure 9). The second resonant mode manifests itself at τ ≈ 0.415 and is a consequence of the convergence of the frequencies of natural vibrations of the drill string structure and the drilling fluid oscillations frequency, caused by the 'operation' of the cavitation generator. Consideration of the theoretical dependences of the swing of vibration accelerations ΔZ on the cavitation parameter τ and experimental data indicates the satisfactory convergence of the results obtained, including in the above resonance modes.

## 2.4 Evaluation of the efficiency of drill string with a cavitation hydraulic vibrator for geological exploration and construction of hydrogeological wells

On the basis of above theoretical and experimental studies, the new typed BSKG-76 hydrodynamic (with a cavitation hydraulic vibrator) drilling assemblies were created for drilling exploration wells with the following specifications [17]:

- ☆ outer tube diameter is 57 mm;
- ☆ the length of the hydraulic vibrator is 400 mm;
- ☆ the diameter of the generator throat section is 4 mm and 6 mm;
- ☆ generator feed pressure from 2.0 to 5.0 MPa;
- ☆ flow rate of working fluid from 19 to 200 l/min;
- ☆ rotational speed of the drill bit is 245 rpm.

The tests of the BSKG-76 type drilling rigs were carried out under the conditions of 'Production Geological Association Stepgeologia' LLP (Kazakhstan) by drilling exploration wells using a drilling rig, including the SKB-5 drilling rig, the ANB-22 pump with a three-stage reduction gear, the RT -1200 turning mechanism. Drill pipes with a diameter of 50 mm of a nipple joint, diamond bits of the 02IZ and A4DP types, and the Shch76k-4 L three-cone bits were used as dril bits.

Water and emulsion solutions were used as a working agent: 3% sulfanol and 3% emulsollenol-32. The tests were carried out in the depth interval from 70 m to 530 m on granites of IX-XI categories in terms of the Protodyakonov drillability scale. The technological parameters of drilling were monitored: the feed force by the load indicator, the flow rate and the fluid pressure by the flow meter and pressure sensor, the power consumption for rotation by the self-recording wattmeter.

The parameters of the well drilling modes in terms of axial load and rotational speed of the drill bit remained identical for the shock-rotational and hydrodynamic methods and alternated after 1-2 runs with the G76VO hydraulic hammer and the BSKG-76 drill string. Comparative analysis of drilling methods was carried out according to the following indicators: ROP, service life of drill bits and power consumption.

For drilling wells by hydrodynamic drilling rig BSKG-76 with coring in comparison with rotary-percussion drilling by the G76VO hydraulic hammer:

- ☆ for the 02IZ drill bits an increase in ROP was obtained by from 16–61%; by the resource of the crown by 18%;
- ☆ for the A4DP drill bits an increase in ROP was established from 27 to 77%, for a bit resource by 12%;
- ☆ for coreless drilling with the Shch76k-4 L roller cone bits an increase in the ROP was obtained by an average of 13.5% and the drill bit resource by 23%.

Analysis of the power consumption for the rotation of the drill bit in all drilling modes showed that for the BSKG-76 drill string is in operation, the power consumption decreases by 30% in compared to the power consumption of the G76VO hydraulic hammer, improves the operation stability of the drill string and drill bit.

A comparative analysis of the BSKG-76 hydrodynamic drill reliability and the G76VO hydraulic hammer reliability during the testing period showed the following: four failures of the hydraulic hammer were noted and ten assemblies were disassembled to adjust and replace the cuffs in the cylinder, O-rings in the splined connector, nozzles and pistons in the striker.

At the same time, during the entire testing period, not a single failure occurred in the operation of the BSKG-76 hydrodynamic drilling rig. The absence of their wear was established by the help of examinations and measurements of the main dimensions of the drill string parts. This indicates that the service life of the hydrodynamic drill string significantly exceeds the service life of the hydraulic hammer.

The drilling rig with a cavitation hydraulic vibrator is characterized by increased reliability and ease of maintenance due to the absence of moving parts, the need for adjustments and assemblies-disassembly with replacement of parts. It does not require additional energy sources other than the energy of the washing solution. A well with a depth of 525 m was drilled by the use of a hydrodynamic drill string and its performance was confirmed to this depth.

To assess the efficiency of large-diameter well drilling by the drill string with the cavitation hydraulic vibrator, it was tested in an industrial environment at the 'Geotechnika' special design bureau (Russia) during the construction of hydrogeological wells.

The geological wells on which the studies were carried out are represented by Quaternary deposits to a depth of 10.5 m and further to a depth of 60 m by limestones and dolomites (weathered in the upper part) of the V-VII category in drillability with interlayers of siliceous and dolomitized limestones with a thickness of no more than 0.5 m each IX- X categories (according to Protodyakonov classification).

The tests were carried out while drilling wells using the hydrodynamic method and rotary drilling was carried out to compare the data in similar geological and technical conditions. The drilling was carried out using an IBA15V drilling rig and an IIGR mud pump with an electric drive. Drill pipes with a diameter of 73 mm sleeve-and-tool joints, heavy weight drill pipes with a diameter of 146 mm and three-ball bits of the "K" type with a diameter of 190 mm were included in the drill string. The experimental model of a hydrodynamic (cavitation) vibrator was built into the central bore of the bit and was closed from above with drill pipes.

The drilling fluid used was water, which was not purified specially.

Technical characteristics of the BSKG-190 hydrodynamic drill string are:

- ☆ tube outer diameter is of 73 mm;
- ☆ the generator length is 400 mm;

- ☆ the diameter of the critical section of the generator is 6 mm;
- ☆ generator feed pressure is changed from 1 to 4 MPa;
- ☆ the flow rate of the working fluid is from 140 to 260 l/min;
- ☆ the drill bit rotational speed is 245 rpm.

To determine the effectiveness of the use of experimental hydrovibrator samples, the two wells with a depth of 60 m were drilled by the hydrodynamic method (with the cavitation hydrovibrator) and one well of the same depth by the rotary method (without the cavitation hydrovibrator) in the same area. The axial static load to drill string structure along the compared intervals of depths was identical for both methods and increased with increasing well depths.

The results of a comparative analysis of drilling the hydrogeological well with the diameter of 190 mm by rotary and hydrodynamic methods are given in Table 2.

**Table 2. Results of the comparative analysis of drilling the hydrogeological well with the diameter of 190 mm by rotary and hydrodynamic methods.**

| Depth drilling intervals, m | Drilling methods | Time, hour | ROP, m per hour | Increase in ROP, % |
|---|---|---|---|---|
| 10÷23.7 | rotary<br>hydrodynamic | 0.69<br>0.36 | 4.42<br>9.72 | 119.9 |
| 23.5÷26.2 | rotary<br>hydrodynamic | 0.22<br>0.12 | 9.54<br>16.67 | 74.0 |
| 25.5÷32.0 | rotary<br>hydrodynamic | 0.99<br>0.69 | 6.69<br>9.42 | 40.8 |
| 32.0÷35.5 | rotary<br>hydrodynamic | 0.72<br>0.6 | 3.56<br>5.83 | 63.8 |
| 49.75÷53.55 | rotary<br>hydrodynamic | 0.47<br>0.3 | 5.85<br>10.0 | 70.0 |
| 52.25÷60.85 | rotary<br>hydrodynamic | 1.48<br>0.75 | 5.51<br>8.87 | 61.0 |
| Average indicators | rotary<br>hydrodynamic | 4.47<br>2.82 | 5.415<br>8.92 | 71.5 |

As can be seen from the Table, during the hydrodynamic drill operation, the average increase in ROP reaches 71.5%, compared to the rotary drilling ROP. At the same time, there was a decrease in the wear of drill bits and energy consumption by up to 30%.

According to the research results, it was found that the highest dynamic loads on the bit produced by the hydraulic vibrator are within the range of $0.2 < \tau < 0.5$.

Taking into account the obtained test data, the hydrodynamic drill string was finalized and the experimental sample with the cavitation generator throat diameter of 8 mm was manufactured. Experimental works on the construction of hydrogeological wells with the diameter of 190 mm and the depth of 300 m at a flow rate of flushing fluid of 300 l/min and at a pressure of up to 3.0 MPa confirmed that hydrodynamic drill strings are an effective means of increasing the ROP in middle and high strength rocks using serial drilling equipment and tools.

## 3. CONCLUSIONS

The sonic drilling technology with the use of a hydraulic cavitation vibrator is an effective means of increasing the penetration rate in rocks of medium and high hardness using commercial drilling equipment and drill bits.

The drilling rig with a cavitation hydraulic vibrator has a number of advantages over other known vibration drilling devices, such as ease of manufacture, the absence of moving parts and the elimination of the transfer of fluid vibrations to the mud pump, which increases its service life. In comparison with the hydraulic hammer drill, the resource of the drill string increases by 5 times, the operating time to failure by 40 times. The cost of one set of a hydraulic vibrator, according to forecast estimates, will not exceed one third of the cost of a set of hydraulic hammer machines (or resonant sonic drill heads).

The cavitation hydraulic vibrator fits organically into the rotary drilling technology, does not require any equipment modifications and allows intensifying the drilling processes at lower specific energy consumption compared to traditional drilling technologies.

Analysis of the results of theoretical and experimental research of the drilling with the cavitation hydraulic vibrator, allows us to draw the following conclusions:

- for borehole drilling in medium and hard rocks using hydrodynamic drilling tools operating in the mode of intermittent-stall cavitation with the fluid pressure oscillations frequency of more than 200 Hz, the increase in the ROP of the exploration wells with the diameters of 76 mm is from 30–50% and for the hydrogeological wells with a diameter of 190 mm is up to 70%,
- the decrease in energy consumption by 25-30% and wear of rock cutting tools by 15-20% was obtained in comparison with traditional drilling methods;
- the drill bit vibrational modes with the basic frequency of cavitation oscillations (rational to achieve the maximum ROP of hard rocks, i.e. from 1.2 kHz to 1.4 kHz) are achieved in the range of values of the cavitation parameter $\tau$ from 0.41 to 0.43.

## REFERENCES

1. Sun Long, Bu Changgen, Hu Peida, Xia Bairu. The transient impact of the resonant flexible drill string of a sonic drill on rock. International Journal of Mechanical Sciences. 2017; 122: 29-36. DOI: 10.1016/j.ijmecsci.2017.01.014

2. Kiselev A.T., Melamed Yu. A. Hydropercussion drilling - results and prospects // Exploration and conservation of mineral resources. - 1996. - No. 9. - pp. 19-22. (in Russian).

3. Gorodilov L.V. Analysis of dynamics and characteristics of main classes of self-oscillating volume-type hydraulic impact systems// Journal of machinery manufacture and reliability. 2018; 1: 22-30. (in Russian). DOI: 10.3103/S1052618818010077

4. Khorshidian, H., Butt S. D., Arvani F. Influence of High Velocity Jet on Drilling Performance of PDC Bit under Pressurized Condition. In: Proceedings of the American Rock Mechanics Association; 2014; Available from: https://www.onepetro.org/conference-paper/ARMA-2014-7465. [Accessed: 2021-05-23].

5. Xiao, Y., Zhong J., Hurich C., Butt S. D. Micro-Seismic Monitoring of PDC Bit Drilling Performance during Vibration Assisted Rotational Drilling. In: Proceedings of the American Rock Mechanics Association; November 13, 2015. Available from: https://www.onepetro.org/conference-paper/ARMA-2015-474. [Accessed: 2021-05-23].

6. Babapour, S., & Butt S. D. Investigation of Enhancing Drill Cuttings Cleaning and Penetration Rate Using Cavitating Pressure Pulses. In: Proceedings of the American Rock Mechanics Association; 18 August 2014. Available from: https://www.onepetro.org/conference-paper/ARMA-2014-7751. [Accessed: 2021-05-23].

7. Thorp N. J., Hareland G., Elbing B.R., Nygaard R. Modelling of a Drill Bit Blaster. In: Proceedings of the 50th US Rock Mechanics / Geomechanics Symposium; Jun 2016; Houston, TX., American Rock Mechanics Association (ARMA); 2016. vol. 4, p. 3443-3449.

8. Fu J., Li G., Shi H., Niu J., Huang Z. A Novel Tool To Improve the Rate of Penetration--Hydraulic-Pulsed Cavitating-Jet Generator. In: Proceedings of SPE Drilling & Completion; April 2013; 27(03):355-362. DOI: 10.2118/162726-PA

9. Li G., Shi H., Niu J., Huang Z., Tian S., Song X. Hydraulic Pulsed Cavitating Jet Assisted Deep Drilling: An Approach To Improve Rate Of Penetration. Society of Petroleum Engineers. DOI: 10.2118/130829-MS. 2013

10. Shi H., Gensheng L., Huang Z., Shi S. Properties and testing of a hydraulic pulse jet and its application in offshore drilling. Petroleum Science, 2014, Volume 11, Issue 3, p. 401-407. DOI: 10.1007/s12182-014-0354-1

11. Wei L., Tie Y., Siqi L., Xiaoning Z. Rock fragmentation mechanisms and an experimental study of drilling tools during high-frequency harmonic vibration. Pet.Sci. (2013) 10:205-211. DOI: 10.1007/s12182-013-0268-3

12. Pilipenko V.V. Cavitation-oscillations. Naukova Dumka Publishing Company: Kyiv; 1989. 316 p. (in Russian).

13. Manko I. K., Nikolayev O. D. The mechanism for converting of drilling fluid high-frequency oscillations into longitudinal vibration accelerations of a drill string with a cavitation hydrovibrator. Mint: Naukovy Bulletin of the NSU, Dnepr, Ukraine, 2004; 10:124-136. (in Russian).

14. Zhulay Yu. A. On the paradox of the influence of the volumetric flow rate of liquid through the cavitation generator on the range of oscillations. Mint: Aerospace Engineering and Technology. 2017; 1:136. p. 29 – 35. (in Russian).

15. Nikolayev O., Zhulay Yu., Kvasha Yu., Dzoz N. Evaluation of the vibration accelerations of drill bit for the well rotative-vibration drilling using the cavitation hydrovibrator. Mint: International Journal of Mining and Mineral Engineering (IJMME), 2020; 2: 102-120. DOI: 10.1504/IJMME.2020. 108643

16. Nikolayev O. Khoryak N., SerenkoV., Klimenko D., Khodorenko V., Bashlij I. Taking into account dissipative forces in mathematical modeling of longitudinal vibrations of the body of a liquid-propellant rocket. Mint: Technical mechanics. 2016; 2: 16 – 31. (in Russian).

17. Zhulay Yu. A., Dzoz N. A. Intensification of drilling processes using hydrodynamic cavitation. Mint: Mining Information and Analytical Bulletin, Moscow State Mining University; 2008; 4: 290-296. (in Russian).

CHAPTER-6

# SFE2D: A HYBRID TOOL FOR SPATIAL AND SPECTRAL FEATURE EXTRACTION

## 1. INTRODUCTION

Global trends show that the number of major mineral discoveries is drastically declined during the last 25 years because the most outcropping mineralization systems are mapped and already excavated [1]. Therefore, a significant challenge for mineral exploration is the deep targeting of hidden resources. The "deep" targets are usually considered as resources as deep as hundreds of meters to thousand meters of depth. However, occurrences of "deep" targets are not limited to the third dimension. They can be seen as complex obscured mineralization systems barely detectable within a large amount of hyper-dimensional geoscientific data. Consequently, advanced data mining methods are needed to extract useful information from large amounts of data sets. Responding to these challenges of integrating multidisciplinary information is the motivation of present research.

Automated interpretation of multiple images is an important topic in large data interpretation and multivariate pattern recognition. No matter how accurate the geoscientific images (geo-images) are, each geo-image is only sensitive to a limited number of geological features. Therefore, different parts of the subsurface geology can be reconstructed from various geo-images. The critical question is how one can put together the interpreted jigsaw puzzles inside a high-dimensional space to rebuild a relevant geological model. This has led us to the topic of feature extraction in the treatment of large data sets.

The fundamental problem in integrated geoscientific interpretation is the proper geological understanding of multiple geo-images, which demands high dimensional techniques for the extraction of geological information from hyperdimensional data sets. Several methods are available for feature extraction in the high dimensional space, which can be seen as a dimensionality increase problem [2]. The problem is that the increased dimensionality due to feature extraction leads to an overload of information that creates difficulties for human visual interpretation as well as machine learning optimization [2]. That is to say; latent patterns are lost in high space as one moves to higher dimensions. Several recent studies, mainly in seismic attributes analysis, have investigated the problem of high-dimensional pattern recognition to extract relevant geological features from broadband seismic data [3, 4, 5, 6, 7]. In mineral exploration, the treatment of multiple non-seismic data also put forth a similar pattern recognition problem, which seeks to extract relevant geological features from potential field and electromagnetic data in the form of multiple images [8].

This study aimed to provide a tool for spatial and spectral feature extraction from multiple geo-images to facilitate the identification of geoscientific features. The study employed a quantitative approach combining different source separation methods for feature extraction and representation. The output is the SFE2D program, which is a standalone 2D spatiospectral feature extraction tool based on unsupervised source separation methods like principal component analysis (PCA), independent component analysis (ICA), continuous wavelet transform (CWT), RGB color processing, and k-means clustering segmentation. The program is made in a MATLAB environment for feature extraction and dimensionality reduction of hyperdimensional geoscientific data sets through variance/kurtosis/negentropy maximization, k-mean clustering segmentation, color pick algorithm, and RGB visualizations (SFE2D ver. 2.0).

## 2. THEORETICAL BACKGROUND OF SOURCE SEPARATION

### 2.1 Feature extraction

The theoretical framework underpinning this study is based on blind source separation (BSS) methods. Generally, BSS aims to recover latent source signals (or images) from a set of highly mixed signals (or images). Consider a mixing model, where every geo-image (gi) is a mixture of several latent features (fj) with different contributions in constructing the observed image. A mathematical description for this model can be formulated as a linear mixing system that links the latent features to the observed geo-image by a set of mixing weights (aij) that determine the contribution of each feature in the geo-image construction:

$$g_i = \sum a_{ji} f_j \tag{1}$$

Where j = 1, 2, ..., n denotes the number of latent features, and i = 1, 2, ..., m indicates the number of geo-images. The vector form of Eq. (1) can be rewritten as:

$$g = Af \tag{2}$$

Where the unknown mixing weights are defined as the matrix [A](j,i)=aji. The observed geo-images g=[g1(x,y),g2(x,y),...gm(x,y)]T are linear mixtures of the latent features f=[f1(x,y),f2(x,y),...fn(x,y)]T. The x and y denote the coordinates on a two-dimensional space in the spatial feature extraction scheme. The problem is to find a separation matrix (W) that tends to unmix the geo-images (g) to recover the hidden features (f):

$$f = Wg = A^{-1}g \tag{3}$$

Where separation matrix (W) is the inversion of the mixing matrix and cannot be directly determined. Nevertheless, it can be estimated adaptively as an optimization problem and setting up a cost function to be minimized iteratively. This is the general formulation of a feature extraction process that iteratively eliminates or at least reduces the effect of feature overlaps (shadow effect) on the observed geo-images (Figure 1).

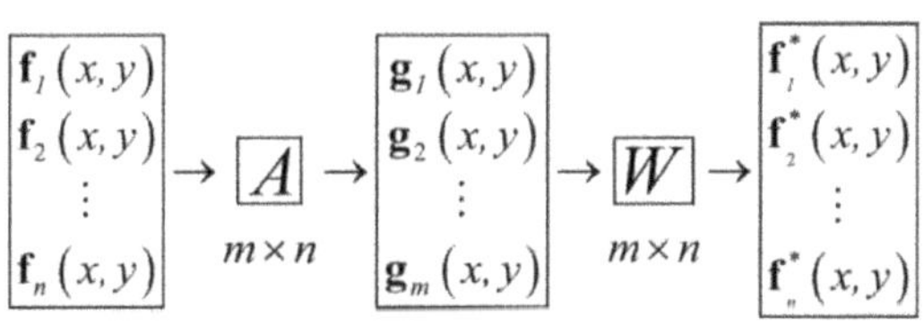

**Figure 1. Schematic of feature extraction model.**

## 2.2 Spatial feature extraction through PCA and ICA

Estimating a relevant separation matrix is possible by making assumptions about the statistical measures such as correlation. In some instances, it is common for two geo-images to be statistically correlated. For example, suppose there is a linear relationship between two gamma-ray concentration images (e.g., K vs. eTh). In that case, the amount of information that the first image provides is as same as the second one. Therefore, one can transform the bivariate data to a univariate form without losing any valuable information. This transformation is called dimensionality reduction, which is the basis of PCA algorithms. PCA algorithms utilize the maximization of second-order statistical measure (variance) for image separation and produce linearly uncorrelated images (Figure 2a). However, when there is a nonlinear form of correlation (dependency) between images, PCA will not work. In this case, ICA is useful to separate the geo-images into nonlinearly uncorrelated images by maximizing non-Gaussianity (Figure 2b).

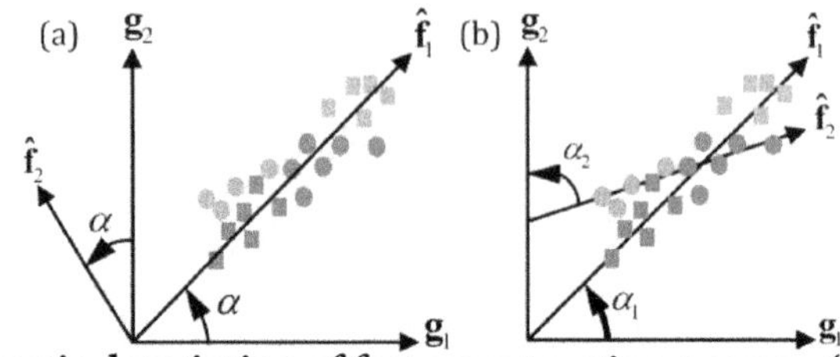


**Figure 2. Schematic description of feature extraction process: (a) PCA through maximization of variance. The correlated bivariate data sets (g axes) are transformed into univariate forms ($\hat{f}$ axes) without losing valuable information. (b) ICA through maximization of non-Gaussianity. The correlated and interdependent (overlapped) bivariate data sets (g axes) are transformed into two separate univariate independent components ($\hat{f}$ axes).**

PCA is, in fact, the first step in the ICA process. PCA looks for a weight matrix D so that a maximal variance of the principal components (yy) of the centered geo-images (gC) are confirmed:

$$y = Dg_C \tag{4}$$

During this preprocessing step, the mean of the input geo-images (gi) is removed (also known as Centering). Then whitening is performed by eigenvalue decomposition, which results in unit variance and identity covariance matrix. The matrix D that is calculated for linear transformation of centered geo-images into whitened images is:

$$D = \lambda^{-1/2} E^T \tag{5}$$

Where λ is eigenvalue and EE is the eigenvector matrix of the covariance matrix of the geo-images [9].

Whitening solves half of the ICA problem. The second step in the ICA is increasing the non-Gaussianity of the whitened images or principal components (yy). The problem is to find a rotation matrix R that during the multiplication with principal components produces the least Gaussian outputs ($\hat{f}$) that are approximations of the latent features (Figure 3):

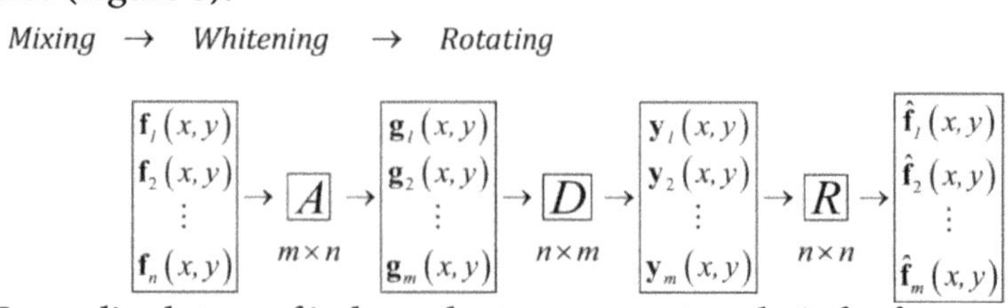


**Figure 3. Generalized steps of independent component analysis for feature extraction.**

$$\mathbf{f} \approx \hat{\mathbf{f}} = R^T y \tag{6}$$

## 2.3 Fast-ICA algorithms

This study has employed two alternative methods to obtain the rotation matrix R based on Fast-ICA through kurtosis maximization and negentropy maximization. Both kurtosis and negentropy maximization methods performed through the Hyvärinen fixed-point algorithm employ higher-order statistics to recover the independent sources [9]. The fixed-point algorithm has a couple of properties that make it superior to the gradient-based methods: (a) It has a cubic speedy convergence criterion. (b) In contrast to gradient-based algorithms, it does not need any learning rate adjustment or parameter tuning, making it easy to implement [9].

### 2.3.1 Fast-ICA through kurtosis maximization

According to the central limit theorem, the distribution of a sum of independent random variables tends toward a Gaussian (normal) distribution [9]. One can use this principle to maximize the non-Gaussianity through kurtosis maximization (kICA). Kurtosis that is the fourth-order cumulant of the whitened images can be expressed as the normalized version of the fourth moment:

$$kurt(\mathrm{y}) = E\{\mathrm{y}^4\} - 3 \tag{7}$$

Where E{.} denotes the expectation over the unknown density of input geo-images. Kurtosis provides a measure of how Gaussian (kurt = 0), super-Gaussian (kurt > 0) or sub-Gaussian (kurt < 0) the probability density functions of the geo-images are. Maximization of the kurtosis of the principal components estimates the latent independent components ($\hat{\mathrm{f}}$). The algorithm for kurtosis maximization in the present SFE2D program incorporates deflationary orthogonalization that estimates the independent components one by one:

**Step 1.** Center and whiten the geo-image data g to give y=DgC, where D=λ-1/2ET.

**Step 2.** Set N as the number of independent components to be estimated and a counter I←1.

**Step 3.** Set randomly an initial vector Ŵ I of unit norm (rows of the separation matrix).

**Step 4.** Let $\hat{W}_I \leftarrow E\left\{\mathrm{y}\left[\hat{W}_I^T \mathrm{y}\right]^3\right\} - 3\hat{W}_I$.

**Step 5.** Rotate by deflationary orthogonalization: $\hat{W}_I \leftarrow \hat{W}_I - \sum_{i=1}^{I-1}\left(\hat{W}_I^T \hat{W}_i\right)\ \hat{W}_i$.

**Step 6.** Normalize: Ŵ I←Ŵ I/‖‖Ŵ I‖‖

**Step 7.** Go to step 4 if Ŵ I is not converged: $\left|\left\langle \hat{W}_I^{k+1},\ \hat{W}_I^k\right\rangle\right| \neq 1$. Otherwise, Ŵ I is row I of the estimated separation matrix.

**Step 8.** If I≤NI≤N go to step 3 and set I=I+1I=I+1 to estimate the next row of the separation matrix.

**Step 9.** Obtain the latent features by $\hat{\mathrm{f}}$ =Ŵ g where Ŵ =[Ŵ 1,Ŵ 2,...,Ŵ I]T.

### 2.3.2 Fast-ICA through fixed-point negentropy maximization

For large-scale studies, kurtosis maximization is time-consuming because of its computational complications. Also, kurtosis is not a robust measure of non-Gaussianity in the presence of unknown noises and image artifacts. Kurtosis is very sensitive to outliers, that is, a single erroneous outlier value in the tails of the distribution makes kurtosis extremely large. Therefore, using kurtosis is well justified only if the independent components are sub-Gaussian and there are no outliers.

Another principle in information theory enables us to obtain the rotation matrix R more efficiently in the presence of outliers. It states that the spatial complexities of the input images are equal to or greater than that of the least complex latent features [9]. This general principle enables us to maximize the non-Gaussianity of multiple geo-images through negentropy maximization (nICA).

Negentropy is based on the information-theoretic quantity of entropy. The entropy (H) of a geo-image (g) with probability density of p(g) is defined as [9]:

$$H(\mathrm{g}) = -\int p(\mathrm{g}) \log p(\mathrm{g}) d\mathrm{g} \tag{8}$$

The more random (unpredictable and unstructured) the variable is, the larger its entropy. Between all random variables, the Gaussian variable has the largest entropy. Negentropy of a geo-image g is normalized differential entropy of g, which is the difference between the entropy of that geo-image g and the entropy of a Gaussian random vector of the same covariance matrix as g ($g_{gauss}$):

$$neg(\mathrm{g}) = H\left(\mathrm{g}_{gauss}\right) - H(\mathrm{g}) \tag{9}$$

Negentropy is always non-negative and is zero when the signal has a Gaussian distribution. In other words, the more random (unpredictable and unstructured) the variable is, the larger its entropy [9]. Negentropy approximated in this study is based on using classical higher order cumulants given as:

$$neg(\mathrm{y}) \approx \frac{1}{12} E\{\mathrm{y}^3\}^2 + \frac{1}{48} Kurt(\mathrm{y})^2 \tag{10}$$

Since entropy estimation is not directly performed on geo-images, and instead, centered/whitened images (principal components) are used for entropy calculations, therefore, g is replaced by y. Replacing polynomial functions y3y3 and y4y4 by another non-quadratic function Gi that does not grow too fast results in robust negentropy estimation (i is an index denoting odd and even functions):

$$neg(\mathrm{y}) \approx k_1 \left[E\{G^1(\mathrm{y})\}\right]^2 + k_2 \left[E\{G^2(\mathrm{y})\} - E\{G^2(\nu)\}\right]^2 \tag{11}$$

Where ν is a standardized Gaussian variable with unit variance and zero mean, and $k_1$ and $k_2$ are positive constants. In the case where only one non-quadratic function G is used, the approximation becomes simpler:

$$neg(y) \approx \left[E\{G(y)\} - E\{G(\nu)\}\right]^2 \tag{12}$$

In this moment-based approximation, we used a slow-growing exponential function for G:

$$G(y) = -e^{(-y^2/2)} \tag{13}$$

The criterion for negentropy maximization is based on bringing an objective function to an approximated maximum value. The algorithm for negentropy maximization in the present SFE2D program is as followed:

**Step 1.** Center and whiten the geo-image data g to give y=DgC, where D=λ-1/2ET.

**Step 2.** Set N as the number of independent components to be estimated and a counter I←1.

**Step 3.** Set randomly an initial vector Ŵ I of unit norm (rows of the separation matrix).

**Step 4.** Let $\hat{W}_I \leftarrow E\left\{yg\left[\hat{W}_I^T y\right]\right\} - E\left\{g'\left[\hat{W}_I^T y\right]\right\}\hat{W}$, where g(y)=ye(-y2/2).

**Step 5.** Rotate by deflationary orthogonalization: $\hat{W}_I \leftarrow \hat{W}_I - \sum_{i=1}^{I-1}\left(\hat{W}_I^T \hat{W}_i\right)\ \hat{W}_i$

**Step 6.** Normalize: Ŵ I←Ŵ I/||Ŵ I||.

**Step 7.** Go to step 4 if Ŵ I is not converged: $\left|\left\langle \hat{W}_I^{k+1},\ \hat{W}_I^{k}\right\rangle\right| \neq 1$. Otherwise, Ŵ I is the row I of the estimated separation matrix.

**Step 8.** If I≤N go to step 3 and set I=I+1 to estimate the next row of the separation matrix.

**Step 9.** Obtain the latent features by f̂ =Ŵ g where Ŵ =[Ŵ 1,Ŵ 2,...,Ŵ I]T.

## 2.4 Spectral feature extraction through wavelet-based PCA and ICA

Spectral decomposition of geo-images provides a unique way for feature extraction in the frequency domain. Although the Fourier transform is a powerful tool for image decomposition, it does not represent abrupt changes efficiently due to the infinite oscillation of the periodic function in any given direction. In contrast, wavelets are localized in space and have finite durations. Therefore, the output of wavelet decomposition effectively reflects the sharp changes in images, and that makes it an ideal tool for feature extraction [10, 11, 12].

Mathematically, the 2D CWT of an image I (x, y) is defined as a decomposition of that image (I) on a translated and dilated version of a mother wavelet ψ (x, y). Thus, the 2D CWT coefficients are given by:

$$C_s = (b_1, b_2, a) = \frac{1}{\sqrt{|a|}} \iint I(x,y)\psi^*\left(\frac{x-b_1}{a}, \frac{y-b_2}{a}\right)dxdy \tag{14}$$

Where $b_1$ and $b_2$ are controlling the spatial translation, a > 1 is the scale, and $\psi^*$ is the complex conjugate of the mother wavelet $\psi$ (x, y).

Analysis of isolated sources in potential field data with CWT was introduced by Moreau [13]. Moreau showed that the maxima lines of the CWT indicate the location of the potential field sources [10]. He also showed that the maxima lines bear the highest signal-to-noise ratios, allowing the treatment of the noisy data sets [14]. An example of a CWT on a geophysical image in which the mother wavelet is shifting and scaling in one direction is shown in Figure 4. The scale is inversely proportional to frequency. Large-scale factors are corresponding to largely expanded mother wavelets (low frequencies).

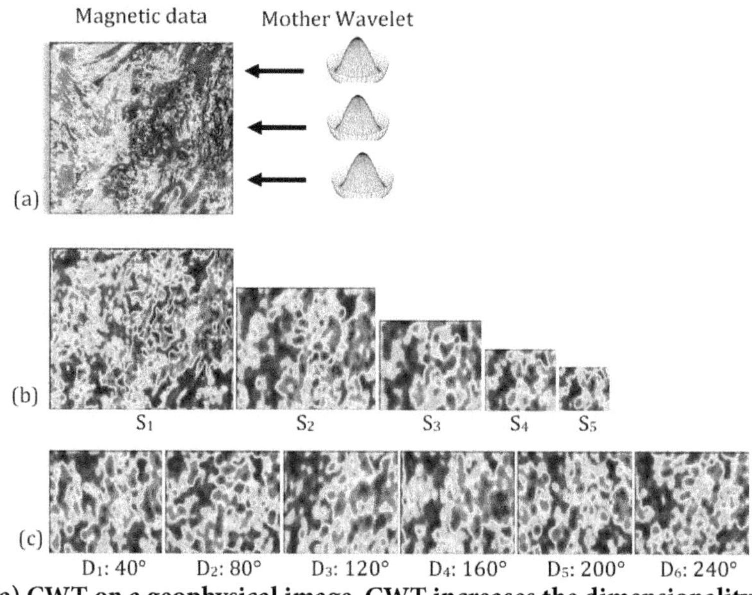


**Figure 4. (a) CWT on a geophysical image. CWT increases the dimensionality depending on the choice of scales (S) and directions (D). (b) CWT Mexican Hat mother wavelet in five scales ($S_1$–$S_5$). (c) CWT with Cauchy mother wavelet in six directions ($D_1$–$D_6$ at $S_4$).**

As can be seen in different frequencies, different features are detectable (Figure 4b). Scaling and shifting the mother wavelet in other directions also reveal other sets of features (Figure 4c). If the mother wavelet is isotropic, there is no dependence on the angle in the CWT. The Mexican Hat mother wavelet used in Figure 4b is an example of isotropic wavelets.

On the other hand, an anisotropic mother wavelet is dependent on the angle in the analysis; therefore, the CWT acts as a local filter for an image in scale, position, and angle. The Cauchy wavelet is an example of an anisotropic wavelet (Figure 4c). To better see the effect of directional transformation, we can use different anisotropic mother wavelets and compare the results.

## 3. THE SFE2D ARCHITECTURE

To separate the spectral features, we created a 2D feature extraction scheme that combines 2D CWT with variance, kurtosis, and negentropy maximization algorithms (PCA, kICA, and nICA) to extract spectral features from wavelet spectra. The algorithm consists of three main stages (Figure 5):

- ☆ Preprocessing step where 2D interpolation and filtering of raw datasets prepare the input images for feature extraction.
- ☆ Spatial feature extraction employs PCA/ICA for spatial source separation and dimensionality reduction.
- ☆ Spectral feature extraction that consists of two substages: (a) continuous wavelet transform (CWT) and (b) spectral PCA/ICA (SPCA/SkICA/SnICA in Figure 5).

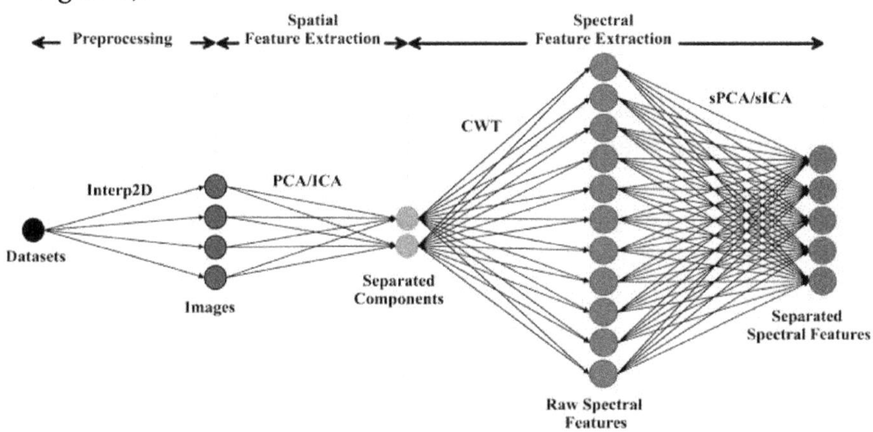


**Figure 5. Schematic view of the SFE2D procedure.**

An effective spectral feature extraction depends on computer hardware specifications, specifically for larger numbers of spectral features produced by increasing the number of scales and mother wavelet's directions. In practice, users can create a larger number of features by changing the CWT parameters in the SFE2D program. For large numbers of CWT features (100–1000 CWT features), PCA/ICA methods provide a way to decorrelate and separate spectral features from CWT images.

If needed, users can also reduce the dimensionality to summarize the features. By running the proposed workflow in the SFE2D program, the redundant frequency volumes could be reduced to a more manageable number of components. Taking advantage of the ICA statistical properties, we can keep the most geologically pertinent information within the spectral decomposed data.

# 4. FEATURE REPRESENTATION

The SFE2D program provides interpretation tools for feature representation in two dimensions:

## 4.1 RGB image compilation and analysis

SFE2D users can select the RGB image compilation method to assemble a colored image from three manually chosen extracted features by PCA and ICA methods. The RGB combination makes it possible to bring out hidden characteristics. To control which extracted features are used for image compilation, the user can graphically set the label number of desired features. For example, in nICA feature extraction, the 1, 2, 3 labels mean the features 1, 2, and 3 are used for image compilation. The user can also change the polarity of the features since PCA/ICA methods distort the polarities randomly. For example, one can set -2, 1, 3 labels for RGB compilation.

A color pick algorithm is also developed to select the region of interest (ROI) based on color intensities. To find objects of a specific color, the SFE2D program assigns the low and high thresholds for each RGB color band with several clicks on the regions of interest. The more users click on the specified zones, the more accurate the thresholding works. Then, the program automatically picks up the minimums and maximums from red/green/blue bands. To reduce the effect of the outliers, only a range of 5 to 95 percentiles are kept, which results in smoother color picking tasks. Figure 6 represents an example of testing the ROI detection method in the SFE2D program to detect the red-colored objects in a standard image.

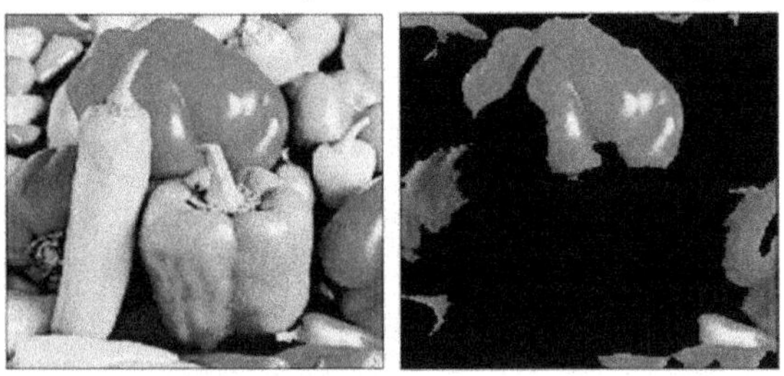

(a) (b)

**Figure 6. Color pick method for extracting the red color objects. (a) Original RGB image. (b) ROI detection.**

## 4.2 The color image segmentation algorithm

SFE2D uses a k-means clustering algorithm for the segmentation of color images. The segmentation helps to reduce the color space size to a manageable number of colors. The process produces a pseudo-geological map based on the spatially extracted RGB features. This eventually helps geologists to detect the hidden geological contacts and structures in geo-images. In addition, segmentation significantly reduces memory usage and speeds up image analysis by focusing on relevant information.

The output of segmentation is a set of k non-overlapping segments {$S_1$, $S_2$, ..., Sk} that comprises the whole segmented representation of a dataset X in the form of [15]:

$$X = \bigcup_{i=1}^{k} S_i \tag{15}$$

For the non-overlapping condition, we should have Si∩Sj=Ø for i≠j, where 1≤i,j≤k which guarantees that each cluster of data belongs uniquely to a segmented centroid.

SFE2D incorporates a k-means segmentation for grayscale or RGB images. The program aims to separate extracted features from an image in different clusters iteratively. The algorithm computes a hyperdimensional centroid for each cluster. Each segment Si is uniquely defined by a center ci:

$$c_i = \frac{1}{|S_i|}\sum_{s \in S_i} s \tag{16}$$

Where |Si| is the number of elements in the ith cluster.

The centroid gets modified interactively through minimizing a cost function that is the distance between data pattern pj and centroid ci:

$$F(c_1, c_1, \ldots, c_k) = \sum_{i=1}^{k} \sum_{p_j \in C_i} d^2\left(p_j, c_i\right) \tag{17}$$

If the image is RGB, the program calculates a 3D Euclidean distance for the RGB color space. The SFE2D program reads data points p and returns k cluster centroids as C={c1,c2,...,ck}. The k-means algorithm for RGB image segmentation in the SFE2D program is as followed:

**Step 1:** Generate k random initial centroids: C←Rand(p,k).

**Step 2:** Repeat the following until Si do not change:

- $S_i \leftarrow \left\{p : \|p - c_i\|^2 \leq \|p - c_{j,}\|^2 \forall j, 1 \leq i, j \leq k\right\}$such that Si∩Sj=Ø..
- $c_i \leftarrow \frac{1}{|S_i|} \sum_{x_j \in S_i} x_j$

**Step 3:** Return all clustered segments as C={c1,c2,...,ck}.

## 5. EVALUATION

Before applying SFE2D algorithms to geoscientific applications, we tested the workflows, including PCA, kICA, nICA, ROI color pick algorithm, and k-mean segmentation in two sections dedicated to grayscale and RGB ICA-based image segmentation.

## 5.1 Spatial feature extraction performance

In grayscale, we tested the performances of kICA versus nICA algorithms and the effect of feature overlaps (shadow effects) on image segmentation. An example of PCA and ICA procedures is presented in Figure 7. We simulated and evaluated the feature extraction processes on an overlapped photo that is mixed with three images: a human face, fruits, and vegetable scenes (features $f_1$, $f_2$, and $f_3$ in Figure 7). The problem can be formulated as the extraction of the human face (feature $f_2$) from the mixed images ($g_1$, $g_2$, and $g_3$) without any prior information from the original face. This simulation helps us to evaluate the performance of the SFE2D algorithm before the implementation on more complex applications.

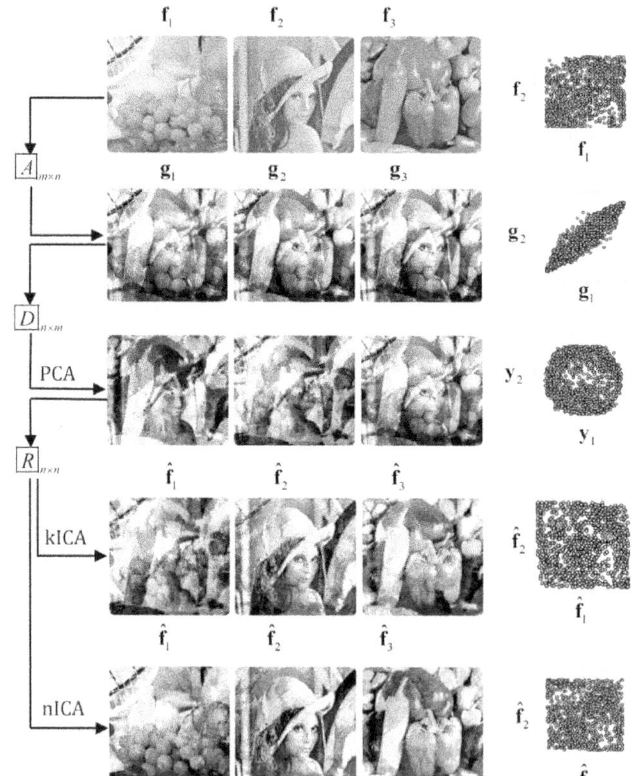


**Figure 7. An example of independent component analysis with kurtosis and negentropy maximization on linear mixtures of three independent images ($f_1$, $f_2$, and $f_3$ with 180 × 180 pixels). ICA goes a step further and rotates the principal components to maximize non-Gaussianity. The results are recovered original images. The column on the right side represents the cross plots of the variables.**

While PCA whitening fails to recover all three features (y1, y2, y3), the Fast-ICA algorithm could separate the latent features inside the mixed images ($\hat{f}$ 1, $\hat{f}$ 2, $\hat{f}$ 3). Further analysis of the non-Gaussianity maximization methods revealed that the

Fast-ICA through negentropy maximization (nICA algorithm) compared to kurtosis maximization (kICA algorithm) is more effective and recovers more details of each original photo. The kICA converges at 50 iterations, while the nICA converges at iteration 5 (Figure 8). The kICA algorithm is prone to outliers and thus fails to converge to an effective solution. However, restarting the kICA each time might improve the results. Therefore, for large images, the efficiency of the nICA method is superior to the kICA, with about 10 times faster convergence and more accurate results.

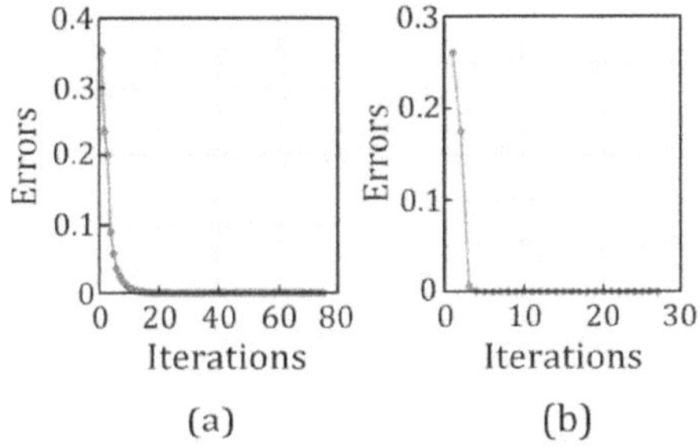


**Figure 8. Performance of kICA algorithm (a) compared to nICA algorithm (b). The kICA results converge at 10 iterations while the nICA results are converged at iteration 5. The nICA method is superior to the kICA, with about two times faster convergence and more accurate results (180 × 180 pixels).**

Another influencing factor with the same level of added unpredictable noise is the sampling interval. This is crucially important in the geophysical sense since the sampling interval directly influences the geophysical survey budget. Large regional-scale data sets are sampled in smaller intervals and give more details about geological structures. As is shown in Figure 9, increasing the number of samples reduces the performance of kICA compared to nICA and indicates that for large datasets with smaller sampling intervals, negentropy maximization is superior to kurtosis maximization.

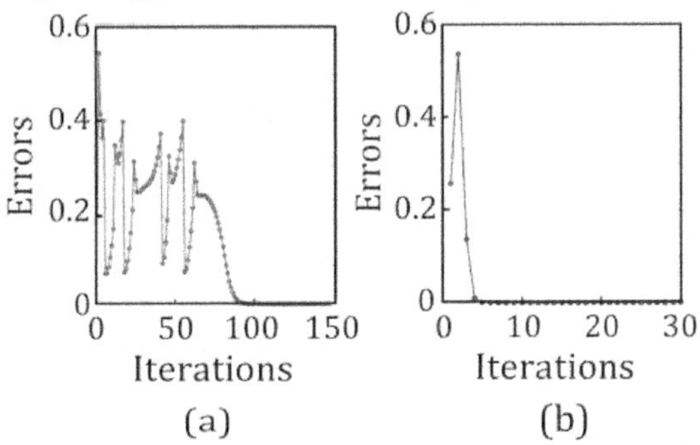


**Figure 9. Performance of kICA algorithm (a) compared to nICA algorithm (b) on large images with 720 × 720 pixels. For the kICA algorithm, a 16 times increase of pixels results in eight times slower convergence with numerous local minima. Therefore, for larger images with smaller sampling intervals, negentropy maximization is superior to kurtosis maximization.**

However, there are two inherent ambiguities in the ICA framework: (1) Ambiguity in permutations of the recovered sources. This problem states that the order of the estimated independent components is unspecified. (2) Ambiguity in the recovered amplitudes of the sources. One can partially solve this problem by assuming unit variance for all sources. However, there is still a 50% chance that the polarities of the sources are not determined correctly. In cases where we have enough prior information, we can multiply sources by -1 to achieve the best results.

The effect of mixing on image segmentation is also explored in Figure 10. ICA significantly reduces the impact of feature overlaps and enhances the performance of image segmentation. The proposed approach integrates information from multiple geo-images and makes sure that the combined images are maximally independent and unique. In other words, the feature overlaps are minimal. This has an important implication in image segmentation since a slight presence of image overlaps and artifacts distort the segmentation output. As shown in Figure 10, the segmentation after negentropy maximization improves the human face detection.

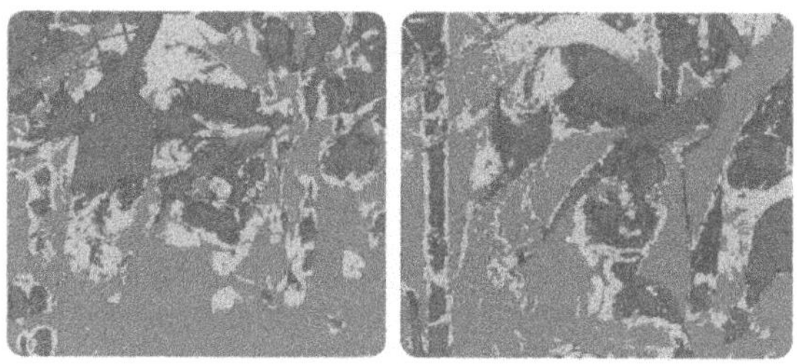

(a) (b)

**Figure 10. Effect of ICA as a preprocessing step before grayscale image segmentation. (a) Segmentation on the mixture image (g2 in Figure 6). (b) Segmentation after negentropy maximization nICA ($\hat{f}$2 in Figure 6).**

## 5.2 Spectral feature extraction

Further feature extraction can be performed on the images to extract spectral features like edges and lineaments inside the photos. Figure 11a shows the results of CWT with Cauchy mother wavelet and 20 scales on the second independent component (recovered human face). As can be seen, different spectral features appear in different CWT scales/directions. Low-level features like edges appear in higher frequencies, and high-level features appear in lower frequencies. However, the transition from each scale/direction is relatively smooth, and that allows some features from each scale/direction leak into the following scale/direction, creating unwanted spectral features' overlap. To reduce these effects, we perform source separation methods like PCA and ICA algorithms again. The results are shown in Figure 11b. As is shown, spectral source separation with nICA has improved the low/high-level features with crisper edges and more visible boundaries.

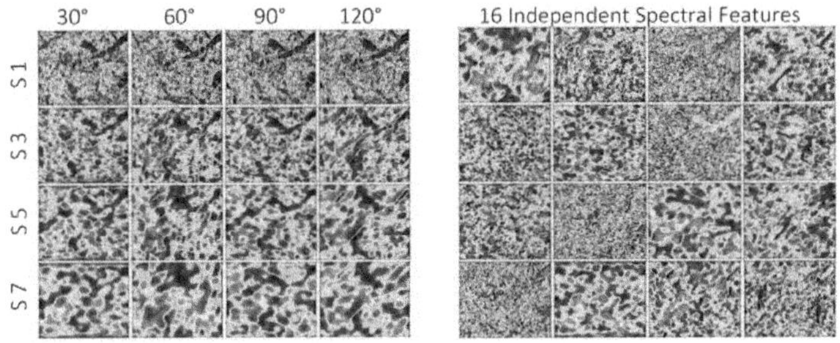


(a) (b)

**Figure 11. (a) Space-frequency representation with Cauchy mother wavelet in four scales on the second independent component (recovered human face). Different spectral features appear in different CWT scales/directions. (b) Separation of spectral features with nICA. The results are crisper and have more distinct features.**

# 6. APPLICATIONS

## 6.1 Integrated interpretation of geophysical data

### 6.1.1 Fast pseudo-geological mapping

Geophysical surveys are essential for fast geological mapping in mineral exploration programs. Nevertheless, there is not necessarily a one-to-one correlation between geophysical responses and contrasts in lithotypes because the rock-forming minerals do not entirely control geophysical properties. For example, in magnetic surveys, most magnetic anomalies are only related to the distribution of rock-forming magnetite inside the rocks. Therefore, a "geological" map created using geophysical data sets should be referred to as a "pseudo-geological" map [16]. However, the integrated interpretation of multiple data types, for example, magnetic, radiometric, conductivity, and so on, helps reduce uncertainty and acquire a more reliable geological model. SFE2D provides such an integration tool for explorations. A geological map of the exemplified region indicates a very complex geological setting along with complex structural faults and fractures (Figure 12).

The geophysical survey of the area is part of a regional program that aims to complete the geological mapping of the southwestern part of James Bay at a scale of 1: 50,000. The region's rocks are mainly of Archean age and belong to the Superior Province, which forms the heart of the Canadian Shield, one of the largest Precambrian cratons exposed from the terrestrial globe. There are also a number of dykes of Neoarchean to Paleoproterozoic diabase [18]. The region is subdivided into five sub-provinces, and the boundaries between the different sub-provinces are based on lithological contrasts, metamorphic, structural, and geophysical information.

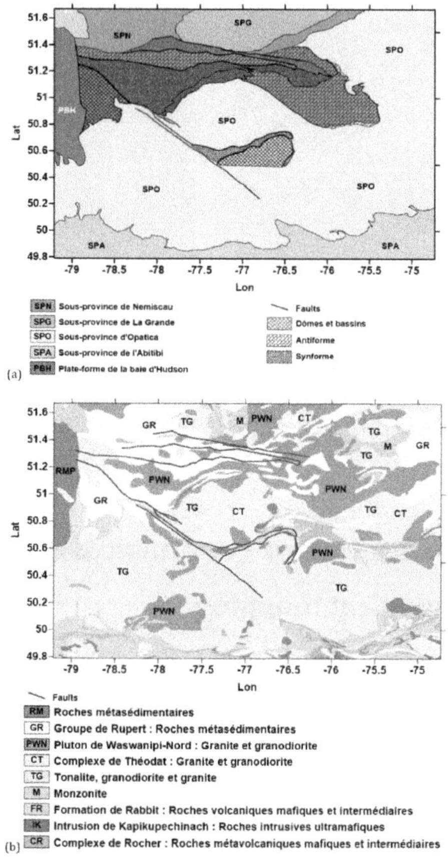


**Figure 12. Geology of the region. (a) Geological sub-provinces and structural features. (b) General geological map of the region. Geological data are compiled from SIGEOM [17].**

However, the geological compilation is subject to varying interpretations due to intrinsic uncertainties in geoscientific data sets. This section provides an example of feature extraction for integrated geophysical interpretation through a PCA and ICA-based color image segmentation by k-means clustering on three sources of geophysical data sets.

GGMplus Bouguer gravity data sets [19], high-resolution airborne magnetic data sets, and digital elevation model exerted from SIGEOM [17] are used as inputs for integrated feature extraction and segmentation (Figure 13).

The program can perform an image segmentation based on the k-means algorithm over the RGB-merged independent components. Unlike traditional segmentation methods, the integrated k-means segmentation algorithm helps calculate segments based on principal or independent components of the original data sets. The results are pseudo-geological maps that integrate extracted features from the three sources of data sets (Figure 14a and b).

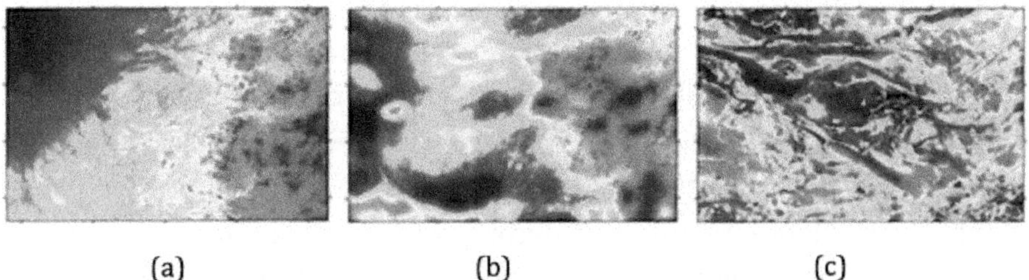


**Figure 13. Three input images. (a) Digital elevation model. (b) GGMplus gravity anomalies. (c) Aeromagnetic data sets.**

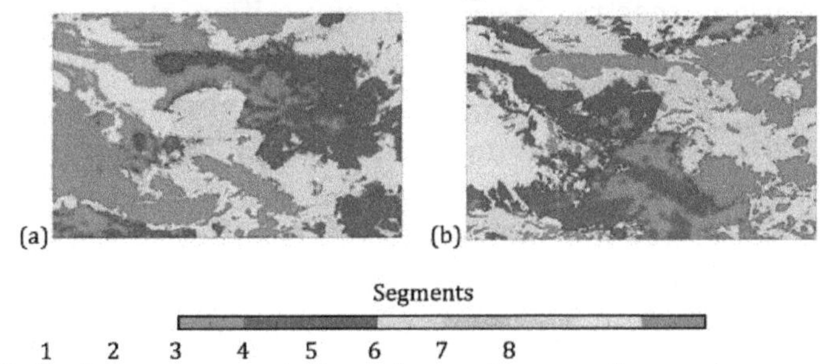


**Figure 14. Color image segmentation after variance and negentropy maximization and RGB image compilation through k-means clustering with eight segments. (a) PCA segmentation with variance maximization. (b) ICA segmentation with negentropy maximization.**

## 6.1.2 Spectral feature extraction

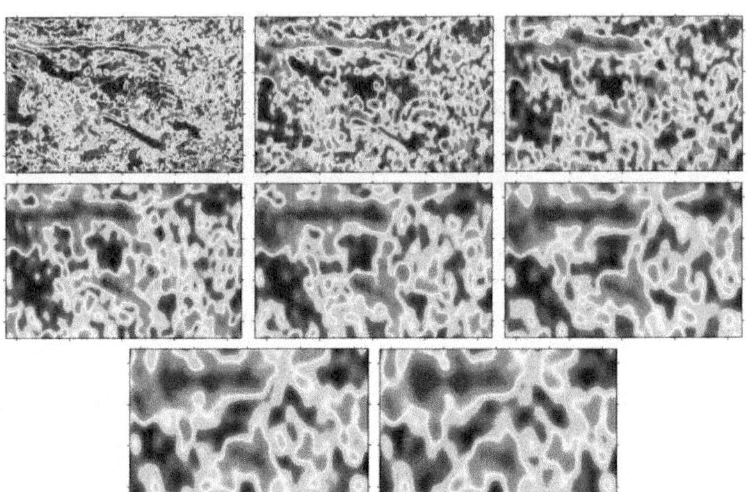

**Figure 15. CWT with Mexican Hat mother wavelet with eight scales over magnetic data sets.**

CWT is performed on the magnetic data sets (Figure 13c). Decomposing the magnetic data sets with CWT forms raw spectral features that eventually increase dimensionality. 2D wavelet coefficients are calculated here for eight scales with Mexican Hat mother wavelet, containing several frequency-dependent raw features (Figure 15). However, the algorithm allows choosing any number of scales and directions (in the case of anisotropic mother wavelets), as long as the computer hardware specifications allow.

As shown in Figure 15, spectral decomposition reveals many latent features that are not properly visible in the spatial domain. The major difficulty arises in extracting and selecting the spectral features due to the statistical interdependence of features in various spectra. Spectral decomposition of images also overloads the computational cost of interpretation and demands a methodology to pick the best spectral representation of images. The SFE2D program tackles this problem with the spectral independent component analysis. We used Fast-ICA through negentropy maximization to separate the eight raw wavelet features to produce the spectral inputs necessary for interpretation. The Fast-ICA algorithm can reduce the dimensionality of the raw features. This is important when we produce a large number of raw features through CWT, and as a result, our computational hardware resources are not enough to handle the inevitable high dimensionality.

We reduced the dimensionality of the raw spectral features and thus produced three independent features (Figure 16). As shown in Figure 16, the program uncovered several low-frequency features in higher wavelet scales related to deep sources and high-frequency features related to shallow sources.

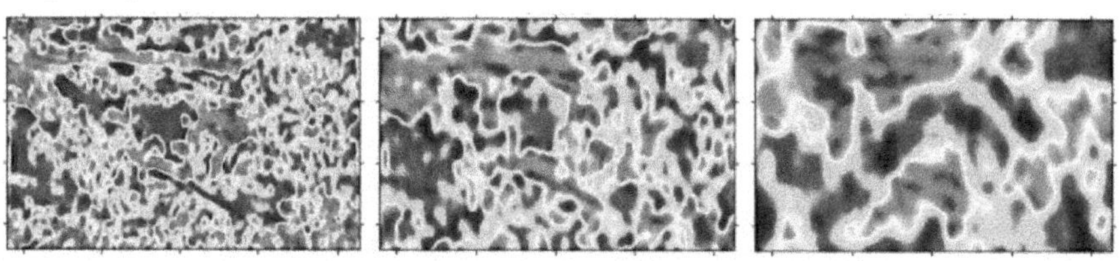

(a) (b) (c)

**Figure 16. Spectral feature extraction and dimensionality reduction by negentropy maximization on CWT results with Mexican Hat mother wavelet. (a–c) Extracted independent spectral features.**

2D wavelet coefficients are also calculated with Cauchy mother wavelet on eight scales and eight directions, producing several directional/frequency-dependent raw features (Figure 17). As can be seen, most of the wavelet spectral content is redundant, and similar features are repeated in 64 subsequent directions/scales. Three independent spectral components are extracted through spectral feature extraction and dimensionality reduction (Figure 18a–c). Therefore, the 64-dimensional hyperspace is reduced to a 3D RGB space to facilitate visual interpretations (Figure 18d). As can be seen, the process helped to uncover several hidden lineaments in the NE–SW direction.

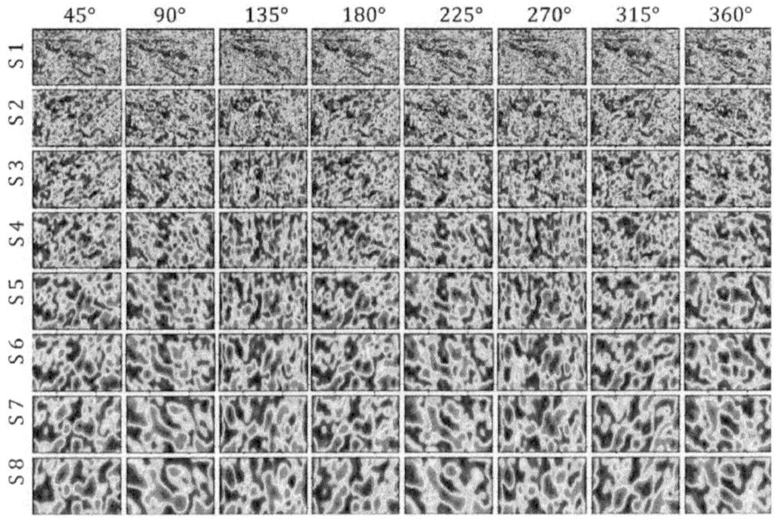


**Figure 17. CWT with Cauchy mother wavelet on eight scales and eight directions over magnetic data sets.**

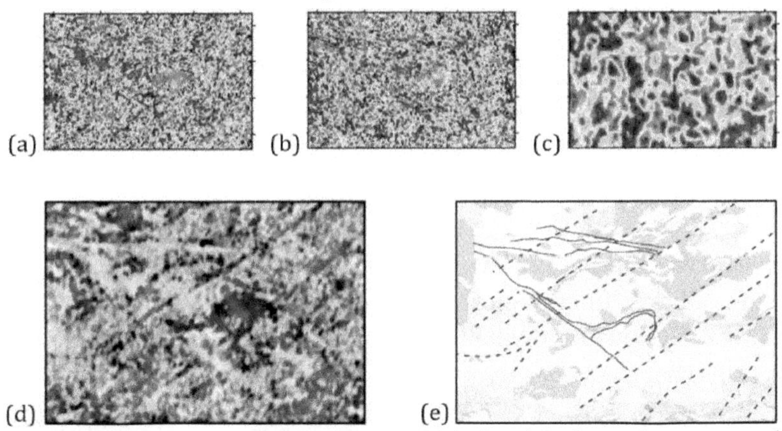


**Figure 18. Spectral negentropy maximization ICA. (a–c) Independent spectral features. (d) RGB image compilation. (e) Extracted lineaments (dashed red lines).**

## 6.2 Microscopic image analysis

Optical microscopy with polarized light microscopes has become one of the most powerful techniques in petrography and mineral exploration. However, due to the complexity of mineral assemblages, acquiring quality images with details of mineral grains and fine textures is a challenging task. Here we present an application of the SFE2D program in the micromorphological characterization of minerals under thin section. An example of an optical microscopic image is presented in Figure 19a. The SFE2D program can separate mineral zones on a highly mixed texture.

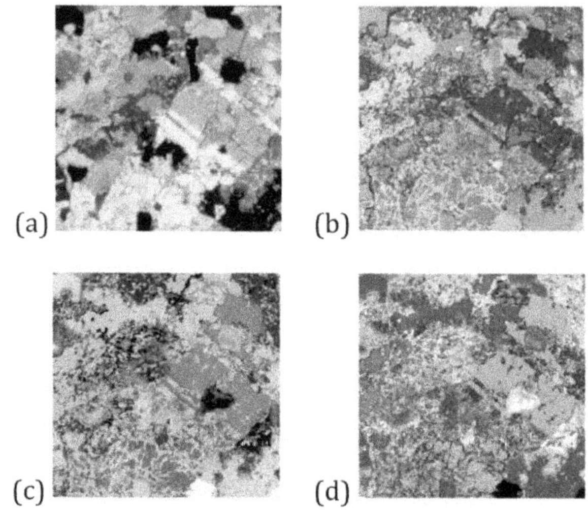


**Figure 19. (a) An example of petrographic thin section imagery used in this study for mineralogical feature extraction. (b–d) Independent components of RGB bands combined to form different representations for enhanced visualization. The thin section image is exerted from Carleton NAGTWorkshops [20].**

The algorithm starts with balancing the colors on the original image based on the normal distribution. Then, source separation on color bands helps extract hidden features in principal or independent components. The RGB compilation of independent components of the image is also shown in Figure 19b–d. As can be seen, different polarities offer different feature representations.

The program also offers a fast detection of the region of interest (ROI) with a color-pick algorithm based on few clicks on specified color zones. As can be seen in Figure 20, subtle mineralogical zones are optimally extracted for geological interpretations. This eventually helps calculate the percentage of specified minerals on thin sections that are very important for mineral exploration studies.

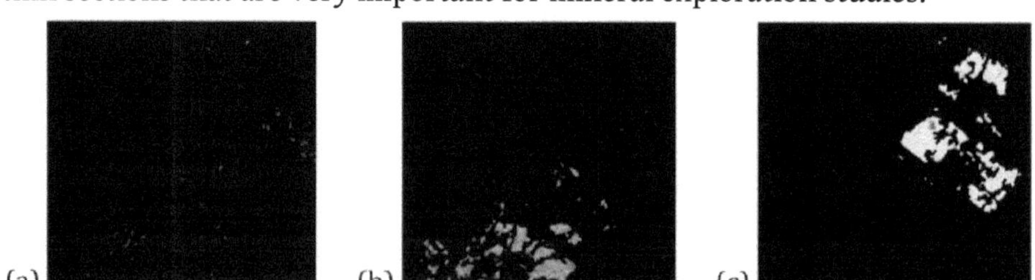


**Figure 20. Regions of interest delineated by the color-pick algorithm in the SFE2D program. (a) First extract mineral. (b) Second extract mineral. (c) Third extracted mineral.**

## 7. CONCLUSIONS

The result presented here illustrates the theory, design, performance, and applications of a standalone mathematical tool (SFE2D) for 2D spatial and spectral feature extraction, based on PCA, ICA, CWT, k-means clustering segmentation, and image processing algorithms. SFE2D provides an integration tool for the interpretation of multiple geoscientific data sets at once. SFE2D has straightforward applications in various geophysical and geoscientific explorations where one needs to add value to observed geo-images by recovering hidden features in hyperdimensional data sets.

The program can perform an image segmentation based on the k-means algorithm over the RGB-merged independent/principal components. The results are pseudo-geological maps that integrate extracted features from multiple data sets. Unlike traditional segmentation methods, the integrated k-means segmentation algorithm helps calculate segments based on principal or independent components of the original data sets. The proposed approach integrates information from multiple geophysical data sets and makes sure that the combined images are maximally independent and unique. In other words, the feature overlaps are minimal. This has an important implication in image segmentation since a slight presence of image overlaps and artifacts distort the segmentation output.

Spectral decomposition of images also provides a unique way for feature extraction in the frequency domain. Deploying the SFE2D algorithms helps eliminate redundant frequency volumes and reduce them to a more manageable number of components. Taking advantage of the ICA statistical properties, we can keep the most geologically pertinent information within the spectral decomposed data. The feature extraction algorithms in SFE2D can also be used in deep learning applications where feature extraction is a primary step in optimizing neural network design.

The SFE2D program can also be used in the micromorphological characterization of minerals under thin sections. The program offers a fast detection of the region of interest (ROI) with a color-pick algorithm based on few clicks on specified color zones.

The SFE2D application is straightforward and for immediate use, as long as users already installed the MATLAB runtime library on their computer.

The SFE2D is provided as a standalone executable program. To use the executable program (SFE2D.exe), users do not need any previously installed Matlab software on the PC. The only prerequisite is installing the latest Matlab 2021a Runtime library, free to download from MathWorks [21]. To do so, users can install the required runtime codes by double-clicking on the offline program installer "Installer_SFE2D (Offline).exe" or the online version of it "Installer_SFE2D (Online).exe" that is a lightweight version in which the program and the runtime codes are going to be installed automatically through downloading from MathWorks server. Users can also directly download the runtime from the MathWorks website [21].

After unzipping the file and installing the runtime, the program should work by simply double click on the SFE2D.exe. It is recommended to copy/paste the SFE2D.exe to a project folder where data sets are located with read/write permission. Running the program for the first time needs activation. To activate the program, one needs to double click on the "Activate.exe" file to create a "Key" file. A dialog box (Password Required) appears that asks to insert the password provided for the user. As soon as typing it and pressing Enter, a "Key" file is going to be generated. The user needs to keep that file and save it in the same project folder where "SFE2D.exe" is copied. When running the SFE2D, the program interface appears as in Figure A1. On the right side, the user can control the program parameters, and on the left, the progress of calculations and possible errors can be tracked with the windows command shell console for execution (black screen on the left).

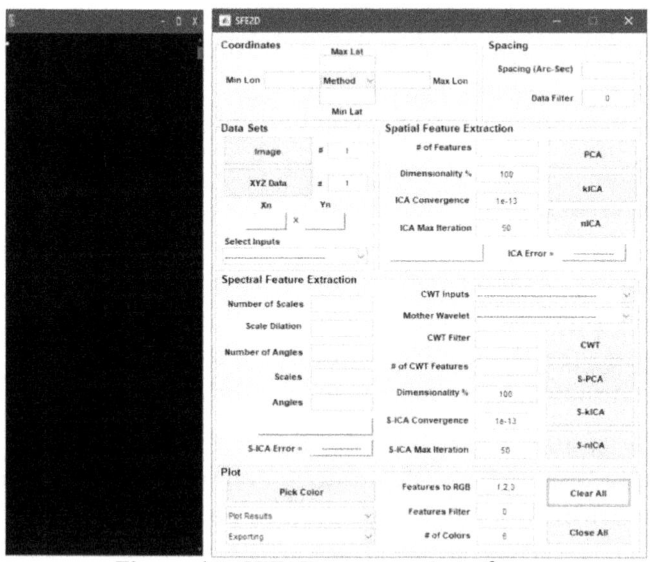


**Figure A1. SFE2D program interface.**

## REFERENCES

1. Barnett C, Williams P. Mineral exploration using modern data mining techniques. First Break. 2006;24(7):295-310

2. Murtaugh F, Starck JL, Berry MW. Overcoming the curse of dimensionality in clustering by means of the wavelet transform. Computer Journal. 2000;43(2):107-120

3. Brown AR. Seismic attributes and their classification. The Leading Edge. 1996;15:10

4. Chen Q, Sidney S. Seismic attribute technology for reservoir forecasting and monitoring. The Leading Edge. 1997;16:445-456

5. Chopra S, Pruden D. Multiattribute seismic analysis on AVO-derived parameters. The Leading Edge. 2003;22:998-1002

6. Lindseth RO. Seismic attributes—Some recollections. Canadian Society of Exploration Geophysicists Recorder. 2005;30(3):16-17

7. Chopra S, Marfurt KJ. Emerging and future trends in seismic attributes. Geophysics. 2008;27:298-318

8. Abbassi B. Integrated imaging through 3D geophysical inversion, multivariate feature extraction, and spectral feature selection [thesis]. Université du Québec à Montréal and Université du Québec en Abitibi-Témiscamingue; 2018

9. Hyvärinen A, Oja E. Independent component analysis: Algorithms and applications. Neural Networks. 2000;13:411-430

10. Moreau F, Gibert D, Holschneider M, Saracco G. Wavelet analysis of potential fields. Inverse Problems. 1997;13:165-178

11. Honório BCZ, Sanchetta AC, Leite EP, Vidal AC. Independent component spectral analysis. Interpretation. 2014;2(1):SA21-SA29

12. Trauth MH. MATLAB® Recipes for Earth Sciences. 4th ed. Berlin: Springer-Verlag; 2015. 436p. DOI: 10.1007/978-3-662-46244-7

13. Moreau F. Méthodes de traitement de données géophysiques par transformée en ondelettes [thesis]. Rennes, France: Université de Rennes I; 1995

14. Moreau F, Gibert D, Holschneider M, Saracco G. Identification of sources of potential fields with continuous wavelet transform: Basic theory. Journal of Geophysical Research. 1999;104:5003-5013

15. Olukanmi P, Nelwamondo F, Marwala T. Rethinking k-means clustering in the age of massive datasets: a constant-time approach. Neural Computing & Applications. 2020;32:15445-15467

16. Dentith M, Mudge ST. Geophysics for the Mineral Exploration Geoscientist. Cambridge: Cambridge University Press; 2014. 516p. DOI: 10.1017/CBO9781139024358

17. SIGEOM. Système d'information géominière of Québec [Internet]. 2021. Available from: https://sigeom.mines.gouv.qc.ca [Accessed: 01 August 2021]

18. Card KD, Ciesielski A. DNAG #1 subdivisions of the superior province of the Canadian shield. Geoscience Canada. 1986;13:5-13

19. Hirt C, Claessens S, Fecher T, Kuhn M, Pail R, Rexer M. New ultrahigh-resolution picture of Earth's gravity field. Geophysical Research Letters. 2013;40:4279-4283

20. Carleton NAGTWorkshops. Optical mineralogy and petrography [Internet]. 2021. Available from: https://serc.carleton.edu/NAGTWorkshops/mineralogy/optical_mineralogy_petrography.html [Accessed: 01 August 2021]

21. MathWorks [Internet]. 2021. Available from: mathworks.com [Accessed: 01 August 2021]

CHAPTER-7

# BLOCK CAVE MINE VENTILATION: RESEARCH FINDINGS

## 1. INTRODUCTION

In the panel caving method, the caving process begins with the ore blasting, then drawing the broken ore from the draw points located at the production level. The extraction of broken ore creates a void volume inside the cave. This void (known as an airgap) and gravity do the rest of the work in breaking the ore in the cave. This rock-breaking process continues as the broken ore is withdrawn from the draw points (Figure 1).

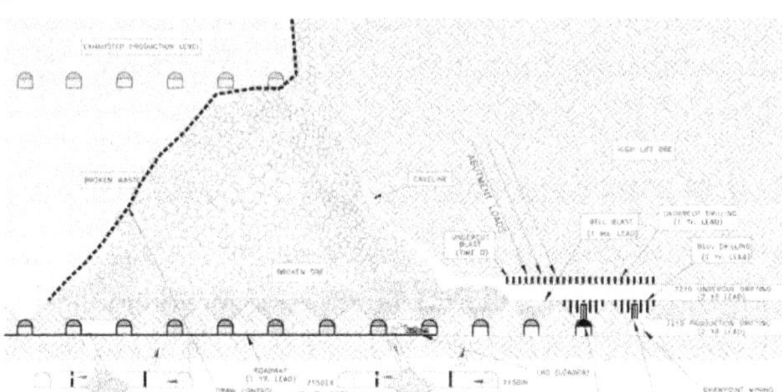

**Figure 1. Panel caving schematic [1].**

The cave initiation is when the caving activity begins, and the hydraulic radius starts to form. As a result of stress increment after the blasting, a stable arch forms in the rock mass. However, the arch cannot resist gravitational stresses indefinitely, and as the cave propagates and the hydraulic radius continues to increase, rock failure will re-initiate. The hydraulic radius at which propagation is achieved can be interpreted as the limit of cavability. However, caving can only actualize when the cave draw starts, and an airgap is created by removing the support provided by the caved rock mass [2].

At the study site (panel cave mine), the panel arches over with a maximum height of 550 m. The ore body rock mass rating (RMR) ranges from 27 to 60, with uniaxial compressive strengths typically ranging from 100 to 275 MPa. Although this is at the high range for caving, there have been minimal problems initiating and advancing the cave because of the lubricating property of the mineral and fillings on the geologic structures [3].

It is already known that gravity and the stress induced in the crown or back of the undercut or cave are the two major factors that trigger the caving event. Caving occurs in two distinct situations—a low-stress environment, where gravity falls due to the lack of confinement is the dominant mechanism; the other extreme, in which the induced tangential stresses are high compared with the compressive and shear strength of the rock mass. This form of caving is often referred to as stress caving [2].

In the caving mining methods, assessing the initiation and growth of caving in rock masses is important to determine the higher-production, lower-cost method. Currently, experience and empirical methods based on the rock mass characterization, such as rock quality designation (RQD), Norwegian Geotechnical Institute's Q system, and rock mass rating system (RMR), are integrated to predict the hydraulic radius for sustained cave growth and the resulting "break" angles and propagation rates of the cave as it grows to the ground surface.

Although this mining method seems most straightforward, it has to be designed carefully; otherwise, the rock will not break properly; hang-ups will develop in the cave. This will result in the development of a large airgap, which can create dangerous conditions in the form of air blasts.

## 1.1 The sequence of operations in a panel cave mining

The sequence of the caving operation starts by advancing the undercut level. A set of parallel and horizontal tunnels is created to develop the upper cavern of broken rock. In the second phase of the production, parallel to the undercut level, the production level is advanced. To collect ore beneath the rock mass, vertical holes are drilled to form funnel-shaped structures called drawbells, which are created above the production level, and extend to the undercut level. The broken ore is extracted from draw points and loaded into the equipment to deliver to the ore passes or an underground crusher.

## 1.2 Panel and extraction layout

The layout of both the panel and the extraction level is one of the most critical tasks in the planning of caving mines. Panel layout design represents a balance between mitigating technical risks and maximizing project value. It aims to minimize surface subsidence risks, minimize abutment stress damage, avoid alignment with major geologic structures, maintain a manageable undercut face length and advance rate and maximize the project's net present value (NPV) Pascoe [4].

The extraction layout seeks to maximize the recovery, minimize the dilution, and increase the efficiency of the ore handling system. In designing the suitable extraction layout, gravitational flow and dilution should be taken into account. However, because of the uncertainty of the in situ rock mass, an accurate gravitational flow evaluation of material movements is not possible. In addition, dilution is a dynamic process and has a self-mixed property, which means that broken ore can easily mix with waste material or low-grade rock that is located in the upper portion of the columns. Since the fine particles move faster to the drawpoints, the percolation of waste material decreases the grade of the drawn material. A schematic sequential drawbell section showing the lateral dilution mechanism is presented in Figure 2.

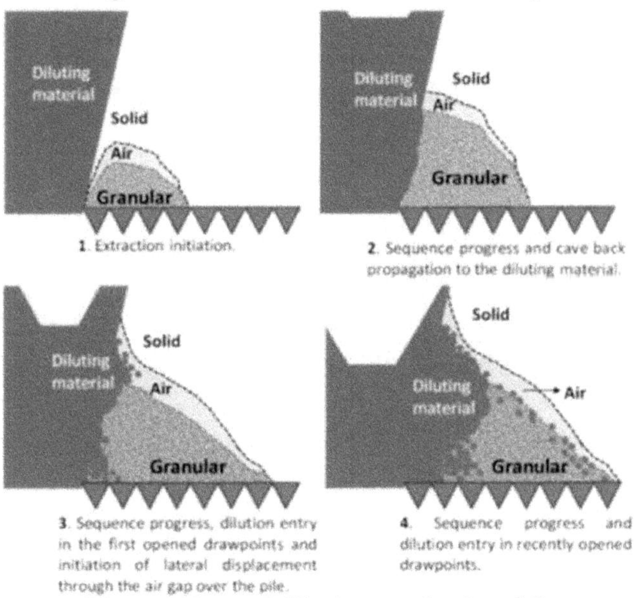


**Figure 2. Lateral dilution mechanism [5].**

## 1.3 Caving zones

Figure 3 depicts the conceptual model of caving consisting of five major zones/ regions. The conceptual model was based on the analysis of data collected at Northparkes Mines' E26 block cave, Australia [6] and consists of the following zones:

- ☆ Caved zone (mobilized zone): This region consists of broken ore blocks that have fallen from the cave back. The material in the caved zone provides support to the cave walls. This is the bottom-most region close to drawbells.
- ☆ Airgap: Extraction of broken ore creates a void volume inside the cave, and this region is called the airgap. During continuous caving, the height of the airgap formed is a function of the extraction rate of the material from the caved zone.
- ☆ Zone of discontinuous deformation (yield zone): This region no longer supports the overlying rock mass and adheres to large-scale displacements of rock.
- ☆ Seismogenic zone: An active seismic front occurs due to slip on joints and brittle failure of rock, mainly due to changing stress conditions caused by the progress of the cave.
- ☆ Surrounding rock mass: Elastic deformation occurs in the rock mass ahead of the seismic front and surrounding the cave.

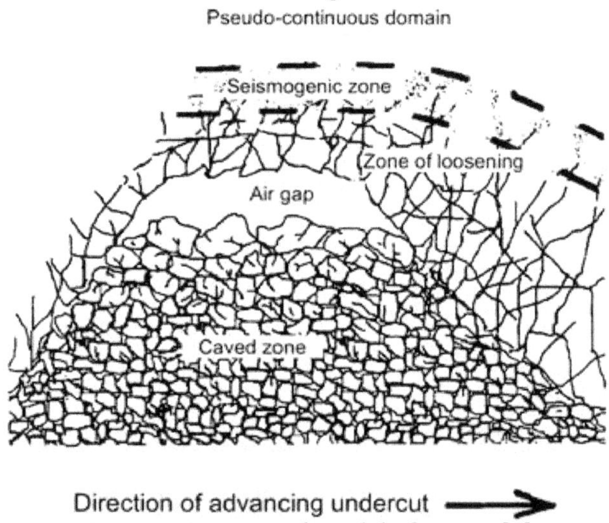


**Figure 3. Conceptual model of caving [6].**

An interesting point to note is that caved zone is the highest porosity region in the cave (if the airgap is not considered). Over time, as the cave evolves and progresses, the caved zone reaches the economic ore boundary, defined as "fully developed" in terms of ore production. The cave is then termed as a "fully developed" or "mature cave." A mature cave consists of different porosity zones consisting of broken ore and waste (based on the degree of dilution) of various sizes in the caved area with zero airgap. The particles' size changes from finer to coarser as we move from caved zone to the surrounding rock mass zone, as shown in Figure 3.

## 1.4 Radon

Radon gas is a major source of ionizing radiation [7] due to the release of harmful radiation during its decay [8]. According to reports from the radon epidemiology subgroup, about 1100 radon-induced lung cancer deaths occur each year in the UK [9]. About 21,000 radon-related lung cancer deaths occur in the US [10]. The severity of these effects on human health prompted multiple investigations that focused on radon mitigation measures. Hence, it is one of the most extensively investigated carcinogens with about 1 million radon-related indoor measurements taken annually in the US [11]. Several measurements and mitigation methods are available to detect and control radon in underground mines [12].

This chapter discusses the recent research investigations related to block or panel cave mines on the following topics—immature and mature cave properties, radon and airflow behavior, radon control measures, cave characteristics, ventilation on demand, blasting fumes, prediction of porosity, and permeability of different cave zones, the effect of undercut ventilation, forcing, exhaust and the push-pull system, the effect of airgap, broken rock porosity and permeability on the cave ventilation system.

# 2. RESEARCH METHODS

The specific objectives of this study include:

- ☆ To develop a better understanding of the effect of airgap geometry on the cave airflow resistance and the radon emission rates from an immature panel cave
- ☆ To predict radon gas emissions from fractured rocks and their control measures in block/panel cave mines
- ☆ To predict the porosity of different cave zones in a typical block or panel cave mine under both cave development and mature cave conditions.
- ☆ To predict cave airflow resistance and gas emission rates from a mature panel cave under varying cave conditions
- ☆ To investigate the blasting fume distribution in a typical block/panel cave mine.

To achieve the stated objectives, the following tasks were completed:

- ☆ Development of a panel cave geometry model.
- ☆ Development of CFD (using continuum approach) models of an immature panel cave with varying airgap geometries.

- Simulation of airflow and radon gas flow in immature and mature panel caves.
- Analysis of the effect of airgap geometry on the cave airflow resistance and radon working levels in a panel cave mine.
- Development of a robust model for predicting radon flux through fractured rocks.
- Development of a numerical model for investigating proactive radon mitigation measures in a developing and developed cave mine.
- Development of a model for predicting airway resistance in cave mines.
- Investigation of the effect of production rate and rock mass strength on the porosity of different cave zones using a continuum approach (FLAC 3D).
- Examination of the effect of particle size distribution and production draw control strategy on the porosity of the mobilized zone (fragmented rock) in a fully developed cave (mature) using a discontinuum approach (PFC 3D).
- Investigation of the behavior of blasting fumes in a block cave mine.
- Analysis of the effect of changes in the cave bulk porosity on the airflow resistance and radon concentration (WL)s found in a panel cave mine.
- Investigation of different ventilation control approaches to minimize the radon flow in an underground mine using a scaled model constructed in the lab.
- Investigation of the airflow behavior through a mature cave under changing cave conditions: cave permeability and porosity, and airgap.
- Examination of the airflow behavior through a single cave column under changing cave conditions: particle size, cave size, and cave porosity.
- Investigation of the airflow behavior through a mature cave under multiple fan configurations and various cave conditions: varying cave permeability and porosity, undercut structures, and different negative pressures on the cave.
- Investigation of the airflow behavior through a mature cave under multiple regulators and changing cave conditions: varying cave permeability and porosity, undercut structures, cave footprint, and regulator combinations.

## 3. RESULTS

This section presents the key findings from the block cave mine ventilation research study that provides valuable information for optimizing the ventilation systems. The findings include the results and observations from numerical simulation studies, scale model studies of the mature and immature block and panel cave mines, mathematical modeling, and field observations.

## 3.1 Finding 1: airgap and airflow resistance of an immature panel cave

Airflow through an immature panel cave was analyzed under four different airgap heights using a 3D panel cave geometry model (Figure 4a and b). Furthermore, CFD simulations were performed to predict the radon emissions from an immature panel cave.

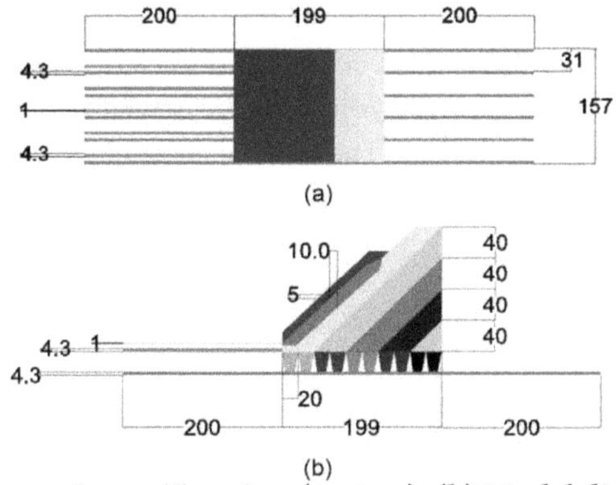


**Figure 4. (a) Model dimensions—Top view (meters). (b) Model dimensions—Front view (meters).**

The analysis of the airflow patterns through the cave indicated that the size and intensity of the recirculation zones change with the change in airgap heights. CFD simulation results show that in the absence of undercut ventilation, radon concentrations in the production level were much lower than those observed when the undercut level was ventilated [13, 14]. This can be attributed to the creation of a low-pressure region in the undercut level, the porous nature of the cave, and the air recirculation (Figure 5) in the cave.

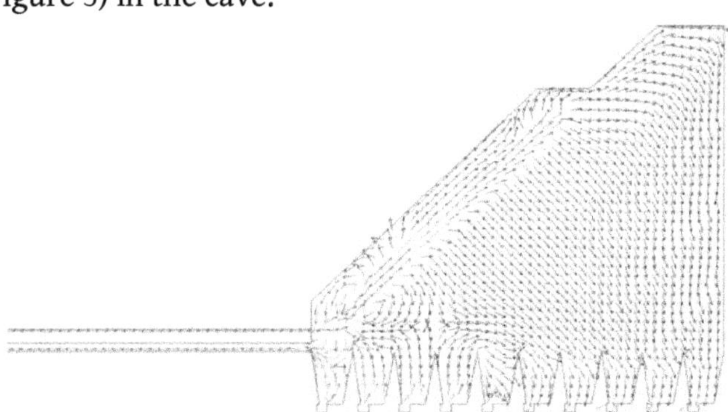

**Figure 5. Velocity vectors.**

## 3.2 Finding 2: cave porosity zone height decreases with an increase in rock mass strength

Porosity values for different cave zones were predicted under both cave development and mature cave conditions using FLAC3D and PFC3D modeling, respectively. FLAC3D simulations were performed first to predict the formation of different zones in a typical block cave mine and then to investigate the effect of rock mass strength (RM) and production rate on the porosity of different cave zones in both block and panel cave mines.

Simulations were performed on two models for both block and panel cave cases by keeping all the model parameters the same except the properties of the rock masses. For both cases, production draw has been simulated with a total height of draw (HD) of 0.6 m by applying the downward velocity of 0.0001 m/s at all the grid points on the roof of the undercut. However, in the case of a panel cave simulation, the applied extraction rates are not the same at all the grid points. Simulated porosity values are shown in Figures 6 and 7 for block and panel cave, respectively.

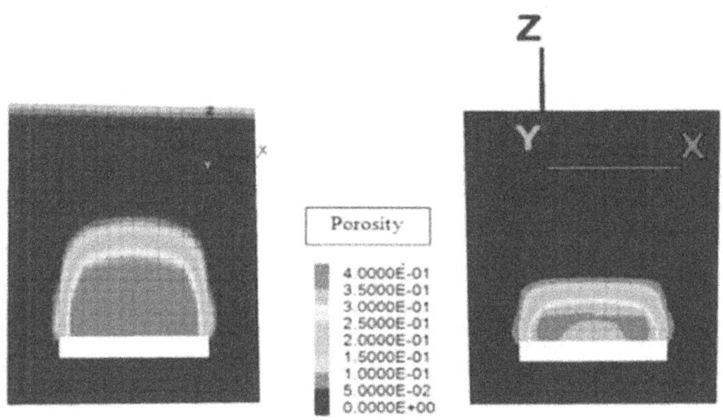


**Figure 6. Porosity value profile for RM1 (left) and RM2 (right) for block cave mine model.**

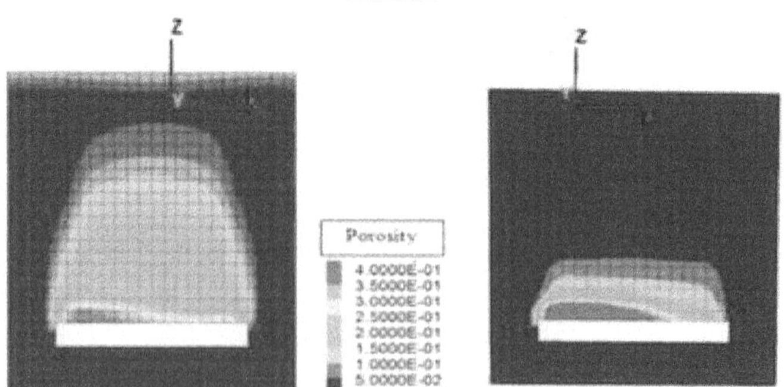


**Figure 7. Porosity value profile for RM1 (left) and RM2 (right) for panel cave mine model.**

It can be seen from Figures 6 and 7 that as the rock mass strength (RM) increases, the heights of the cave porosity zones decrease for both block and panel cave models. This is because the propagation rate decreases as rock mass strength increases. For both cases, the porosity value for the mobilized zone ranges from 0.35 to 0.40. Further, the zone heights for different cave zones are relatively higher for RM1 than RM2.

Similar trends were observed for the panel cave case, except that the cave zone profile is inclined toward the right due to the nature of the extraction for the panel cave mine.

## 3.3 Finding 3: cave porosity zone height decreases with a decrease in extraction rate

Four different scenarios were simulated with increasing velocities from 0.0001 to 0.0004 m/s by keeping the same rock mass properties (RM2). For the block cave model, the same velocities (extraction rates) are assigned at all the grid points, whereas in the panel cave model, different velocities are applied at grid points due to the inherent nature of the caving process. An increase in velocity value means an increase in material extraction rates. The simulated porosity values for different zones under different extraction rates for both block and panel cave models are shown in Figures 8 and 9.

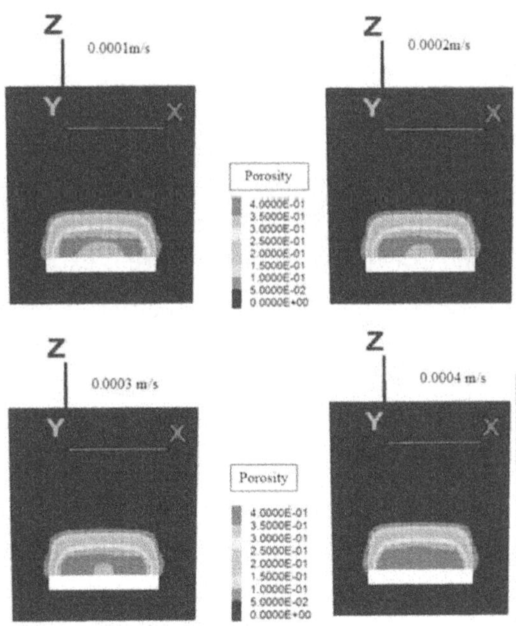


**Figure 8. Porosity value profile for RM2 under four different extraction rates (0.0001–0.0004 m/s) for block cave model.**

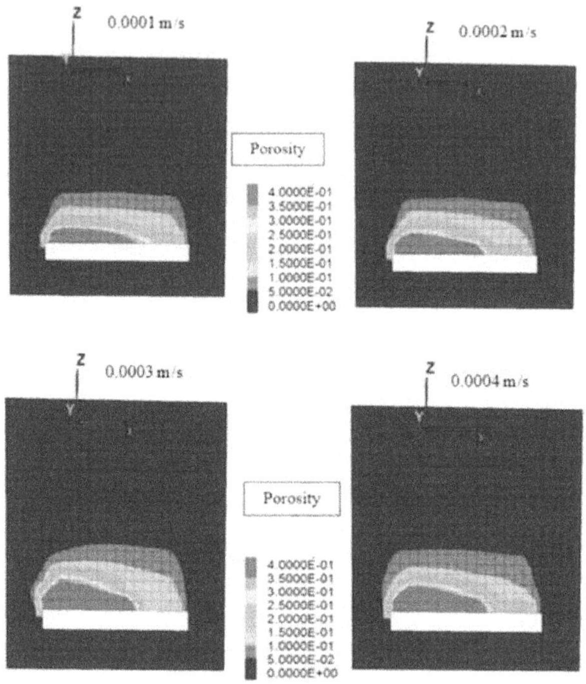


**Figure 9. Porosity value profile for RM2 under four different extraction rates (0.0001–0.0004 m/s) for panel cave model.**

In the real-world scenario, in a propagating cave, the cave height increases with increased production. It was evident from Figures 8 and 9 that when the ore extraction rate was increased, the cave zones height was increased. The mobilized zone porosity tends to be higher as it is the actively flowing region in the cave. In both block and panel cave models, the mobilized zone porosity value ranges from 0.35 to 0.40. The height of this zone is relatively high compared to the other zones due to its proximity to the drawpoints where the ore is extracted from the cave.

In the block cave model, when different velocities, from 0.0001 to 0.0004 m/s, were applied at the drawpoints, the porosity values in the mobilized zone were observed to be from 0.30 to 0.35. This could result from stagnant flow in the cave that subjected the material to re-compaction. If the extraction rate of material is not equal to the rate of cave propagation, the material will stagnate, re-compacted, and result in lower porosity.

## 3.4 Finding 4: cave porosity is affected by the fragmentation size

Material extraction is simulated in a block cave model by opening drawpoints to extract a targeted mass of 100,000 metric tons. As soon as the drawpoint is open, due to gravity, the spheres (broken rock) will start flowing toward the drawpoints.

Measurement locations are strategically placed to measure the porosities as the material flows through the cave. Porosity measurement histories are recorded at all the measuring locations (spheres) while extracting the material from the cave through the drawpoint. From the simulation results, it was found that the porosity change in the isolated extraction zone (IEZ) ranges from 0.39 to 0.56. In comparison, in the isolated draw zone (IDZ) insignificant porosity change (0.38–0.42) was observed. The random spike(s) seen on the graph shows the change in the porosity while the material is drawn from the cave.

To study the effect of particle size distribution on the porosity change, two fragmentation distributions with different mean particle sizes and standard deviations are applied for the block cave mine. Table 1 illustrates the particle distributions considered for the simulations.

**Table 1. Gaussian particle size distributions for fragmentation #1 and #2.**

| Layer | Mean particle size in meter | | Standard deviation in meter | |
|---|---|---|---|---|
| | Fragmentation #1 | Fragmentation #2 | Fragmentation #1 | Fragmentation #2 |
| 1 | 1 | 1.5 | 0.1 | 0.5 |
| 2 | 2 | 2.5 | 0.1 | 0.5 |
| 3 | 3 | 3.5 | 0.1 | 0.5 |
| 4 | 4 | 4.5 | 0.1 | 0.5 |

Scenario #1 is simulated by consecutively opening the six drawbells. When the target discharge mass is reached the assigned value in the system, the next drawpoint will open immediately as shown in Table 2.

**Table 2. Discharge mass criteria for opening the drawpoints for two scenarios.**

| Mass discharged in kg (in million) | Scenario #1 drawpoint id opened | Scenario #2 drawpoint id opened |
|---|---|---|
| 0 | 1 | 1 |
| 1 | 2 | 6 |
| 5 | 3 | 2 |
| 10 | 4 | 5 |
| 20 | 5 | 3 |
| 30 | 6 | 4 |

Scenario #2 is conducted by opening the six drawbells randomly. The discharged mass is applied to control the opening of the drawbells for the random opening. A summary of discharge mass criteria and the drawbells are provided in Table 2.

The numerical model of porosity assessment using a discontinuum approach successfully modeled change in porosity associated with the fragmented rock mass flow in a mature cave. It was found that during material extraction, the porosity changes relatively higher in IEZ than in IDZ. These changes for IEZ range from 0.39 to 0.56 for a block cave and 0.38–0.48 for a panel cave.

The sensitivity analysis on particle size distribution concluded that fragmentation size affects cave porosity. In the case of Fragmentation #1, the change in porosity ranges from 0.40 to 0.48 in IEZ and from 0.38 to 0.56 for Fragmentation #2. Similarly, the draw control strategy also affects cave porosity. In the case of Scenario #1, the change in porosity ranges from 0.38 to 0.52 in IEZ and from 0.38 to 0.48 for Scenario #2 in IEZ.

## 3.5 Finding 5: in a fully developed cave, undercut level ventilation increases the radon concentration in the production drift

Figure 10 shows the velocity contours through a section of the model (the production drift and draw points). The velocity magnitude through the first and second drift is similar; however, it is higher in the third drift due to the influence of the undercut ventilation. Based on the proximity of the undercut drift to the third drift, most of the airflow from the undercut duct flows out through the draw bells in the third drift, creating a significant difference in the magnitude of velocity.

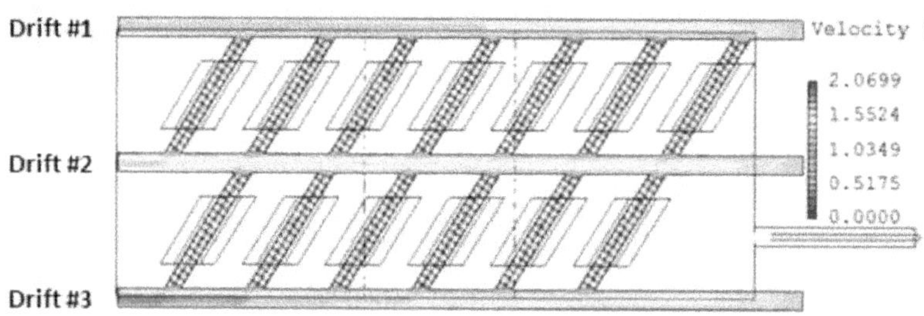


**Figure 10. The magnitude of velocity through the production drift.**

The static pressure decreases down the production drift due to wall friction and shock losses through the draw points. The drawpoint—drift configuration is similar to a "T-junction" with orientation, which introduces flow separation [15]. Therefore, the number of drawbells (shock loss sources) in each drift affects the total pressure drop in the drift. In addition, for each drift, the distance between the inlet and the first draw bell affects the developing flow due to momentum loss from the drawbells. Therefore, the static pressure is maximum in the third drift based on the distance.

In addition, we analyzed the static pressures in the localized regions (Figure 11a) and the shock losses for both sides of the second drift (Figure 11b). We observe a notable variation in pressure around region "B" compared to region "A"; hence the shock loss is greater for region "B" due to the orientation of the drawbells. Since air flows from right to left, the flow makes a 56° turn to get into drawbells around region "B," and a 24° turn into region "A." Therefore, as the bend angle increases, shock loss increases [16], hence the airflow pressure is more efficient with drawbell that requires a less angle of airflow rotation (Region A of the second drift, and the first drift).

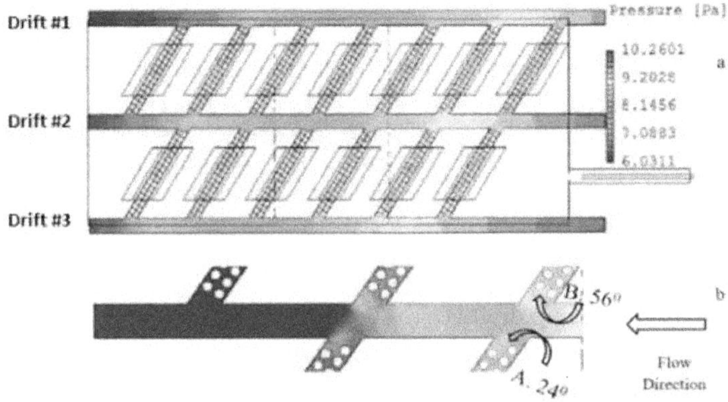


**Figure 11. (a) Static pressure contours through the production drift; (b) localized pressure distribution from a section of the second drift.**

Figure 12 shows the working level through the three production drifts, and based on the number of radon sources, the second drift (with 13 sources) has the largest region with high concentrations compared with the first drift (with seven sources), and the third drift (with six radon sources).

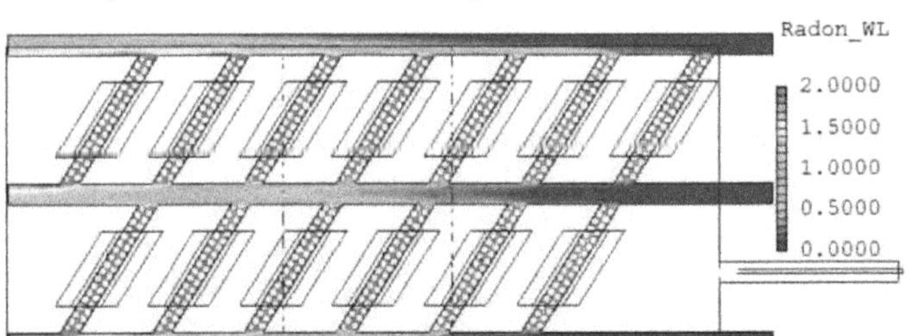


**Figure 12. Radon concentration through the production drift presented in working levels to represent the concentration of harmful radon daughters.**

The concentrations are lowest in the third drift due to the combined effects of the pressure distribution, the number of radon sources, and the undercut ventilation. However, there are small regions with a high concentration around the last drawbell due to the impact of undercut ventilation. Most of the airflow from the undercut duct flows out through the third drift with a high radon concentration from the cave. Figure 13 shows the working level through a section of the cave along with the undercut drift. The positive pressurization due to the undercut ventilation effectively prevents the influx of radon into the undercut drift. Therefore, personnel working in the undercut drifts are not exposed to high concentrations with this ventilation design.

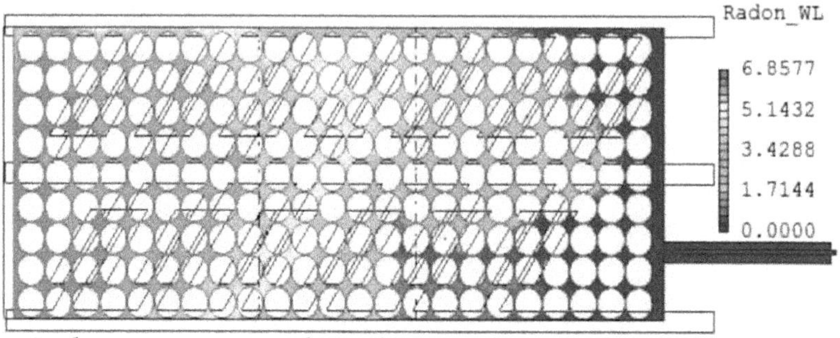


**Figure 13. Radon concentration through a section of cave presented in working levels.**

Figure 14a shows a plot of radon concentration along the center of the first, second, and third production drifts to understand the changes in radon concentration through the production drift. The concentrations increase non-linearly as the number of radon sources increases down the drifts. However, there is a drop in concentration for the first drift due to the distance from the last source of radon, which is the farthest. Hence, based on the drift layout/configuration, specific locations other than the outlet might have higher radon concentrations. As observed in Figure 14a, the non-linear increase is due to the differences in radon sources (drawbells) compared to the wall sources, which increases linearly from previous studies [17]. For further investigation, Figure 14b compares the concentration at the outlet of the three production drifts at different times. The concentrations increase with time, but the rate decreases after about 4 hours as the flow develops. The results presented in Figure 14a and b are from the center of the production drifts; however, radon concentration varies across the drift cross-section for a fixed location.

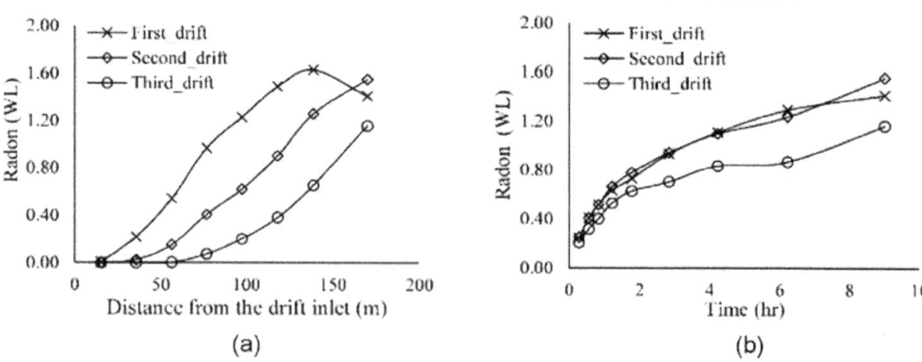


**Figure 14. (a) Growth of radon along the center of the production drift for the first, second, and third, after 9 hours. (b) Radon concentration at the end of the production drifts w.r.t time.**

## 3.6 Finding 6: with undercut ventilation, negative pressure on the cave top effectively reduces radon concentration through the production drifts

In some instances, a regulator is used along with the exhaust fan to maintain negative pressure on top of the cave to remove pollutants from the cave due to the pressure difference. We conducted an independent study to understand the impact of negative pressure (300 Pa) [18] on top of the cave for the result presented in Figure 12. Figure 15 shows a significant reduction in radon concentration through the production drift. Therefore, imposing a negative pressure on the cave top, positive pressurization of the production, and undercut drifts effectively reduce radon concentration through the production drifts.

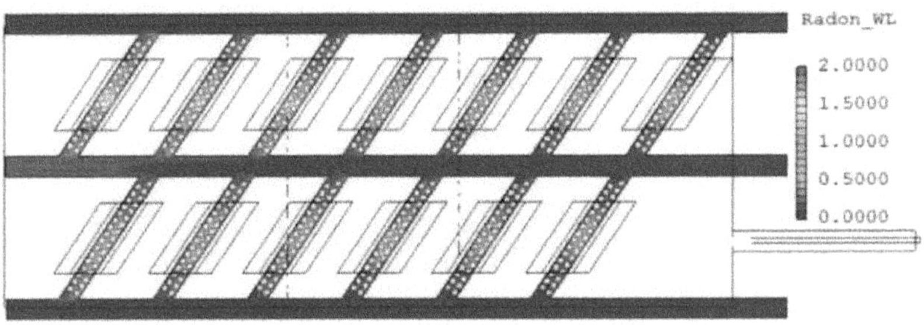


**Figure 15. Effect of negative pressure (boundary condition for cave top) on radon concentrations in the production drifts.**

## 3.7 Finding 7: relationship between pressure drop and airflow

The study investigated two ventilation stages of a fully developed panel cave: with and without undercut ventilation using discrete and continuum CFD models [19]. With active undercut ventilation, we found that—(1) the cave act as a unique form of porous media, which influences flow through the production drifts such that the pressure drop model (in the production drifts) does not agree with either the existing models, hence, a unique model is required for the ventilation design, which provides opportunities for further research; and (2) increase in cave porosity decreases the drift's resistance to airflow. Without the undercut ventilation, the cave has less effect on the production drift ventilation as the pressure drop model agrees with the turbulent model; and an increase in cave porosity decreases the drift's resistance to airflow as shown in Figures 16 and 17 (Tables 3 and 4).

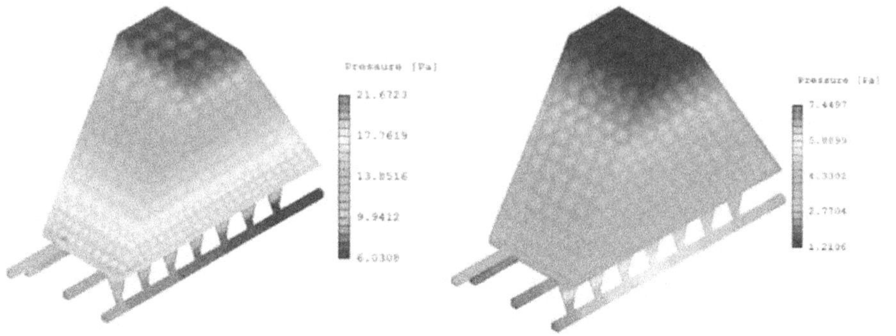


**Figure 16. Static pressure distribution under undercut ventilation (left) and without undercut ventilation (right) using a discrete model.**

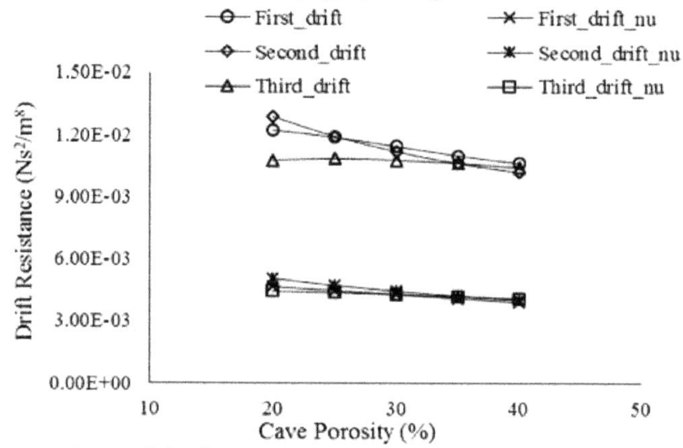


**Figure 17. Comparison of drift resistance with and without the undercut ventilation (nu—no undercut).**

**Table 3. Comparison of pressure drop equation for model with undercut ventilation.**

| Drift | Discrete model | Continuum model |
|---|---|---|
| First drift | Δp=0.0127Q1.7725,R2=0.999 | Δp=0.0102Q1.8201,R2=0.9998 |
| Second drift | Δp=0.0122Q1.8064,R2=0.9994 | Δp=0.0106Q1.8468,R2=0.9999 |
| Third drift | Δp= 0.0106Q1.8437,R2=0.9995 | Δp=0.0099Q1.8547,R2=0.9999 |

**Table 4. Comparison of pressure drop equation for model without undercut ventilation.**

| Drift | Discrete model | Continuum model |
|---|---|---|
| First drift | Δp=0.0052Q1.9585,R2=1 | Δp=0.0046Q1.9878,R2=1 |
| Second drift | Δp=0.0053Q1.9816,R2=1 | Δp=0.005Q2.0042,R2=1 |
| Third drift | Δp=0.0047Q2.0155,R2=1 | Δp=0.0047Q2.0142,R2=1 |

### 3.7.1 Effect of porosity on cave pressure drop

For a given porosity of the cave and airflow in the production drifts, the pressure difference across the cave was calculated and then plotted against the airflow quantity flowing through the cave, as shown in Figure 18. For example, five different air quantities were simulated for a bulk cave porosity of 35%. Therefore, for six different bulk cave porosities, a total of 30 simulations were performed to develop the pressure-quantity (P-Q) characteristic curves for a mature panel cave mine. Figure 18 shows the variation of the airflow resistance value with respect to the bulk cave porosity.

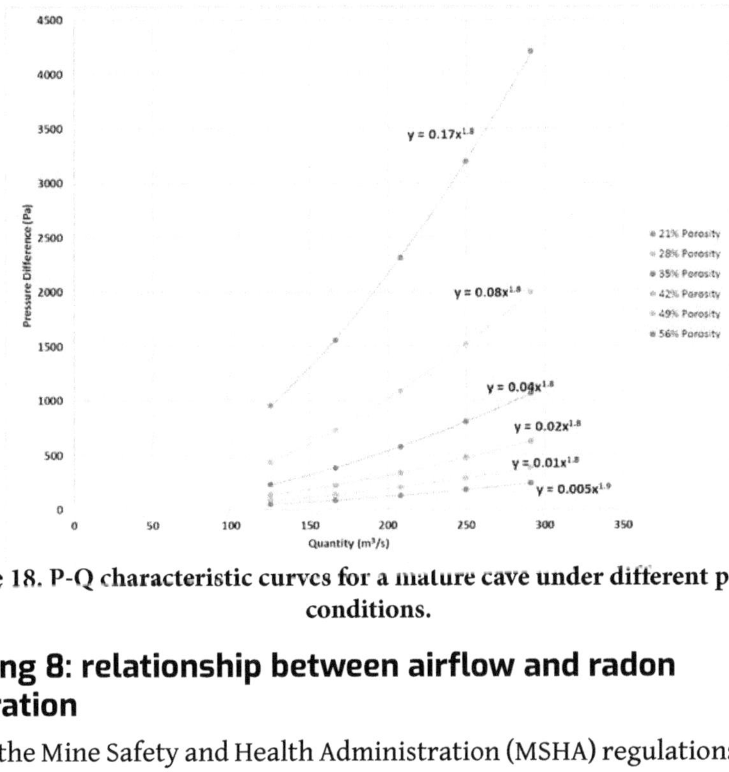


**Figure 18. P-Q characteristic curves for a mature cave under different porosity conditions.**

## 3.8 Finding 8: relationship between airflow and radon concentration

As per the Mine Safety and Health Administration (MSHA) regulations, personnel shall not be exposed to air-containing concentrations of radon daughters exceeding 1.0 WL. No person shall be permitted to receive exposure over 4 WLM (Working Level Months) in any calendar year. 30 CFR 57.5005 suggests dilution with uncontaminated air to mitigate radon exposure. Therefore, we studied the effect of airflow on radon concentration [20, 21]. The airflow through the production drifts is increased, and radon concentration at the outlets of the drifts is measured after 8 minutes. Figure 19 show radon concentrations with airflow at the outlets of the first, second, and third drifts.

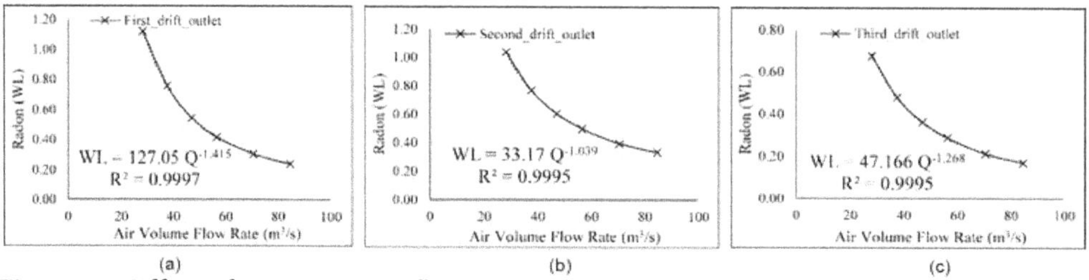


**Figure 19. Effect of increasing airflow on working level at the outlet of the (a) first drift; (b) second drift; (c) third drift.**

McPherson (1993) stated that if an airway is supplied with uncontaminated air and the rate of radon emanation remains constant, then the exit working level of radon daughter is proportional to the residence time (tr) raised to the power of 1.8 Eq. (1).

$$WL \propto (t_r)^{1.8} \quad (1)$$

The results show that the radon concentration decreases with increased airflow, and an empirical relationship is developed for each drift. Due to the difference in the number of radon sources, the relationship varies for the three drifts. Therefore, based on the drift's configuration, the empirical relationship between the working level and airflow might be different, unlike in Eq. (1).

## 3.8.1 Comparison of discrete and continuum model

The airway characteristics are analyzed with the help of a discrete and continuum model [19, 22]. Both models show that radon growth through the production drift is non-linear; however, the continuum model does not replicate the significant variation in radon concentration with time compared to the discrete model [23]. Basically, the continuum model indicates that, beyond a specific time, consistent airflow keeps the concentration constant with respect to time. This is further verified in Figure 20, which compares the radon concentration at the outlet of the second production drift for both models.

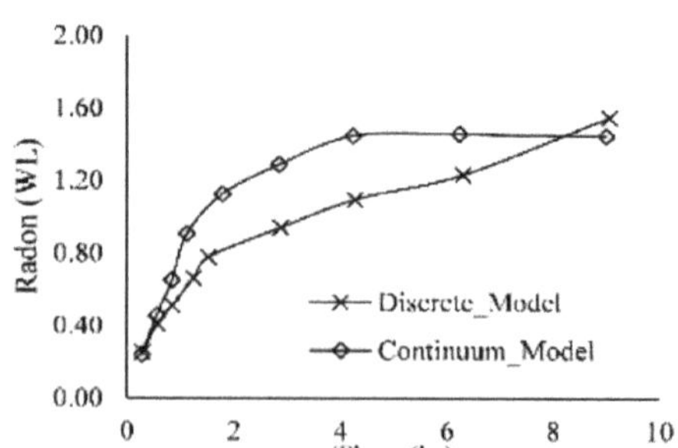


**Figure 20. Comparison of the discrete and continuum models for predicting radon levels at the outlet of the second drift with time.**

The discrete model demonstrates that the concentration increases with time, unlike the continuum model, which shows that after about 5 hours, the radon concentration is almost steady. In addition, we replicated the study on the effects of airflow using the continuum model. The empirical relationships developed are compared with the discrete model in Table 5, and both models suggest that different relationships are required for the drifts based on their configuration.

**Table 5. Empirical relationships—Effect of airflow on radon concentration for the first stage of a fully developed cave.**

| Drift | Discrete model | Continuum model |
|---|---|---|
| First drift | WL=127.05Q-1.42,R2=0.9997 | WL=845.87Q-2.01,R2=0.9918 |
| Second drift | WL=33.17Q-1.04,R2=0.9995 | WL=85.86Q-1.57,R2=0.9962 |
| Third drift | WL=47.17Q-1.28,R2=0.9995 | WL=24.07Q-1.20,R2=0.9998 |

## 3.9 Finding 9: characteristics of model with no undercut ventilation

This section considers the fully developed panel cave without the undercut ventilation (second stage). This is usually after the whole panel is developed, and the undercut level no longer exists. No flow is assigned to the undercut inlet duct and outlet to represent this condition, but all other conditions presented in the previous section are used. Figure 21 shows the velocity contours through the drifts without the undercut ventilation. Unlike in Figure 10 (with undercut ventilation), the velocity magnitude through the three drifts is more uniform. However, based on the number of pressure loss sources (drawbells), the magnitude of velocity through the first (seven shock loss sources) and third (six shock loss sources) drifts are pretty similar.

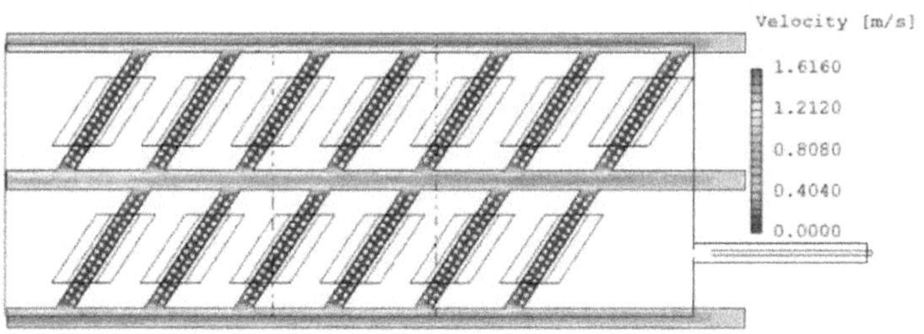


**Figure 21. The magnitude of velocity through production drift without undercut ventilation.**

Figures 22 and 23 show the concentration through the production and undercut drifts, respectively, after 9 hours. The concentration through the production drift (Figure 22) is significantly lower than in the first stage with undercut ventilation (Figure 12).

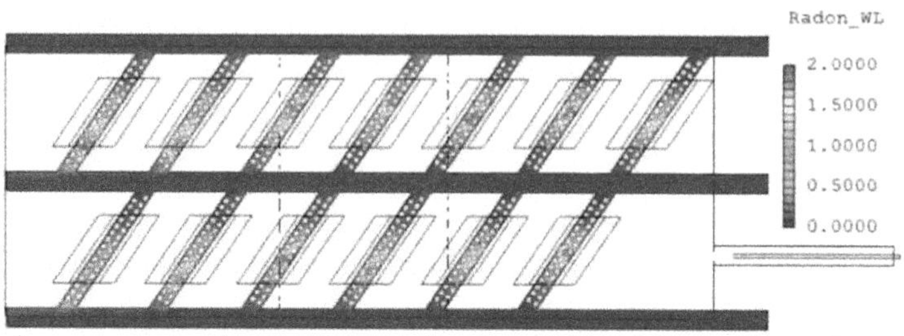


**Figure 22. Radon concentration in the production drift without the undercut ventilation.**

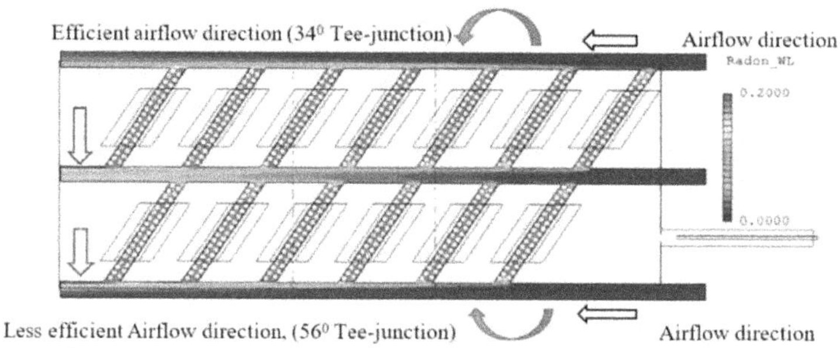


**Figure 23. Radon concentration through the production drift is limited to 0.2 WL.**

This suggests that the undercut ventilation increases radon concentration in the production drift by transporting radon generated within the cave into the drifts. Even though the airflow is almost uniform through the production drifts, the locations of the maximum concentration vary inside the drawbells—Figure 22. To investigate this, Figure 23 shows a localized image of the concentration with a 0.2 WL limit. The drawbells are oriented in two directions (340 and 560) to the flow based on the flow direction. The shock loss is greater with the 56° orientations; hence the airflow is less efficient in this region, as indicated in Figure 23.

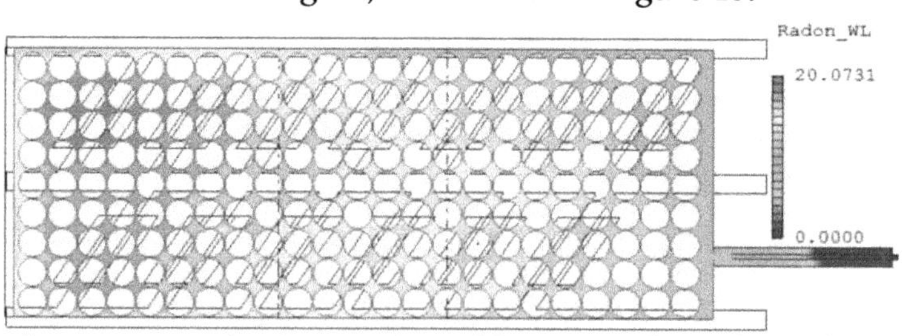


**Figure 24. Radon concentration in a section of the cave without the undercut ventilation.**

Therefore, due to shock losses, the orientations of the drawbells affect the efficiency of the airflow in mitigating radon exposure. Since there is no notable airflow inside the cave, Figure 24 shows that the concentration inside the cave increases significantly. In this case, the maximum concentration is about 20 WL, though mine personnel is not usually exposed to the higher levels in these regions. This agrees with previous studies that the working level in abandoned mines or caves can be as high as 81 WL [24]. Therefore, without undercut ventilation, radon accumulates significantly within the cave.

Without undercut ventilation, negative pressure on top of the cave might have a negative impact on the radon concentration in the production drift.

We studied the effect of maintaining a negative pressure on top of the cave without undercut ventilation. Figure 25a shows radon concentrations before imposing the negative pressure condition, and Figure 25b shows the concentrations after imposing the condition.

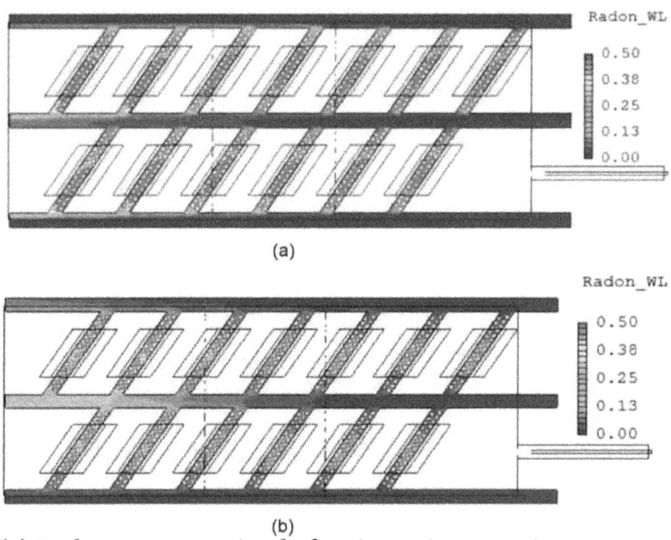


**Figure 25. (a) Radon concentration before imposing negative pressure; (b) radon concentration after imposing negative pressure condition.**

The effectively imposed negative pressure condition reduces radon concentration in the drawbell; however, radon concentration increases toward the end of the production drifts. This is due to significant air loss through the porous drawbells to satisfy the condition imposed. Therefore, the magnitude of air flowing through the drifts decreases, and the radon concentration increases. Although in most cases, the cave is not as porous as the discrete model (47%), this scenario is possible for a very porous cave or drifts with one or two hang-ups close to the drift's inlet. Hence, without the undercut ventilation, maintaining a negative pressure on top of the cave might have a negative impact on the radon concentration in the production drift. Therefore, mitigation measures should be appropriately investigated before implementation because the system might respond differently based on the mine condition. In addition, since there is no more undercut level, one can consider increasing the airflow through the drifts instead of imposing a negative pressure condition on top of the cave.

## 3.10 Finding 10: ventilation shutdown causes variation in radon concentration at the production drifts

In most underground mines with radon sources, the ventilation is continuous to ensure radon concentration is within the permissible levels. However, certain situations such as maintenance or mechanical malfunction could lead to the shutdown of the ventilation system. This study investigates the effects of shutting down the ventilation system for a period of time using the discrete model without the undercut ventilation. Figure 26a shows the radon concentration contours for the model after about 1 hour without ventilation.

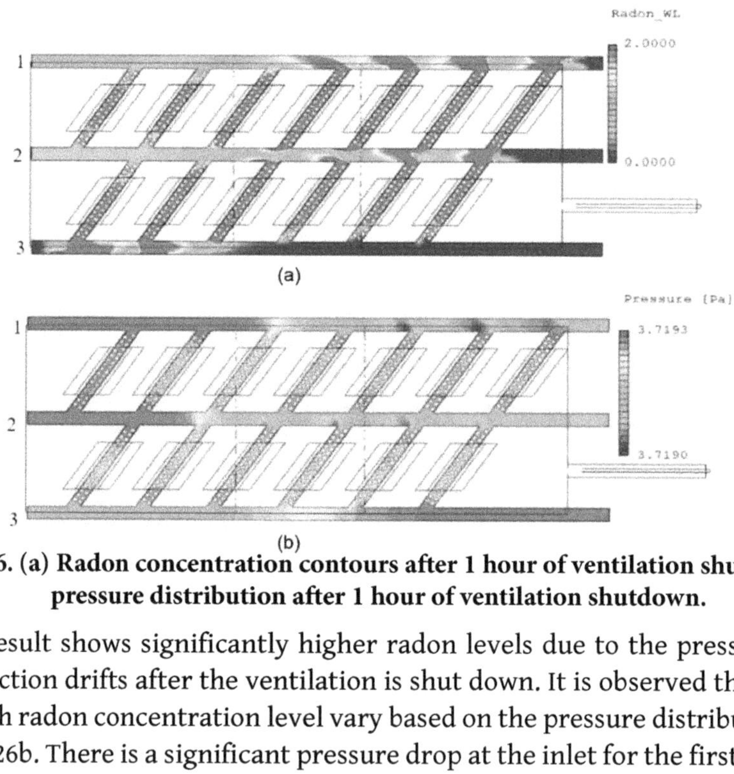


**Figure 26. (a) Radon concentration contours after 1 hour of ventilation shutdown; (b) pressure distribution after 1 hour of ventilation shutdown.**

The result shows significantly higher radon levels due to the pressure drop in the production drifts after the ventilation is shut down. It is observed that locations with a high radon concentration level vary based on the pressure distribution shown in Figure 26b. There is a significant pressure drop at the inlet for the first and second drift as the airflow stops. Therefore, radon concentration increases suddenly toward both inlets due to the pressure difference. However, for the third drift, the trend is different. The third drift develops the maximum pressure due to the distance between the inlet and the first source of pressure loss (drawbell). Hence, after shutting down the ventilation of a mine, the pressure around the inlet of the third drift is still high enough to keep radon concentration low. Therefore, in the event of a ventilation shutdown, there might be a considerable variation in radon concentration through the drifts.

## 3.11 Finding 11: radon daughter concentration is a function of the air quantity supplied to the production drift, the emanating power, and the porosity of the broken ore

A CFD study to investigate the effect of changing cave porosity (Ø), air quantity (Q), and radon emanating power (B) on radon daughter emissions from a cave in a block/panel cave mine was conducted [25] {Bhargava, 2019 #10}. The concentration of radon daughters was measured at the exit of the panel cave (458 m from the inlet) for production drifts 1, 3, 5, 7, and 9. Figure 27 shows the concentrations of radon daughters (on the same scale for ease of comparison) for 18.5 $m^3/s$ air quantity, for 21% cave porosity with emanating powers of 6, 90, and 180 $pCi/m^3s$, respectively. A summary of average radon concentration in drift # 5 (458 m from the inlet) was given in Table 6; similar data were also collected for the other drifts. The results were analyzed using R statistical software to develop the relationship between radon daughter concentration (WL), porosity, emanating power, and quantity supplied to the production drifts. The relationships were summarized in Table 7, where B represents the emanating power, Q is the quantity supplied, and Ø represents the porosity of the cave.

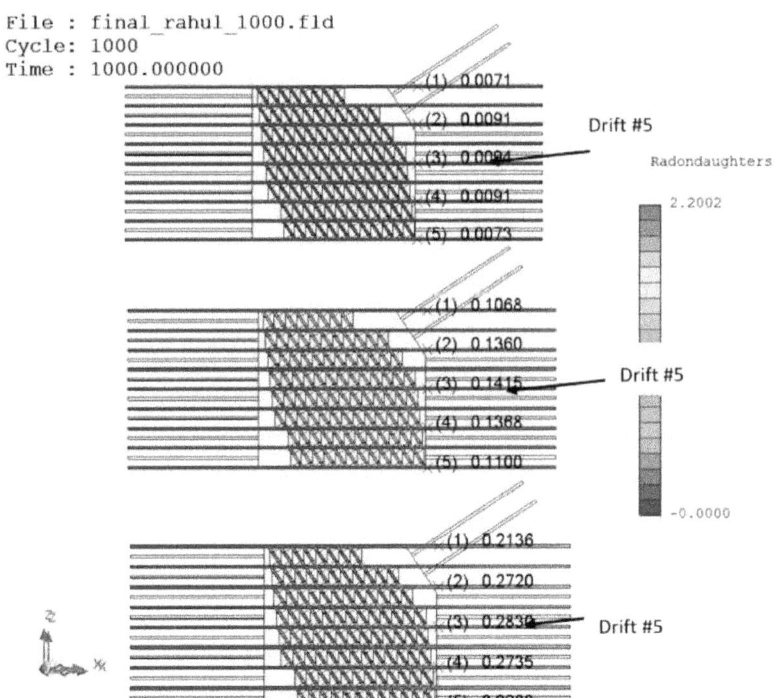


**Figure 27. Radon daughter concentrations (WL) in production drifts with simulation time of 1000 s at Q = 18.5 $m^3/s$, B = 6, 90, 180 $pCi/m^3s$ (top to bottom), Ø = 21%.**

**Table 6. Summary of average radon daughter concentrations in drift # 5.**

| | | B = 6 pCi/m³s | B = 90 pCi/m³s | B = 180 pCi/m³s |
|---|---|---|---|---|
| Q (m³/s) | Ø (%) | WL | WL | WL |
| 18.5 | 21 | 0.009 | 0.142 | 0.283 |
| 23.1 | 21 | 0.007 | 0.097 | 0.194 |
| 27.7 | 21 | 0.005 | 0.071 | 0.142 |
| 32.3 | 21 | 0.004 | 0.055 | 0.100 |
| 18.5 | 28 | 0.010 | 0.153 | 0.306 |
| 23.1 | 28 | 0.007 | 0.105 | 0.211 |
| 27.7 | 28 | 0.005 | 0.078 | 0.155 |
| 32.3 | 28 | 0.004 | 0.060 | 0.120 |
| 18.5 | 42 | 0.013 | 0.197 | 0.394 |
| 23.1 | 42 | 0.009 | 0.138 | 0.276 |
| 27.7 | 42 | 0.007 | 0.104 | 0.207 |
| 32.3 | 42 | 0.005 | 0.082 | 0.163 |
| 18.5 | 56 | 0.018 | 0.270 | 0.540 |
| 23.1 | 56 | 0.013 | 0.193 | 0.387 |
| 27.7 | 56 | 0.010 | 0.148 | 0.310 |
| 32.3 | 56 | 0.008 | 0.119 | 0.237 |

**Table 7. Equations developed for predicting radon daughter concentrations in the production drifts.**

| Production drift | Radon daughter concentration (WL) |
|---|---|
| Drift #1 | WL=e-1.12Q-1.86Ø0.13B0.99 |
| Drift #3 | WL=e-0.71Q-1.64Ø0.69B1.00 |
| Drift #5 | WL=e-0.68Q-1.62Ø0.73B0.99 |
| Drift #7 | WL=e-0.78Q-1.67Ø0.59B1.00 |
| Drift #9 | WL=e-1.28Q-1.83Ø0.05B0.99 |

From Table 7, we can deduce the following equation [26]:

$$\text{WL in Drift\#} \propto \frac{\phi^{a} B}{Q^{b}} \qquad (2)$$

(where) $0.05 \le a \le 0.65$ and $1.62 \le b \le 1.86$

From Eq. (2), we can infer that the radon daughter concentration is directly proportional to the emanating power and porosity of the broken ore (raised to power a) and inversely proportional to the quantity (raised to the power b) supplied to the production drift.

## 3.12 Finding 12: radon diffusivity depends on the fracture sets, fracture orientations, and rock's engineering properties

We introduced the concept of diffusivity tensor in fractured rocks [27], similar to permeability tensor [28, 29, 30, 31]. We have developed a method for predicting the diffusivity tensor and fracture porosity for fractured rocks using a discrete fracture network (DFN) analysis. This method applies to fractured rocks and mines if data such as fracture sets, fracture orientations, and radon generation rates are available. The following are the observations/conclusions from this study—(1) the concept of diffusivity tensor has been developed and implemented; (2) each of the DFN models established a representative elementary volume (REV), but at different DFN scales due to differences in fracture length distribution which emphasizes that the short diffusion length of radon affects the DFN scale to establish a REV; (3) radon diffusivity for the fractured rock increases with an increase in fracture density due to increased porosity; (3) fracture porosity can be related with the diffusivity tensor and used to predict radon flux emanation; (4) radon diffuses at about an equal rate in both directions since, the principal and cross diffusivity are numerically close due to the consistent generation of radon within the rock mass and; (5) the value of radon generation significantly affects radon diffusivity; hence, for the prediction of radon emissions, the site-specific data should be considered.

In the case of a particular field study, discontinuity data from boreholes, rock cores, and scanlines can be processed to identify fracture sets and their orientations used to tune the stochastic model to suit site-specific in situ conditions better. Therefore, this model predicts radon flux from fractured rocks, and it is beneficial for predicting radon flux from the rocks that are not easily accessible for field measurements.

From this study, we found that—(1) the proposed model predicts radon flux from the fractured rocks; (2) the model can be applied to specific locations if the site data such as fracture sets, fracture orientations, and rock's engineering properties are available; (3) the model is very sensitive to the advection velocity model, and aperture model implemented; (4) incorporating the effect of stress into the model shows more heterogeneity related to radon transport as observed from field studies; (5) an increase in fracture density increases radon flux, and an empirical power law relationship is found to relate both parameters; (6) the empirical relationship can be used with measured radon flux from field studies to predict the rock's fracture density; (7) radon flux increases with increase in radon generation rate, but not as sensitive as the fracture density, hence, increase in fracture density of a rock sample with uniformly distributed radon generation rate (q) increases radon flux more than another rock sample with an equivalent increase in radon generation rate.

## 3.13 Finding 13: additional fan increased cave airflow resistance and decreased the exponent n value

This study developed a 1:100 scaled experimental model (Figures 28 and 29) to determine the effects of the change in porosity and particle size of caved materials, undercut structure, and additional fan operation on the cave airflow behavior by developing P-Q curves and equations [32, 33, 34, 35].

**Figure 28. Experimental model showing production drift inlets.**

**Figure 29. Arrangement of drawbells and drawpoints with an El Teniente layout.**

As shown in Figure 30, our scaled block cave model has a caved zone, production level, drawbells, undercut level, and multiple ducts connecting with two exhaust fans. Initially, the wood model had eight rigid windows, and the caved zone dimensions were 244 cm × 229 cm × 122 cm (width × length × height); while in our modified version, they are 244 cm × 229 cm × 81 cm without windows. The production level consists of nine parallel drifts with a cross-section of 5 cm × 5 cm, a center-to-center distance of 30 cm between the drifts, and 188 drawpoints with an El Teniente layout. The caved zone and the production level are connected by 94 drawbells (shown in yellow, red, and green colors). Three 5 cm diameter PVC pipes (shown in blue color in Figure 30) are attached to the caved zone to simulate three undercut drifts. A 10 cm diameter PVC duct (shown in cyan color) is connected to the production drift outlets, and it is fitted with a fan (bottom fan shown in magenta color) to pull the air through production drifts. Another 20 cm diameter steel duct (shown in cyan color) is connected to the cave top, and it is also fitted with another fan (top fan shown in magenta color) to pull the air through the caved zone. The caved zone was divided into three vertical regions: Region 1, Region 2, and Region 3. Nine production drift inlets are shown in white color, and three undercut drift inlets (shown in white color) can be sealed with duct tape or opened during the experiment.

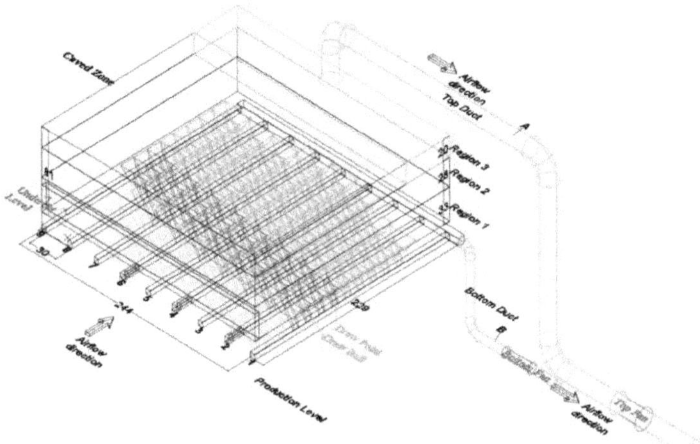


**Figure 30. Schematic diagram of the experimental setup (unit: cm).**

Four different conditions for the top fan to develop a single P-Q curve, three different settings for the bottom fan to check the effect of an additional fan, and two undercut structures (closure and opening) to explore the airflow behavior change [36]. Each data set was repeated to obtain two replications, and the average value was used for data analysis.

Table 8 summarizes the cave characteristics under various conditions in terms of P-Q equations ($P = RQ^n$). Undercut drift openings escalated the value of exponent n from 1.55 to 1.78, while the increase of bottom fan power abated the value from 2.17 to 0.71 in the experimental results. Typically, the value of n is around 1.8 for uniform airflow distribution in a regular porous media, and it is 2 for turbulent airflow through mine openings. Thus, in this study, the value of n represented the combination of airflow through an irregular cave and mine openings.

**Table 8. Average values of exponent n.**

| Undercut drifts | Bottom fan condition | Experimental value n | Undercut drifts | Bottom fan condition | Experimental value n |
|---|---|---|---|---|---|
| Closed | No fan | 2.17 | Open | No fan | 2.24 |
| | Half-open | 1.13 | | Half-open | 1.45 |
| | Full-open | 0.71 | | Full-open | 1.17 |
| | Overall | 1.55 | | Overall | 1.78 |

As shown in Table 9, the effect of three undercut drift openings on the exponent n value was not noticeable, but the increment of top fan power lowered the value.

**Table 9. Average values of exponent n with the top fan.**

| Undercut drifts | Top fan condition | Value n | Undercut drifts | Top fan condition | Value n |
|---|---|---|---|---|---|
| Closed | 0 | 2.16 | Open | 0 | 2.07 |
| | 70 | 1.85 | | 70 | 1.91 |
| | 90 | 1.80 | | 90 | 1.85 |
| | Overall | 1.93 | | Overall | 1.94 |

## 3.14 Finding 14: regulators and cave footprint changes the cave resistance

This study investigated the effects of cave footprint, and regulators on the cave airflow resistance. Regulators were able to distribute airflow rates through the caved zone and extraction drifts. Bends and regulators made it challenging to obtain constant air velocity within the ducts.

Both the experimental and CFD simulation results demonstrated (Figure 31) that the increment of porosity and particle size in the caved materials increases the area available for flow within the cave (decreased airflow resistance) and increased airflow distribution percentage through the cave system under a given regulator combination. The shrinkage/reduction of cave footprint decreases the area available for flow within the cave (increased cave airflow resistance) significantly. The use of regulators increased the fan head pressure, decreased the overall airflow rate, and changed the distribution of airflow rates through the cave system and extraction drifts. The increase of airflow rate through the system is favorable for gas dilution regardless of the source locations; while the regulated airflow system might deteriorate gas dilution performance, especially when the source is located at the extraction level (Tables 10 and 11).

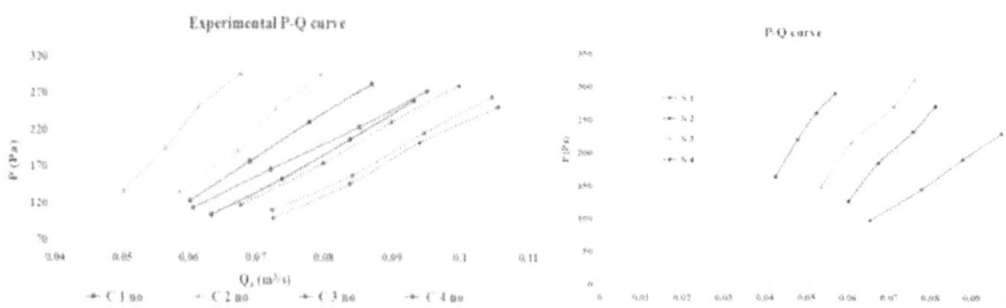


**Figure 31. P-Q curves under various regulator combinations (left) and cave footprints (right).**

**Table 10. Regulator combinations.**

| Combination | Up regulator | Down regulator |
|---|---|---|
| C1 | 100% | 100% |
| C2 | 100% | 50% |
| C3 | 25% | 100% |
| C4 | 6.25% | 100% |

Note: % is the ratio of the open area over the regulator's cross-sectional area.

no—no undercut drifts; three—three undercut drifts.

**Table 11. Cave footprint combinations.**

| Scenario | Drawbells (O—open) | Drawbells (C—closed) |
|---|---|---|
| S1 | 94 | 0 |
| S2 | 72 | 22 |
| S3 | 52 | 42 |
| S4 | 21 | 73 |

## 3.15 Finding 15: blast fumes dispersion in undercut and drawbell development

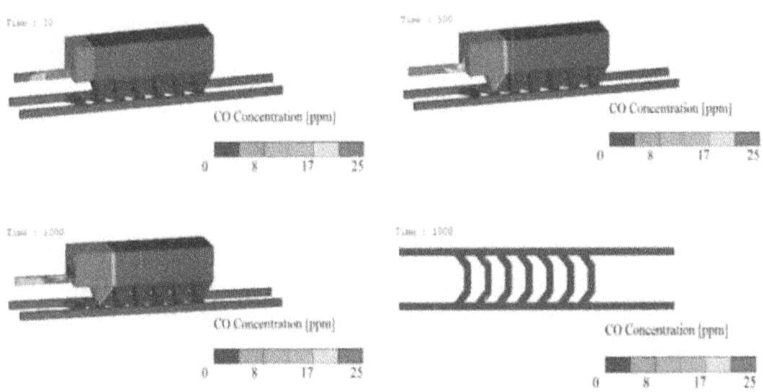


**Figure 32. CO diffusion characteristics in undercut blasting.**

CFD techniques were used to investigate CO diffusion characteristics in two common cases in an immature cave system, assuming CO is contained within the blasting zone [37]. The first case is undercut blasting with multiple ventilation structures (Figure 32). This study aims to find contaminated areas, potentially affected zones in the system, and develop CO concentration curves with respect to time at certain positions, and investigate the effects of broken rock size, porosity, and entrapping percentage on the gas diffusion characteristics in the muckpile. The second case is drawbell blasting (Figure 33) to investigate fume distribution and find possible zones that are likely to be filled with high concentration CO. All findings and observations provide helpful information to understand CO diffusion characteristics in block caving mines.

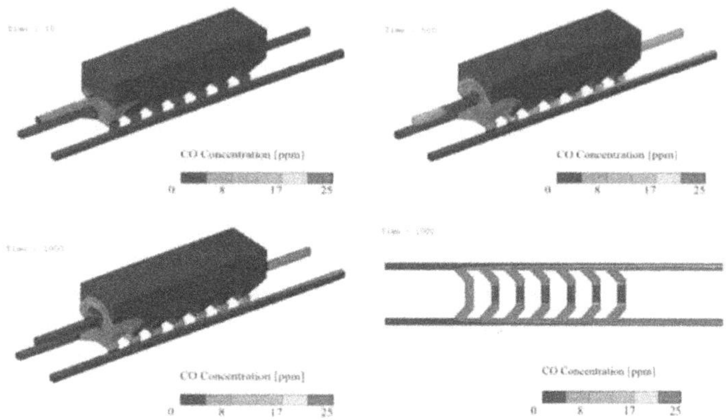

**Figure 33. CO diffusion characteristics in drawbell blasting.**

## 4. CONCLUSIONS

This study provides valuable information for designing and optimizing an effective ventilation system for panel/block cave mines. The key findings are listed below.

- ☆ The analysis of the airflow patterns through the cave indicated that the size and intensity of the recirculation zones change with the change in airgap heights. CFD simulation results show that in the absence of undercut ventilation, radon concentrations in the production level were much lower than the radon concentrations observed when the undercut level was ventilated which can be attributed to the creation of a low-pressure region in the undercut level, the porous nature of the cave, and the air recirculation in the cave.
- ☆ Rock mass strength (RM) increases the heights of the cave porosity zones decreases for both block and panel cave models. This is because the propagation rate decreases as rock mass strength increases. When the ore extraction rate was increased, the cave zone height increased. The mobilized zone porosity tends to be higher as it is the actively flowing region in the cave.
- ☆ The numerical model of porosity assessment using a discontinuum approach successfully modeled change in porosity associated with the fragmented rock mass flow in a mature cave and it was found that during material extraction,

the porosity changes relatively higher in Isolated Extraction than in the Isolated Draw Zone. The sensitivity analysis on particle size distribution concluded that fragmentation size affects cave porosity.

- ☆ In a fully developed cave, the radon concentration is high without undercut level ventilation and high in production drift with undercut ventilation. With undercut ventilation, negative pressure on the cave top effectively reduces radon concentration through the production drifts.
- ☆ Radon concentration in the drifts was studied with a discrete and continuum model. Empirical equations developed using both models suggested that different relationships are required for the drifts based on their configuration. The numerical study also indicated that the undercut ventilation increases radon concentration in the production drift by transporting radon generated within the cave into the drifts. Even though the airflow is almost uniform through the production drifts, the locations of the maximum concentration varied inside the drawbells. The result showed significantly higher radon levels due to the pressure drop in the production drifts after the ventilation is shut down. It is observed that locations with a high radon concentration level vary based on the pressure distribution.
- ☆ Without the undercut ventilation, the cave has less effect on the production drift ventilation as the pressure drop model agrees with the turbulent model; and an increase in cave porosity decreases the drift's resistance to airflow.
- ☆ By statistical analysis of the numerical results, we inferred that the radon daughter concentration is directly proportional to the emanating power and porosity of the broken ore and inversely proportional to the quantity supplied to the production drift. Radon Diffusivity depends on the fracture sets, fracture orientations, and rock's engineering properties.
- ☆ From the experimental and CFD analyses, it was concluded that the reduction in porosity and particle size of caved materials elevated cave airflow resistance. At the same time, the existing undercut openings decreased the airflow rate through production drifts, increased the overall airflow through the cave system, reduced the overall cave resistance, and increased the exponent n value in the P-Q equation.
- ☆ The use of an additional fan increased cave airflow resistance and decreased the exponent n value. The use of regulators increased the fan head pressure, reduced the overall airflow rate, and changed the distribution of airflow rates through the cave system and extraction drifts.

## REFERENCES


1. Rech W, Keskimaki K, Stewart D. An update on cave development and draw control at the Henderson mine. In: Proceedings of the MassMin. 2000. pp. 495-505
2. Potvin Y, Hudyma M. Interpreting caving mechanisms using microseismic monitoring data. In: Proceedings of MassMin. 2008. pp. 971-981
3. Callahan M, Keskimaki K, Fronapfel L. Constructing and operating Henderson's new 7210 production level. In: Proceedings of Massmin. 2008. pp. 15-24
4. Pascoe C, Oddie M, Edgar I. Panel caving at the resolution copper project. In: Proceedings Fifth International Conference and Exhibition on Mass Mining. 2008
5. Castro R, Paredes P. Empirical observations of dilution in panel caving. Journal of the Southern African Institute of Mining and Metallurgy. 2014;114(6):455-462
6. Duplancic P, Brady B. Characterisation of caving mechanisms by analysis of seismicity and rock stress. In: 9th ISRM Congress. International Society for Rock Mechanics; 1999
7. Nadakavukaren A. Our Global Environment: A Health Perspective. Illinois, USA: Waveland Press; 2011
8. Mc Pherson MJ. Subsurface Ventilation and Environmental Engineering. California, USA: Springer Science & Business Media; 2012
9. HPA. Radon and Public Health: Report Prepared by the Subgroup on Radon Epidemiology of the Independent Advisory Group on Ionising Radiation, Documents of the Health Protection Agency. UK: Health Protection Agency; 2009
10. O. O. I. US EPA. Health Risk of Radon. Available from: https://www.epa.gov/radon/health-risk-radon [Accessed: 2 August 2017]
11. George AC. World history of radon research and measurement from the early 1900's to today. AIP Conference Proceedings. 2008;1034(1):20-33
12. Tukkaraja P, Bhargava R, Jayaraman Sridharan S. Radon in underground mines. In: Mining Technology. 2021
13. Erogul D, Ajayi K, Tukkaraja P, Shahbazi K, Katzenstein K, Loring D. Evaluation of cave airflow resistance associated with multiple air gap geometries during cave evolution. In: 16th North American Mine Ventilation Symposium, Golden. 2017

14. Erogul D, et al. Effect of the air gap associated with cave evolution on cave resistance. In: 15th North American Mine Ventilation Symposium, Blackburg. 2015. pp. 193-199

15. Hager WH. Losses in flow. In: Wastewater Hydraulics. Berlin, Heidelberg, Germany: Springer; 2010. pp. 17-54

16. Liu H. Pipeline Engineering. Boca Raton, USA: CRC Press; 2003

17. McPherson MJ. Radiation and radon gas. In: Subsurface Ventilation and Environmental Engineering. California, USA: Springer; 1993. pp. 457-487

18. D. Loring and E. Meisburger IV, A discussion of radon and the mitigation strategy at the Henderson Mine, 2010.

19. Ajayi KM, Shahbazi K, Tukkaraja P, Katzenstein K. Prediction of airway resistance in panel cave mines using a discrete and continuum model (in English). International Journal of Mining Science and Technology. 2019;29(5):781-784

20. Ajayi K, Shahbazi K, Tukkaraja P, Katzenstein K. Numerical investigation of the effectiveness of radon control measures in cave mines (in English). International Journal of Mining Science and Technology. 2019;29(3):469-475. DOI: 10.1016/j.ijmst.2018.07.006

21. Ajayi K, Tukkaraja P, Shahbazi K, Katzenstein K, Loring D. Computational fluid dynamics study of radon gas migration in a block caving mine. In: 15th North American Mine Ventilation Symposium. 2015. pp. 341-348

22. Baysal A, Ajayi K, Tukkaraja P, Shahbazi K, Katzenstein K, Loring D. Prediction of airflow resistance of a matured panel cave. In: 16th North American Mine Ventilation Symposium, Golden. 2017

23. Ajayi KM, Shahbazi K, Tukkaraja P, Katzenstein K. A discrete model for prediction of radon flux from fractured rocks (in English). Journal of Rock Mechanics and Geotechnical Engineering. 2018;10(5):879-892

24. DixonD. Exposure to radon in caves and abandoned mines. In: IRPA9: 1996 International Congress on Radiation Protection. Proceedings. 1996

25. Bhargava R, Tukkaraja P, Shahbazi K, Katzenstein K, Loring D. CFD analysis of the effect of porosity, quantity and emanating power variation on gas emissions in block/panel cave mines. In: Proceedings of the 11th International Mine Ventilation Congress, Singapore. Singapore: Springer; 2019. 838-849

26. Bhargava R, Tukkaraja P, Adhikari A, Sridharan SJ, Vytla VVS. Airflow Characteristic Curves for a Mature Block Cave Mine. London: CRC Press; 2021. pp. 56-64

27. Ajayi KM, Shahbazi K, Tukkaraja P, Katzenstein K. Estimation of radon diffusivity tensor for fractured rocks in cave mines using a discrete fracture network model (in English). Journal of Environmental Radioactivity. 2019;196:104-112

28. Fanchi JR. Directional permeability. In: SPE Reservoir Engineering Evaluation and Engineering. 2008. pp. 565-568

29. Klimczak C, Schultz RA, Parashar R, Reeves DM. Cubic law with aperture-length correlation: Implications for network scale fluid flow. Hydrogeology Journal. 2010;18(4):851-862

30. Ren F, Ma G, Fu G, Zhang K. Investigation of the permeability anisotropy of 2D fractured rock masses. Engineering Geology. 2015;196:171-182

31. Zhang X, Sanderson D, Harkness R, Last N. Evaluation of the 2-D permeability tensor for fractured rock masses. International Journal of Rock Mechanics and Mining Science and Geomechanics Abstracts. 1996;33(1):17-37

32. Jha A, Pan Y, Tukkaraja P, Sridharan SJ. Scale Model Investigation of Ventilation Parameters in a Block Cave Mine. London: CRC Press; 2021. pp. 556-562

33. Pan Y. Investigation of gas and airflow characteristics in block cave mines [Ph.D. thesis]. Rapid City: South Dakota School of Mines and Technology; 2020

34. Pan Y, et al. An investigation of the effects of particle size, porosity, and cave size on the airflow resistance of a block/panel cave. In: Proceedings of the 11th International Mine Ventilation Congress, Singapore. Singapore: Springer; 2019. pp. 82-91

35. Ajitha SS. Fragmentation analysis of a propagating cave in a block/panel cave mine [MS thesis]. Rapid City: South Dakota School of Mines and Technology; 2018

36. Pan Y, Tukkaraja P, Jayaraman Sridharan S, Jha A. Investigation of airflow characteristics under parallel fan conditions in a block cave mine. CIM Journal. 2021;12(4):169-178

37. Pan Y, Tukkaraja P. Numerical investigation of blasting fume characteristics in a block cave underground mine. Journal of Explosives Engineering. 2021;38(6):32-38

# INDEX

S



T



U



V



W

www.ingramcontent.com/pod-product-compliance
Ingram Content Group UK Ltd.
Pitfield, Milton Keynes, MK11 3LW, UK
UKHW021327190726
13845UKWH00004B/59

9 788197 559464